PASSION OF ISRAEL:

Jacques Maritain, Catholic Conscience, and the Holocaust

D1520558

PASSION OF ISRAEL:

Jacques Maritain, Catholic Conscience, and the Holocaust

Richard Francis Crane

University of Scranton Press
Scranton and London

Library of Congress Cataloging-in-Publication Data

Crane, Richard Francis.
  Passion of Israel : Jacques Maritain, Catholic conscience, and the Holo-
caust / Richard Francis Crane.
     p. cm.
  Includes bibliographical references.
  ISBN 978-1-58966-193-6 (pbk.)
  1. Maritain, Jacques, 1882-1973. 2. Jewish question. 3. Antisemitism. 4.
Catholic Church--Relations--Judaism. 5. Judaism--Relations--Catholic
Church. 6. Holocaust, Jewish (1939-1945) I. Title.
  B2430.M34C69 2010
  261.2'6092--dc22

                                                        2009048497

Distribution:
University of Scranton Press
Chicago Distribution Center
11030 S. Langley
Chicago, IL 60628

PRINTED IN THE UNITED STATES OF AMERICA

In memory of my grandfather
Francis Joseph Karpinski
(1910–1985)

CONTENTS

ACKNOWLEDGMENTS

My research for this book involved personal visits to libraries and archives as well as long-distance requests for books, articles, and copies of shorter documents. While visiting the *Cercle d'Etudes Jacques et Raïssa Maritain* in Kolbsheim, France, I benefited from the wisdom and hospitality of that institution's director, René Mougel. The since-retired director of the Maritain Center at the University of Notre Dame, Ralph McInerny, along with his assistant Alice Osberger, introduced me to another important Maritain collection. I received assistance from archivists whom I have not yet had the privilege of meeting at Seton Hall and Georgetown Universities, the YIVO Institute for Jewish Research, and the American Jewish Archives. Finally, this book evidences a particular debt to the successive interlibrary loan specialists at my own college, reference librarians Jennie Hunt and Michael Simmons.

For reading parts of the manuscript and offering helpful critiques, Oscar Cole-Arnal, David Bell, John Conway, Donald Dietrich, Richard Scott Jones, Jonathan Judaken, Paul Mazgaj, Philip Rolnick, Karl Schleunes, Paul Teed, and especially Bernard Doering, all receive my heartfelt thanks. I also learned much from suggestions offered by Joel Blatt, Vicki Caron, John Hellman, and David Roskies. At Greensboro College, my colleagues in the Department of History, Michael Sistrom and April Najjaj, as well as my academic dean, Paul Leslie, encouraged and aided my scholarship in every way possible. Another of my colleagues, philosopher John Woell, read all the finished chapters, and Nancy McElveen, who is a professor of French, reviewed translations and quotations.

During a 2006–07 leave from Greensboro College, I received a Christopher Browning Research Fellowship from the Holocaust Educational Foundation led by Theodore "Zev" Weiss, and took up residence as Hoffberger Family Fellow at the United States Holocaust Museum's Center for Advanced Holocaust Studies (CAHS). This study does not necessarily embody the views and opinions of Mr. Weiss and the Holocaust Educational Foundation, or those of the Hoffberger family, the CAHS, and the United States Holocaust Memorial Museum, but it does bear the indelible imprint of their generous support. The CAHS director, Paul Shapiro, along with the director of the Visiting Fellows Program, Lisa Yavnai, and the Staff Director for Church Relations, Victoria Barnett, helped me make the most of my residency, as did another staff member, historian Suzanne Brown-Fleming.

I also want to acknowledge the courtesy shown to me by both the Catholic University of America Press and Routledge for permitting me to incorporate into this book some material from articles I have published in their respective scholarly journals, *The Catholic Historical Review* and *Patterns of Prejudice*. I am grateful, too, to Richard and Jane Levy for subsidizing the permission fees to obtain the use of the cover image, Marc Chagall's painting "Yellow Crucifixion," which is housed at the Centre Pompidou in Paris. The Director of the University of Scranton Press, Jeffrey Gainey, has been helpful, patient, and supportive as I have worked to complete this book.

Lastly, and most importantly, I bear a cherished debt to my wife Piper, daughter Delaney, and son Rory, as well as to my parents, Bonnie and Richard Crane, for loving and supporting an often preoccupied, sometimes absent, but always very grateful author.

RFC, Greensboro, October 2009

INTRODUCTION

On the ninth of January 1943, *Reichsführer* Heinrich Himmler visited the Warsaw Ghetto and decided to deport another 8,000 of its remaining Jewish inhabitants.[1] That same day, in the vastly different setting of New York's Waldorf-Astoria Hotel, one European expatriate paid tribute to another. The Russian Jewish painter Marc Chagall spoke of his friendship with the French Catholic philosopher Jacques Maritain at the latter's sixtieth birthday celebration: "Though I have followed a different religious path, I nevertheless felt a kind of union with Maritain, and I asked myself: Could not what is possible in the spiritual realm be realized between men in the political field, in the social field, in the world where one war succeeds another, where among all the misunderstandings there is the gravest misunderstanding of all—the two-thousand-year-old misunderstanding which lies behind anti-Semitism, and has led to persecution, and finally the extermination of a people?"

Chagall saw in Maritain not only a courageous Gentile but also a sorrowful exception, whose tireless efforts on behalf of persecuted Jews had sparked more heated controversy than concrete changes in Christian responses to antisemitism: "He was one of the first men in France who broke the troublesome embarrassed silence which surrounded the 'Jewish Question.' It seemed then — and alas! — it still seems today, as if good breeding compels silence on this point, always and everywhere. Why?"[2]

With the Nazi Final Solution finally an open secret, Chagall implored the birthday celebrants to tell him why his fellow Jews had been so honored as to be "eternally persecuted, eternally hunted, without a home," and why "Europe, if not the whole world, has submitted not only to a military invasion, but a moral one as well," with the enemy continuing to "deal mortal blows to our home front."[3] Chagall may have discomfited the assembled guests at the Waldorf, but in his anguished appraisal of the Christian conscience, and in his reiteration of at least one version of the Jewish Question — that is, the question of the "place" of Jews in an overwhelmingly Gentile modern world — he clearly spoke both for himself and his friend Maritain.

The question of course long preceded what we today call the Holocaust.[4] For nearly two thousand years, Christian attitudes toward Jews had juxtaposed denigration with veneration, disavowal with acknowledgment, and sometimes limitless hatred with limited gestures of love. The Holocaust has profoundly exacerbated and embittered, and arguably given a new opening to a historically troubled relationship. In the middle of the twentieth century, Maritain pondered deeply how he and other Christians needed to put an end to hatred against the Jewish people. Given his outspoken rejection of antisemitism, he since has been lauded both as a sign of health within the Body of Christ and as a dissident voice that throws the alleged silence of figures such as Pope Pius XII into sharp relief.[5]

France's Catholic bishops themselves have cited Maritain's fight against antisemitism in their 1997 "Declaration of Repentance," read aloud at the former Drancy internment camp outside Paris: "Why is it, in the debates which we know took place, that the Church did not listen to the better claims of its members' voices? Before the war, Jacques Maritain, both in articles and in lectures, tried to open Christians up to different perspectives on the Jewish people. He also warned against the perversity of the anti-Semitism that was developing."[6]

But some interpretations of the case of Maritain, including recent assertions that he resigned his late-1940s post as French ambassador to the Vatican as a protest against papal silence in the aftermath of the Holocaust,[7] run the risk of oversimplifying his own attitudes toward Jews. Even Maritain, who could write of "The Impossible Antisemitism,"[8] might fall short of the standard that retrospectively has been set for him, and by extension, his fellow Christians. As the extent of the emerging genocide became known during the Second World War, Maritain, writing and speaking from American exile, wondered aloud whether or not the fate of European Jewry, or the "passion of Israel"[9] as he described it, was part of God's saving plan, with six million innocent Jewish victims following the path of one innocent one almost two millennia earlier.

Maritain's response to antisemitism before, during, and after the Holocaust can best be understood, then, not simply *in contrast to* a prevailing blindness within the Christian world during this time, but also *as indicative of* the ambiguous, conflicted, and still unresolved attitudes of Christians toward their Jewish neighbors, particularly as regards the soteriological question — that is, regarding the salvation of non-Christians. Maritain's ambivalent philosemitism, encapsulated in his theological probing of what many Christians have, since the time of Saint Paul, called the mystery of Israel, points to a personal struggle that touched the center of his life of faith and reason.[10]

In this book, I trace Maritain's developing opposition to antisemitism and analyze the Catholic philosemitism[11] that both animated that stance and sought to give meaning to the unprecedented tragedy of the Shoah. In order to accomplish these historical tasks, I focus on three main questions. First, what is the basis for Maritain's reputation as an opponent of antisemitism before and after the Holocaust, and, are all the claims that support this reputation justified? Second, how did Maritain frame the Jewish Question between the 1920s and 1960s, and, what were his historical, philosophical, and theological reference points? And third, in what ways can Maritain be seen as influential upon and indicative of changing Christian perceptions of Jews and Judaism? Answering these questions promises to shed important light not only upon Maritain, but also on the issue of Christian-Jewish understanding as an ongoing project in the wake of the Shoah.

This book reexamines Maritain's spiritual and intellectual biography in light of his Christian response to antisemitism. After the first chapter, we follow a Catholic conscience into exile. Wrested by war from his place within the French Catholic intelligentsia, Maritain would live the rest of his professional life (for the most part, not by choice) outside his native land. In studying Maritain's lifelong encounter with the Jewish Question, I concentrate on his efforts to make sense of the traumatic turning point in Christian-Jewish relations evident in the Holocaust. His framing of the Jewish Question as the mystery of Israel underwent important changes, and most of these changes can be noted between 1937 and 1945. But in the midst of evolving notions of pluralism and tolerance on his part, Maritain's Jewish Question always had at its heart an abiding and sometimes agonizing concern with the place of Jews in the economy of salvation as understood by Christians. As a Catholic thinker in the Aristotelian-Thomistic tradition, Maritain naturally viewed God not only as the first cause, but also the final goal of human existence. Seeing all human ends leading ultimately to the divine, Maritain's approach to the mystery of Israel drew its primary motivation from a life lived in the light of his own conversion. "I am a man," Maritain explained to the writer Jean Cocteau, "whom God has turned inside out like a glove."[12]

Born in Paris in 1882, Maritain grew up in an *haute-bourgeois* setting far removed from Catholic piety, and this was by design. His roots lay in France's secular republican elite; he was the grandson of Jules Favre, one of the founders of the laic Third Republic, and entered the Sorbonne as a socialist and an anticlerical Dreyfusard.[13] When at age twenty-four he embraced the Catholic faith, he provoked "lamentations, reproaches, and bitter accusations" within his family.[14] His Russian-born wife Raïssa paid for her choice in a similar fashion, as her mother could only associate Christianity with the cross brandished high above the pogroms that drove her from her homeland.[15] But Maritain, like his wife, saw his conversion to Catholicism as a product more of grace than of his own volition, and his view of grace at work in the world followed a Thomistic appreciation of grace fulfilling nature, rather than destroying it.

In an analogous sense, Jacques Maritain, along with Raïssa, saw what we might call Jewish conversion to Christianity as a fulfillment of Judaism itself and a prefiguring of Israel's messianic redemption and "reintegration."[16] But how could he reconcile this assessment of Christian-Jewish relations with the coming of the Shoah, the destruction of the European Jews at the hands of—or in the face of the indifference of — their Gentile neighbors? If the Church represented the future of the Jews, then what did the "crucifixion of the Jews" mean for the future of the Church? Maritain's challenge to his own Catholic conscience and to the consciences of other Christians to work toward a fuller understanding of the mystery of Jewish identity, suffering, and destiny, an understanding refracted through the horror and hope of the "passion of Israel," forms the substance of this book.

CHAPTER ONE

A METAPHYSICAL NECESSITY:
MARITAIN'S JEWISH QUESTION, 1921–1937

It is necessary to add that an essentially messianic people such as the Jews, from the instant when they reject the true Messiah, inevitably will play a subversive role in the world; I do not mean through some premeditated plan, but rather because of a metaphysical necessity, which makes of messianic Hope, and a passion for absolute Justice, when they are brought down from the supernatural to the natural level, and are falsely applied, the most active ferment of revolution. That is why, as Darmsteter and Bernard Lazare have pointed out candidly, Jews, Jewish intrigues, and the Jewish spirit can be found at the origin of most major revolutionary movements in the modern era. I will not dwell on the enormous role played by Jewish financiers and Zionists in the political evolution of the world during the war and in the working out of what is called the peace.

Jacques Maritain, July 1921

"The working out of what is called the peace" preoccupied a great many minds at this time. In a Europe in upheaval after the explosions of nationalism and internationalism known respectively as the Great War and the Russian Revolution, anti-Jewish imagery held an undeniable explanatory power. Léon Poliakov describes this power and the hostility aimed at European Jews identified with revolutionary violence: "In December 1918 the attacks against the Jews revived and soon intensified by the Communist seizure of power in Bavaria and Hungary, and by violent strikes in France itself. The fear of a social upheaval, which for a few weeks seemed imminent, was propitious to variations on the thesis of Jewish Bolshevism, that national tradition more readily than elsewhere described as Judeo-German or even (by Charles Maurras) as Wilsonian Judeo-German. But France had a strong government."[1] Thus a historian of antisemitism narrates a specific historical moment and captures the protean nature of a more-or-less respectable (and manageable) antipathy toward Jews in the western world immediately after the Great War.

Not for the first time, the "Spectral Jew"[2] offered a name — or in this case, an inchoate, hyphenated tag such as "Judeo-German" — to place upon an otherwise nameless fear. Poliakov also might have mentioned that this *grande peur* of late 1918 situates itself at the chronological midpoint of two vitally important dates in the history of antisemitism in France and Europe as a whole. Twenty-four years earlier, in December 1894, the French General Staff charged Captain Alfred Dreyfus with selling military secrets to Germany; almost twenty-four years hence, in July 1942, 12,884 Jewish objects of a French police roundup would be held in the stifling heat of *Vélodrome d'Hiver* in Paris or brought directly to the transit camp at Drancy — France's "antechamber to Auschwitz."[3]

In the five decades separating Dreyfus and Drancy, the Jewish Question remained a fixture in French national discourse. The legacy or legacies of 1789, the omnipresent vagaries of modernization and its discontents, the recurrent conflict with a reborn German Reich, the Russian Revolution and consequent rooting of a Communist International in Moscow served as important contexts for this national discourse. The putative *Guerre des Deux France* — progressive, secular democratic, cosmopolitan, Dreyfusard France versus traditionalist, clerical, authoritarian, nativist, anti-Dreyfusard France, a myth no less potently divisive for being mythical — provided yet another context. All served as present memories for contemplating the national future. And the Jewish Question embraced them all, the question of the place of native-born and immigrant Jews within the French body politic taking as interrelated points of departure both the Jewish emancipation set in motion by the 1789 Revolution and a widespread sense of incipient national decline — that is, decadence — that became common currency by 1900.[4] This chapter begins to engage the complex, polyvalent nature of the Jewish Question in the early twentieth century, not simply by citing the most extreme antisemites of the era (which tends to sensationalize the subject of anti-Jewish prejudice at the expense of historical understanding), but rather by following closely the evolving ideas of an intellectual who eventually emerged from his association with figures such as the aforementioned Maurras to offer a sustained and vehement rejection of antisemitism, a rejection itself almost unheard of in respectable circles before the Holocaust.

Jacques Maritain has been identified as an extraordinarily philosemitic member of the Catholic intelligentsia in interwar France. For Michel Winock, Maritain exemplifies a growing openness to "the democratic spirit and tolerance" among French Catholics by the end of the 1930s, "because this philosopher went from the Action Française to a militant humanism that excluded all forms of totalitarianism and refuted all justifications of antisemitism."[5] Indeed, as will be seen in subsequent chapters, Maritain's outspoken and principled opposition to antisemitism would provoke attacks by French fascists before the Second World War,[6] complicate his relations with Pope Pius XII when he served as French ambassador to the Vatican after 1945,[7] and merit posthumous praise by France's Catholic bishops in their "statement of repentance" issued at Drancy in 1997.[8]

Maritain's severing of his early ties with the anti-democratic and antisemitic Charles Maurras in 1927 brought recognition as well as notoriety. Employing his pen as the preeminent apologist for the papal condemnation of the Action Française,[9] he asserted the "primacy of the spiritual" against *politique d'abord* and assumed a leading role within what Philippe Chenaux describes as a new category of Catholic intellectual increasingly more open to democratic pluralism.[10] But how much and in what ways had Maritain's views on Jews in the modern world changed as a result of his ostensible political realignment? While his writings about the Jewish Question inevitably carried political implications, he always framed the question philosophically and above all theologically. Accordingly, and particularly given Maritain's designation as perhaps the most influential figure in the intellectual world of interwar French Catholicism, the development of his philosemitism — from the publication of his first essay specifically devoted to the Jewish Question in 1921 to the appearance of his second one in 1937 — merits further attention.

These two essays, written in very different historical contexts, reveal both an increasing opposition to racist antisemitism on Maritain's part, and at the same time a persistent, even intensified, essentializing of Jews, their author exhibiting not only an undeniable "anti-antisemitism"[11] but also an ambivalent philosemitism based on Jewish stereotypes both positive and negative. A devout Catholic who had broken with the radical right, Maritain strove to advance a metahistorical understanding of what might be called the Sacred Jew in an era when the racially hygienic construct of the Dirty Jew threatened to prevail in contexts ranging from the gutter to the drawing room to the classroom. But Maritain's recasting of the timely Jewish Question as the timeless mystery of Israel — which he took from his reading of Saint Paul — amounted to just as much of an expression of the political-cultural anxieties of the interwar period as its racist and ever more eliminationist counterpart, articulated as the so-called Jewish Problem. After all, both the mystery of Israel and the Jewish Problem removed the Jewish object of the question from the perspective of visible mundane reality and uncovered — or recovered — hidden secrets, arriving at apocalyptic answers. Maritain's vision of Jewish identity in the modern world, as it developed in the 1920s and 1930s, thus proved inseparable from his negotiation of the personal and public crises of his time.

REGARDING THE JEWISH QUESTION

In "À propos de la question juive," drawn from a lecture delivered to an audience at the *Semaine des écrivains catholiques* (Catholic Writers Week) and published in *La Vie spirituelle* in July 1921, Maritain scarcely denied the existence of a "Jewish problem," even if he avoided the term. Some Jews, particularly those wounded in the Great War, had demonstrated their assimilation to France or another country, but by and large European Jewry remained apart "even as Providence decreed would be the case throughout history, as witness to Golgotha." Therefore, "one should expect from the Jews something other than a real attachment to the common good of western, and Christian, civilization."[12] Worse, their historical rejection of Christ and the resultant temporalization of eschatological hopes — that is, an earthly corruption of the promise of God's kingdom — made at least some of them agents of revolution, not "through some premeditated plan, but rather because of a metaphysical necessity, which makes of messianic Hope, and a passion for absolute Justice, when they are brought down from the supernatural to the natural level, and are falsely applied, the most active ferment of revolution."[13]

However much these "Jewish intrigues" troubled him, Maritain rejected the kind of antisemitic conspiracy theory ("I do not mean through some premeditated plan") and attendant incitement to violence exemplified by the *Protocols of the Elders of Zion*, in which, as he puts it, "'the Jew' appears in a sort of simplistic mythology as the *unique* cause of the evils from which we suffer." But he conceded (in a formulation hardly uncommon for the time) "the evident necessity of a struggle for public safety against secret Jewish-Masonic societies and against cosmopolitan finance."[14] Exactly what this struggle entailed remained unclear and problematic in a post-Christian political order, and Maritain wished that Jews could be required once and for all "to opt, some of them, for French, English, Italian, etc., nationality . . . others for Palestinian nationality." Unfortunately the latter *patrie* did not (before 1948) exist. However frustrating he might find this practical problem, Christian faith and practice demanded a veneration of the people of Israel, for as Maritain articulated it, updating Saint Paul's Epistle to the Romans: "However degenerate carnal Jews may be, the race of the prophets, of the Virgin and the apostles, the race of Jesus is the trunk onto which we are grafted. Let us recall chapter eleven of the Epistle to the Romans."[15]

But if Maritain prescribed a reading of Saint Paul to curb antisemitic excess, his contemporary sources pointed to the Jew as inveterate schemer. The most striking argument he encountered to this effect came from the pen of a French Jewish writer. Bernard Lazare made his reputation as an anarchist writer and maverick Dreyfusard (in fact the very first Jewish Dreyfusard according to Robert Wistrich) who associated closely with Maritain's early mentor Charles Péguy before dying prematurely in 1903. His 1894 book *L'Antisémitisme, son histoire et ses causes*, cited by Maritain in his essay, represented an early, provocative stage of Lazare's ever-evolving thought. What evidently resonated most with Maritain in this work was the idea that "it would seem that the grievance of the antisemite were well founded; the Jewish spirit is essentially a revolutionary spirit, and consciously or otherwise, the Jew is a revolutionist." Still, Maritain could not embrace the rest of this thesis, refracted through an anarchist-socialist perspective that foresaw the simultaneous destruction of antisemitism and capitalism.[16] With considerably less enthusiasm, Maritain saw Christian civilization, not capitalism, as the real object of the revolutionary upheaval associated with what both he and Lazare termed "the Jewish spirit."

Maritain's willingness to simultaneously ascribe holiness and degeneracy to the Jewish people — citing Jewish writers such as Lazare, and elsewhere in the essay the *fin-de-siècle* antisemite Marquis René de la Tour du Pin — placed him in an awkward position to render judgment upon antisemitism. Hence, he proceeded to render an awkward judgment. Directly addressing his fellow Catholic writers, Maritain cautioned against, but by no means categorically rejected, antisemitism: "However antisemitic he might be in other respects, a Catholic writer, it seems evident to me, must in his faith refrain from any hatred and any contempt as regards the Jewish race and the religion of Israel considered in and of themselves."[17] Not only should one keep in mind "the number, relatively large, and in any case truly impressive, of Jews who for some time have been converting to Catholicism," but one should recognize also the "extraordinary *élan* of prayer that manifests itself within the Church, for Israel, and of which these conversions are precisely the fruit."[18] Above all, and in keeping with an Aristotelian-Thomistic understanding of virtue-based ethics,[19] one must prudentially distinguish between the theological virtue of *caritas* and the cardinal virtue of justice in one's dealings with Jews in the world: "Even as they must denounce and combat those depraved Jews who, along with apostate Christians, are leading the anti-Christian Revolution, so too they must guard against closing the door to the Kingdom of Heaven before souls of good will, before those *true Israelites* of whom Our Lord said *in whom there is no guile*. [John 1: 47] Charity toward the latter does not invalidate the justice the former deserve, nor the other way around."[20] This injunction at once advocates judging Jews on an individual rather than collective basis, distinguishes between good and bad ones (the parallel between Jewish depravity and Christian apostasy evidently pointing to the perils of secularization), and warns against closing the "door" of Christian conversion to "true Israelites."

At least one historian, John Hellman, has branded the "early Maritain" an antisemite.[21] But antisemitism — "best defined as unprovoked and irrational hatred toward Jews"[22] — hardly manages to contain Maritain's complex, fluid, and even hopeful view of a Jewish Question framed in worldly parameters and pointing to an otherworldly resolution. Hellman's anachronistic application of the term — applied pejoratively and begging clarification — would have to apply as well to the pacifist Socialist Jean Jaurès, who during the Dreyfus Affair could group together "cosmopolitan Jews without country, [and] conservatives without conscience," not to mention Georges Clemenceau, whose paper *l'Aurore* had published Zola's "*J'accuse*," yet could also write in the same year, 1898, about how "the Semite tried to come back and to fulfill himself by the domination of the earth." As distasteful as post-Holocaust readers will find such utterances, this kind of anti-Jewish discourse pervaded western culture to the extent that merely assigning to it the label *antisemitic* fails to differentiate between this level of unreflective prejudice — fortified by cultural presuppositions — and a pathological hatred of Jews increasingly activated in the interwar period by the biological imperative of racial hygiene.[23]

In the context of the 1920s, Maritain's construction of the Jewish Question, with its reference points of the "anti-Christian Revolution" and the "door to the Kingdom of Heaven," differs essentially from the ostensibly impersonal and political Maurrasian *"antisémitisme d'état,"* with its identification of French Jewry as one of the four solid pillars of "Anti-France" (along with foreigners, freemasons, and Protestants), an antisemitism which, according to Maurras, "should be defined as the premier organic and positive idea, the premier counterrevolutionary and naturalist idea."[24] As a reflection of the Action Française chief's overall mindset and his hostility toward Jews as an unassimilated and literally foreign body within the French body politic, this viewpoint opposes a reactionary positivism to what a recent study calls Maritain's "mystic modernism,"[25] while lending itself to influencing forthcoming "organic and positive," "counterrevolutionary and naturalist" ideas about Jews. Given the prevalence of a Christian supernaturalism in Maritain's approach to the Jewish Question, one can more readily perceive the enduring imprint of his godfather, the Catholic mystic novelist Léon Bloy.

The preeminence of Bloy's influence over that of Maurras in Maritain's framing of the Jewish Question, if not his confrontation with modernity, drew in part on chronological precedence, as the former association anticipated the latter by several years. Bloy had played a decisive role in Maritain's transformation of lifestyle and world view, superseding passing masters Péguy and Henri Bergson.[26] The last of these living mentors, Bloy stood as godfather in June 1906 as Maritain — finally rejecting his republican, *libre-penseur* upbringing — and his Russian Jewish émigré wife Raïssa, along with her sister Véra, received Catholic baptism. This amounted to a dramatic, even traumatic, conversion on Maritain's part. He had been born the scion of a solidly Republican and nominally Protestant family. His mother Geneviève, who reverted to her maiden name after divorcing *avocat* Paul Maritain, was the daughter of one of the founders of the Third Republic, Jules Favre. As a teenager, Jacques Maritain considered himself both an atheist and a socialist, vowing to "live for the Revolution."[27] But he subsequently experienced a different kind of revolution.

By 1901 he had become the "disciple" of poet, essayist, and editor Péguy, an unorthodox socialist who also extolled France's national *mystique* and the legacy of Joan of Arc, and who would eventually himself embrace Catholicism before dying on the battlefield in the opening weeks of the Great War.[28] Maritain inhabited Péguy's bookshop, and assisted with the editing of the *Cahiers de la Quinzaine* journal with which the shop shared a name. This work involved not only literary tasks, but actively supporting various human rights causes. In fact, he met Raïssa Oumansov later in 1901 while seeking signatures for a petition on behalf of imprisoned students in Tsarist Russia. During this time, Maritain backed Péguy in the fight to have Dreyfus finally and fully exonerated, a combat, as Bernard Doering describes it, that for Péguy had more to do with French justice than an abiding affection for the Jews, "some of whom he loved for their spirit of poverty, their fidelity and friendship, others of whom he despised for their degrading avarice, their willingness to sell one of their own (Dreyfus) in exchange for a little peace and economic security."[29] As he entered into this apprenticeship, and assimilated Péguy's mixed messages regarding Jews, Maritain also pursued his university studies in the sciences at the Sorbonne, along with Raïssa.

But an intellectual and spiritual crisis led him to reject the positivism and scientism of the Sorbonne and ultimately turn toward the very Catholicism that he had hitherto associated with all things reactionary.[30] As Raïssa, who would marry Jacques in 1904, later recalled, they shared an almost suicidal despair at the prevailing intellectual climate: "Through some curious *de facto* contradiction, they [their professors] sought to *verify* everything by processes of material learning and of positive verification, and yet they despaired of *truth*, whose very name was unlovely to them and could be used only through the quotation marks of a disillusioned smile. . . . All in all, the only practical lesson to be had from their conscientious and disinterested instruction was a lesson in intellectual relativism, and — if one was logical — in moral nihilism."[31]

Péguy, whose bookstore almost defiantly faced the Sorbonne,[32] advised the couple to attend the lectures of Bergson, the philosopher of intuition (who was himself Jewish), who held a chair in philosophy at the *Collège de France*. Bergson's philosophy offered an inspiring alternative to what the Maritains both saw as a mechanistic dead end in modern thought, even if Jacques would later publicly criticize his former teacher for inclining toward pantheism. Reinvigorated by *élan vital,* but still dissatisfied, Jacques and Raïssa increasingly wanted to ascertain the source of Being itself, and this finally brought them in 1905 to Montmartre, and the very doorstep of Bloy, the "Pilgrim of the Absolute," who lived there at the edge of poverty with his wife and daughters.

Bloy's "apocalyptic vision," as Stephen Schloesser writes, "stirred the passions of a younger elite bitterly contemptuous of the received order in both politics and religion" and "made suffering not merely a *privileged* path to redemption, but in fact the *exclusive* mode of participation in the supernatural."[33] Preoccupied with society's outcasts and victims, he particularly focused on Jews, whom on the one hand, he venerated, as if in doing so he were prophetically calling to account the decadent modern bourgeois world around him: "The Jews are the first-born of all peoples, and when all things are in their final place, their proudest masters will think themselves honored to lick the Jewish wanderers' feet. For everything has been promised them, and in the meantime they do penance for the earth. The right of the first-born cannot be annulled by a punishment however rigorous, and God's word of honor is unchangeable, because 'His gifts and vocation are without repentance.'" [34] No wonder he could denounce an antisemite such as Édouard Drumont, author of *La France juive* (1886) and editor of *La Libre Parole* with an almost frenzied contempt, ascribing to him the same cold-blooded mercenary cynicism with which the antisemite typically adorned his prey. [35]

But then Bloy also could find Jews guilty of the worst kinds of anti-human avarice. Perhaps no passage better demonstrates this taint than one particularly hallucinatory part of Bloy's book *Le Salut par les Juifs*. The author encounters a trio of Jewish merchants on the streets of Hamburg, his eyes widening as they transform themselves into Abraham, Isaac, and Jacob (re)incarnate, a primordial vision of "three incomparable blackguards whom I can still see in their putrid cloaks, bent forehead to forehead over the opening (*l'orifice*) of a fetid sack that would have horrified the heavens, in which were accumulated, for the exporting of typhus, the unspeakable objects of such arch-Semitic commerce." [36] Originally published in 1892, but with most of its copies mislaid by a bankrupt publisher, the 1905 edition of this forgotten, disturbing book saw the light of day thanks to the Maritains' subsidy, and opened with Bloy's dedication to his Jewish-born goddaughter: "To Raïssa Maritain. I dedicate these pages written for the Catholic glory of the God of Abraham, of Isaac, and of Jacob." [37] As for Jews in general, Bloy held that their obstinacy kept Christ perpetually suffering on the cross: "They have Him nailed strongly enough that He cannot come down without their permission." [38]

Of course, both of the Maritains found Bloy's angriest declamations troubling, but they tried to explain them away, Jacques insisting that "it would be unjust to sketch of Bloy a hideous caricature," and Raïssa rather serenely concluding, "To this man among all others much will be forgiven, because he loved so much. . . . We pardoned him his dross by virtue of the grandeur of his intentions and the magnificence of his language." [39] Most importantly, Jacques Maritain remained deeply impressed with the theological-historical implications of Léon Bloy's writings, ever returning to the latter's representation of a Jewish people that "obstructs the history of the human race as a dam blocks a river, to raise its level." [40] If Péguy had already taught Maritain that "the whole of Israel's *mystique* demands that Israel should pursue its painful and resounding mission throughout the world,"[41] Bloy's tutelage influenced him to envision and articulate that mission in predominantly otherworldly, even salvific, terms.

ANTIMODERN/ULTRAMODERN

Maritain never repudiated the Dreyfusard convictions of his youth, and like Bloy he considered the Jews an always-chosen people. But still he allowed himself to be drawn toward the milieu of the inveterate anti-Dreyfusard Maurras. This affinity developed despite the fact that Maritain never embraced Maurras' coldly political *antisémitisme d'état* let alone the more virulently biological *antisémitisme de peau* that still awaited widespread popularity. So if outright antisemitism had little or nothing to do with Maritain's *rapprochement* with the Action Française, what common ground presented itself?[42] The answer lies in Maritain's philosophical engagement with modernity,[43] which one recent biographer rather dramatically deems a *Kulturkampf*.[44]

In 1909, after Maritain had spent 1907–08 in postgraduate studies in Heidelberg, his new spiritual director, Father Humbert Clérissac, introduced him to the thirteenth-century Scholastic Saint Thomas Aquinas and also exhorted him to read the *Action française* newspaper,[45] at a time moreover when writers such as André Gide and Marcel Proust read it as well, and when Maurras' literary fame — for his criticism as well as his poetry — still exceeded his political notoriety. Historian Bruno Goyet correctly states that "classic historiography has run up against the positioning of Maurras between literature and politics."[46] Reading history backwards indeed has its perils: before the Republic convicted Maurras of treason (1945), he succeeded in getting himself elected to the *Académie française* (1938).

Maritain, from 1914 a professor at Paris's *Institut catholique*, never joined the Action Française in any case, but he did serve as philosophy editor at an affiliated publication called the *Revue universelle*, a journal moreover that he and Maurras had co-founded. He spent the rest of his life regretting this association, and a lingering defensiveness permeates Maritain's letter many years later, from August 1941, to his friend and one-time student Yves Simon. In it, he pleads that "the cause of this error was my obedience to the advice of Father Clérissac, for whom I have so much veneration and to whom in addition I owe so much. How is one to make sense of these things on the morrow of one's conversion? . . . I never read Maurras' books, and I relied on the wisdom of my director. I paid a high price for this mistake."[47] But later protestations of a youthful lapse of judgment belie how his antipathy toward what he saw as bourgeois liberal modernity led him to a logical alliance with the royalists.[48] This alliance drew on three motives: a working partnership with and hoped-for Catholicization of Maurras and the Action Française; a shared preoccupation, as evidenced by their adherence to Henri Massis' 1919 *Pour un parti de l'intelligence* manifesto, with a continued intellectual mobilization against Germanism and a rejection of art-for-art's-sake; and finally, the practical necessity of disbursing and utilizing the one million francs bequeathed to Maurras and Maritain jointly by a fallen soldier named Pierre Villard.

Perhaps the very question of the degree of Maritain's adherence to the Action Française's program distorts the historical picture — in simply asking how close Maritain approached Maurras' political outlook. We might also ask to what extent, at least from Maritain's perspective, Maurras seemed to be approaching *his* philosophical, if not spiritual outlook. As Oscar Arnal notes, "In 1917 Charles Maurras wrote a book called *Le Pape, la guerre, et la paix*. Included in its contents were contrasts of Latin Catholicism and German Lutheranism which paralleled those drawn by Jacques Maritain and others."[49] Nor should one forget that the convert Maritain also sought to save the souls of others, the celebrated conversion of Jean Cocteau in summer 1925 serving as but one example of those who found their hearts lastingly, or in Cocteau's case as well as that of Maurice Sachs, fleetingly, warmed by the spirit of Meudon, where the Maritains lived, worked, and prayed outside Paris. And even though in retrospect it is clear that Maurras always extolled Roman Catholicism as a functional bulwark of western (that is, Latin) civilization, why would Maritain not think, or at least hope, that the workings of grace might effect a spiritual transformation of the deaf *maître* and his movement. However mistaken Maritain may have been about Maurras' likely conversion, his hopes in that regard, and his not unrelated hopes to influence a movement and newspaper which thousands of Catholics had joined and/or subscribed to, should not be ignored or discounted.

Maritain had found common ground with Maurras during and after the Great War in seeing Germany as an enduring if not inveterate enemy, even if he did so from a philosophical perspective more than a political one. Maritain's 1914–15 public lecture series rejected the thesis that there were two Germanies, as Martha Hanna puts it, "one lofty and creative, the other base and destructive."[50] For Maritain, German atrocities against civilians and the ruination of cathedrals both followed as naturally from *Kultur* as from Prussianism. Writing in November 1915 to his friend Absalom Feinberg, a native of Turkish Palestine whom he had known years earlier in Paris and who would soon lose his life working to free his native land from the Germans' Ottoman allies, Maritain portrayed the European conflict as a culture war, managing an analogical reference to the ultimate conversion of Israel:

> This is the clash of two enemy forms that have issued from the great European Revolt of which Luther marked the first victory: on one side the revolution (I mean by that the substitution of man for God), the imperialist, authoritarian revolution monstrously organized by pride in carnal Domination, on the other side, the liberal, idealist, disorganizing, utopian, democratic revolution that leads to anarchy under the pretext of Liberty and Equality. For I firmly believe that Protestantized Germany has devoted itself body and soul to this spirit, to the European revolution (reread the second *Faust* if you have the time, quite suggestive at this moment), whereas an atheistic France is not truly France; God loves France and He holds on to her (France enjoying in the economy of Providence a role analogous to that of the Jewish People under the Old Law — *waiting* for the Jewish people, returned to the Light, to retake its place, which is the first).[51]

A decade later, Maritain still could show himself quite capable of mining this rich vein of national essentialism, colored by a vibrant anti-Protestantism: "Happy the nation whose supreme incarnation of her own genius is not a mere individuality of flesh but a personality radiant with the Spirit of God! If we want to set off against Luther's egocentrism an example of true personality, let us think of that miracle of simplicity and uprightness, of candour and wisdom, of humility and magnanimity, of loss of self in God — Joan of Arc."[52]

The Great War devastated much of France and took from Maritain close friends such as Péguy and Ernest Psichari. But it also indirectly gave him some measure of financial independence. When the aforementioned Villard, with whom Maritain corresponded at length during the war, died at the front in June 1918, he left over a million francs to be spent by Maritain "conjointly" with Maurras. Maurras apparently directed most of his half to the Action Française, Maritain purchased the house at Meudon which would serve as the center for the Thomist Circle and annual retreats of the 1920s and 1930s, and the two legatees would each contribute 50,000 francs to found *La Revue universelle*.[53] Maritain privately reflected at the time: "Here I am charged with a responsibility which I alone can fulfill. In order to contribute to the renewal [the spiritual renewal of the French nation] which Pierre Villard has in view, weapons will have to be wielded freely. Maurras and I will each have to use them for the undertaking for which he [Villard] has devoted his life."[54] Rightly or wrongly, and this seems obvious in the case of their differing approaches to the Jewish Question, Maritain thought he could associate with Maurras on an autonomous if not equal footing, preserving a sense of philosophical and spiritual integrity while advancing the renewal of Christian civilization.

After all, in the 1920s, the devout, contemplative Maritain also asserted himself as an ascendant and confident public intellectual who relished the prospect of philosophical confrontation.[55] The very title of his 1922 book *Antimoderne* sounded a battle cry, even if its contents were more nuanced—for example, extolling Catholicism as both a challenge to modernity and *the* truly ultramodern world view, for "Catholicism is as antimodern in its immutable attachment to tradition as it is ultramodern in how boldly it adapts itself to new conditions arising in the world."[56] *Trois Réformateurs (Three Reformers*, 1925) offered a history of the deformation of western thought — as a turn to the subjective self as the determiner of all meaning and value, thanks to Luther, Descartes, and Rousseau.

According to Maritain, Luther banished reason "to the foulest place in the house," teaching future generations of Germans and others that "the swollen consciousness of self is essentially a consciousness of will."[57] Descartes should be held responsible for repudiating reason's reliance on the past and irremediably rupturing the relationship between "intelligence and Being."[58] Finally, Rousseau exalted the ego by detaching himself from everything save his own "exorbitant Individuality": "A stupendous perverter, Rousseau aims not at our heads but a little below our hearts."[59] Having thus slain the fathers of modernism, Maritain could seek a constructive engagement with modernity, but he also named the terms, to be found in the Catholic tradition. And he further strengthened his hand through his *rapprochement* with the Action Française, a movement popular among French Catholics despite the agnosticism of its leader.

THE PRIMACY OF THE SPIRITUAL

But stresses within both Maritain's understanding of the *question juive* and his overall relationship with the Action Française began to tell even before the papal condemnation forced a wholesale reevaluation of his temporal application of philosophical and theological positions. In June 1925, Maurras wrote an open letter to Interior Minister Abraham Schrameck, threatening to shoot him "like a dog" for having taken measures to suppress the Action Française street battalions called the *Camelots du Roi*.[60] While Maurras faced criminal charges, *Camelots* found an opportunity to assail Schrameck with antisemitic catcalls. In Maritain's *Réponse à Jean Cocteau*, published in 1926, he found no problem with "booing an unfit minister," but he objected strongly to "outraging Heaven by soiling the name of the immense Saint in whose paternity all believers are enveloped. *Abraham begat Isaac, and Isaac begat Jacob* [Matthew 1: 11–17] . . . The Genealogy of our God."[61]

In his letter to Cocteau, Maritain proceeded to evoke the emphasis on suffering so typical of Bloy as well as the Jew/Israelite opposition seen for example in the Johannine Gospel: "I have known prideful and corrupt Jews. Above all I have known magnanimous ones, with great and guileless hearts, born poor and dying poorer still, having neither the sense of lucre nor economy, happier to give than receive. If there are always carnal Jews, there are also true Israelites, *in whom there is no guile* [John 1: 47]."[62] Nor did Maritain apparently think Maurras possessed any guile, having testified in his defense at a trial that resulted in a suspended two-year sentence.

Apparently, as far as Maritain was concerned, in giving his testimony, he spoke solely as a philosopher, defending the principle of principled free speech without himself intervening in matters political. But biographer Jean-Luc Barré rightly concludes that this culminating act of Maritain's Maurrasian *dérive* shows how far he had deluded himself: "Maritain thus accepted, without any inordinate concern, to align himself with the most overtly antisemitic intellectual milieu that one could find. He had managed to distance himself so far from comprehension that in 1925, during a trial initiated by Minister of the Interior Abraham Schrameck, whom Maurras had threatened to 'shoot like a dog,' he testified in favor of the offender in the name of 'resisting unjust laws.'"[63]

Maritain's disquietude with Action Française Jew-baiting coincided with his failure, in concert with Orientalist Louis Massignon, to enlist papal support for Zionism (it will be remembered that for Maritain the establishment of a Jewish state promised a resolution to the question of Jewish national identity). The October 1925 report for Pius XI, prompted by an August visit to Meudon by Doctor Victor Jacobson, the Paris representative of the Zionist Organization's European Executive,[64] also extolled Catholic collaboration with Zionists as an avenue for evangelization: "Given the great historical importance of the Zionist movement, due above all to the religious vocation of Israel . . . it seems desirable that Catholics, in their capacity as private persons, follow closely, and sympathetically, the efforts of the Zionists, and keep in contact with them, so as to allow for the possibility of Catholic penetration [*pénétration catholique*] among the newly reunited Jews, and in order to permit those among them whom grace attracts an easier return to the light of Christ."[65] Maritain addressed a preparatory note to Father Edouard Hugon, an intimate of Pius XI, as a preface to the proposal. Despite the reference to "Catholic penetration" in the larger document, Maritain's enthusiasm for Zionism appears more than tactical here: "There is in this a historical phenomenon of the highest significance, in which spiritual forces, an energy, perhaps even a heroism worthy of admiration, are being mobilized (for momentarily earthly and national purposes). Israel is coming back to life."[66]

One cannot conclude from Maritain's evident excitement over Zionism, as has one historian, that he simply "saw the good — even world-historical—Jew as the convert."[67] It should be noted that this restrictive and pejorative use of the word *good* would be essentially foreign to the Thomist, and it further bestows a coldness upon Maritain that contradicts his basic character and his specific relations with Jews, converts to Christianity or not. This simplification of Maritain's attitude toward Jews — equating missionary zeal on his part with a disrespect for Judaism or worse — ignores his close relationship with Jews such as Feinberg who gave him firsthand news of Zionist ventures in Palestine.

Renée Nehem-Bernheim stresses the consistent open warmth and occasional muted tensions inherent in such relations: "If Maritain's understanding of what he will call 'the mystery of Israel' came to him above all from his affection for Raïssa (an understanding in no way contradictory with his desire to convert Jews), his sympathy for the National Homeland, then for the State of Israel, these he certainly owed to Absalom. Even though Absalom and his aunt Sonia showed themselves impervious to any attempt at conversion, Maritain held for them a true tenderness."[68] In any case, after reading Maritain's supplication extolling Catholic support for Zionism, Pius demurred, inclining instead to "prudence" and "reserve."[69] Maritain thus found himself discouraged from further pursuing the Zionist "answer" to his Jewish Question in the immediate future. And as would prove the case with the impending Action Française crisis, Maritain reluctantly bowed to the Holy Father's will.

Bowing to the papal interdict of Maurras and his movement would prove far more painful than relinquishing immediate hopes for the Vatican's blessing, even a discreet one, of Jewish national statehood. The papal condemnation would embroil him in a bitter, protracted controversy. But even before the pontiff forced the issue at the end of 1926, Maritain questioned the degree to which Maurras' integral nationalism encroached upon Catholic universalism. His letters to Massis, as the latter worked on the book later published in Maritain's *Roseau d'Or* series as *Défense de l'Occident*, illustrate how, well in advance of the condemnation, he sought to warn his friend away from some of Maurras' fundamental theses. Maritain wrote, in October 1925, "If your Defense of the Christian West is confused with a defense of Latinity in a nationalist or racialist sense, in a strictly Maurrasian sense, then the whole undertaking will have been for nothing."[70] He would make this critique more explicit in March 1927 shortly after the papal ban took effect, taking a swipe at Maurrasian antisemitism and classicism, by invoking "Christ himself, Jewish and 'Oriental'" and concluding, "Our culture is Greco-Latin, but our religion is not."[71]

After a preparatory barrage begun by the French Cardinal Paulin Andrieu, Pius XI condemned several of Maurras' books and the *Action française* newspaper in December 1926, offering a counterthrust to the Action Française's political co-opting of French Catholics and forbidding the faithful to retain membership in the movement.[72] Maritain's book *Une Opinion sur Charles Maurras et le devoir des catholiques*, appearing the previous September, had tried to demonstrate the positive aspects of Maurras' fervent patriotism, love of order, and invocation of Catholicism as a force behind social cohesion, and Maritain urged his readers to consider "what writer during the war laid greater stress upon it than Maurras?"[73] But in the eyes of the Vatican, times had changed. In his recent study of Maritain's political thought, Guillaume de Thieulloy deems *Une Opinion* a "quite naïve brochure"[74] in any event made moot by the climactic papal blow and the *Action française*'s defiant "*Non possumus!*" banner headline of 24 December 1926.

On 11 January 1927, as the Action Française crisis entered its bitter final phase, Maritain concluded a letter to Maurras as follows:

> I am appealing to something more profound than your reason. No one knows if the faith is dead or simply sleeping in your soul. . . . In a human sense, you find yourself alone, tragically alone between God who is testing you and your followers who obey you. . . . Is it possible to serve the common good until the very

end . . . without also recognizing and serving . . . the Chief of the entire universe, who loves you and who created you? I think that is the big question before you. I too love your soul, and that is why I speak to you thus.[75]

Abandoning further attempts at mediation and mollification in the face of an *Action française* antipapal press barrage, Maritain undertook to offer a philosophical support for the condemnation, and in the process, save Thomism as a viable school of thought, vulnerable as it was to charges by fellow Catholic philosopher Maurice Blondel and others that in Maritain's hands nature and grace had become separated due to Maurrasian contamination.[76] Completed in May 1927 and published in July, *Le Primauté du Spirituel* (English translation, *The Things That Are Not Caesar's*)[77] asserted the imperative of spiritual authority making itself felt in the temporal realm in times of moral crisis, but drew as much on medieval precedents as it did on the particulars of the current crisis of the Action Française. The Pope wanted more from Maritain.

After two private audiences with Pius XI in September 1927, in which the pontiff disabused the philosopher of any further wishful thinking regarding Maurras,[78] Maritain led a group of clerics in drafting a more categorical rejection of Catholic collaboration with the Action Française and an explanation of "why Rome had spoken." Even if the papal audiences carried an aftertaste of correction, Maritain could count the commission as a publicly visible honor, for centuries had elapsed since the last time a layperson presided over the drafting of a major doctrinal statement on behalf of the Catholic Church.[79] Maritain introduced and contributed the final chapter of *Pourquoi Rome a parlé*, describing the innocent participation in the movement by Catholics in unmistakably autobiographical terms:

> They nevertheless lent their support to this movement, because they believed the dangers could be remedied, [they could] find a useful support in the zeal for the civic good and in the important partial truths that Maurras reestablished in their spirits, and they hoped that grace would one day transfigure this movement of thought by completing it and rectifying it in the light of faith. [But they were] ready to denounce, at the first word from their supreme leader, alone competent to appreciate the real gravity of the dangers in question, the alliance thus concluded by them for honest reasons. . . . Nothing was more loyal and more logical than such a disposition.[80]

The remainder of his intervention argued for the inherently non-political nature of the papal ban, while offering stinging inversions of the very core aspects of Maurras' self-fashioning. Maritain mocked "men of order" who "bring an anarchic agitation into the bosom of the Church of France," indeed calling this "the very height of liberalism"; he identified the Action Française leadership with the "prevaricating judges filled with a schismatic spirit" who condemned Joan of Arc (the icon of the Action Française); and finally, he cited the most dangerous Jew in all history to undercut the Action Française's claim on French Catholic consciences: "The 'Hebrew Christ,' the Word made flesh, reminds her [France] that He is her king, reminds her at the same time of what makes her strong, and of the demands of her vocation."[81] Maritain had burned his bridges; a further volume he wrote with the other contributors to *Pourquoi Rome a Parlé*, titled *Clairvoyance de Rome* (1929),[82] only finalized the separation after the fact.

Maritain's very public break with Maurras and championing of the papal condemnation earned him the enmity of erstwhile friends such as Massis and, at least for a time, the novelist Georges Bernanos, whose first novel *Sous le soleil de Satan* Maritain published in 1926 in the *Roseau d'Or* series.[83] In an April 1928 letter, Bernanos vilified Maritain as a hypocritical collaborator in cynical Vatican politics, whose arguments — "such bullshit!" — merited only "the enthusiastic cries of a tiny number of esthetes and epileptic Jews," and who stood guilty of leading his fellow Catholics spiritually astray: "You speak well, you speak too well, you speak like the friends of Job. . . . You have dishonored with useless palinodes the very idea of the humble submission of hearts."[84] Bernanos, a dissenter from the Vatican volte-face more than a defender of Maurras, almost gleefully infused such angry declamations with antisemitic slurs, an increasing tendency among Maritain's enemies.

In 1931, the same year Maritain oversaw the *Roseau d'Or* publication of the Egyptian-born Jewish Catholic convert Jean de Menasce's *Quand Israël aime Dieu*, Bernanos published a book that contained a paean to the foundational antisemite Drumont. Bernanos sneered at Maritain's objections to *La Grande Peur des bien-pensants*: "My dear friend, what a phobia of anti-Semitism! God knows after all the very small place I have given it in my book! But when you write that my book 'wounds Christ from the very beginning,' I find this a very human view, a truly Jewish view of the Mystery of the Incarnation. It is precisely for just such flesh and blood reasons that your friends ended up putting Christ on the cross."[85]

This sufferer from an antisemitism "phobia" would reconcile with Bernanos later in the decade, after an estrangement that apparently Massis did much behind the scenes to foment and Raïssa did much to heal.[86]

In the meantime, Maritain also contracted new alliances, such as that with spiritual revolutionary Emmanuel Mounier, perhaps the best-known representative of a new generation of *nonconformiste* intellectuals, whom he first welcomed to Meudon in 1928, and who founded the personalist journal *Esprit* in 1932 with Maritain's support.[87] He also further solidified his reputation as a Catholic philosopher. The early 1930s saw the completion of what has been cited as Maritain's quintessential exposition of Thomism, *Les Degrés du savoir* (*The Degrees of Knowledge*, 1932),[88] as well as the polarization of European politics against the backdrop of the Great Depression, the 1933 Nazi seizure of power, and France's own 6 February 1934 antiparliamentary riots, in which the Ligue d'Action Française figured prominently.

Maritain led a group of five Catholic intellectuals in drafting the 19 April anti-fascist manifesto *Pour le bien commun* (*For the Common Good*).[89] For Maritain and his friends, and the fifty-two signatories, a sterile separation between the temporal and spiritual violated the vocation of Christians in the earthly city:

> Neither a sulky nor fearful prudence nor a lax and opportunistic one has anything to do with Christian prudence. The Jewish people did not understand the depth of what was demanded of them at the moment when Christ brought them a *new* Testament which was to fulfill and not abolish the old Law. With all due proportion kept, a similar demand is made of men at each visitation of God in their history. The promises made to the Church, and which concern the spiritual and supernatural order, do not dispense its children from vigilance in the temporal order. . . . We have done with the separations and the exclusionism of the preceding age. Religion and politics, while remaining distinct, must be vitally united.[90]

Other manifestos necessarily would follow, but on the moral-political dimensions of the burgeoning European crisis, not on a historic Jewish obliviousness to the significance of the Christian message. Nonetheless, maintaining "all due proportion" when writing about the Jews continued to present a challenge for Maritain.[91]

Impossible Antisemitism

Maritain wrote his second essay on the Jewish Question, "*L'impossible an-tisémitisme,*" for Daniel-Rops's edited collection *Les Juifs*, published in 1937.[92] An earlier sketch of this essay appeared in 1936 in the German Catholic publication *Die Erfüllung* and also drew on his lectures in Buenos Aires in October of that year. His presentation "*Science et Sagesse*" ("Science and Wisdom") at the *Sociedad Hebraica Argentina* provoked an antisemitic backlash in parts of the Argentine press, to the extent that Maritain felt compelled to respond when, six days later, he lectured on Léon Bloy at the *Cursos de Cultura Católica*:

> Because I am speaking about Le Salut par les Juifs . . . I will take advantage of the occasion to clarify in a few words my position as regards antisemitism. I do not make it a habit to respond to newspapers, and moreover, I take no responsibility for either the criticisms or adulation they would like to direct toward me. . . . An elementary sense of courtesy prevents me, moreover, from saying what I think, myself, a foreigner, of such and such of your country's periodicals, even certain ones which, claiming to be Catholic, by their blindly violent spirit, do more harm to Catholicism than many of the anticlerical journals. . . . I must say that one is mistaken if one confuses moderation on my part with weakness, for I have never given ground either before calumnies or bad faith.[93]

Maritain's consciousness of taking what he saw as a truly Catholic position against antisemitism, but one that stood in conflict with that of many of his fellow Catholics, could only have been increased by reading some of the other essays in *Les Juifs*. Maritain differed with the most renowned of his fellow contributors, Paul Claudel, on whether Jewish involvement in modern unrest stemmed from their divine vocation (Claudel did not think so).[94] A more serious difference, however, arose between Maritain and his friend René Schwob, a Jewish convert to Catholicism. Maritain could not accept, or at this point could no longer accept, Father Schwob's equivocal hope "for France to defend itself against the Jewish venom, but by means other than Hitlerian demagoguery."[95]

Maritain's own contribution, "*L'impossible antisémitisme,*" demonstrated the distance traveled since 1921 and "*À propos de la question juive.*" Its author now stressed the inanity of approaching the question racially or nationally, arguing instead that "Race, People, Tribe, all these words used to describe them must be sacralized."[96] Sacralization entails mystery. Holding to Paul's teaching that the mystery of Israel can only be resolved eschatologically, he averred that "what is called the *Jewish problem* is a problem *without a solution*." One must acknowledge this temporal insolubility of such a problem, the German case proving for example the folly of placing one's faith in assimilation.[97] Continued attempts at worldly solutions could only lead to a "carnal war directed at the extermination, the deportation, or the enslavement of the Jews, a war of the world and the *animalis homo* against Israel."[98] Only a *"pluralist and personalist"* willingness to accept Jewish distinctiveness in the framework of a common humanity, the "opposite of the absurd Hitlerian medievalist parody," stood a chance of preventing ongoing tragedy from devolving into total disaster.[99]

Yet as much as Maritain deplored this "tragic" predicament of European and world Jewry, seeing in it "the tragedy of humanity itself . . . of man in his fight with the world and the world in its fight against God," he still could not separate it from the age-old sin of the fathers, "priests of Israel, bad keepers of the vineyard, killers of the prophets, who for good reasons of political prudence had opted for the world, and to that choice all the people are henceforth bound — until they change of their own accord."[100] Maritain offered the mystery of a chosen people bound to a fatal choice: "The Jews chose the world; they have loved it; their suffering comes from having been held by their choice. They are prisoners and victims of this world that they love, and of which they are not, will never be, cannot be."[101]

Here Maritain does not relinquish his old view that Jews have a mission to disturb the world; he sanctifies it. One recent study looks back on Maritain's first essay on the Jewish Question and asserts that its author would never disavow nor take up again this early "critique of revolutionary messianism," a *"hapax* [an isolated utterance] within his *oeuvre*," even though he would "ceaselessly meditate on the mystery of Israel."[102] Yet this scholarly assessment confuses the point that he subsequently offered a transcendent update of Jewish "revolutionary messianism," renegotiating a series of anti-Jewish stereotypes even as he repudiated antisemitism itself. Where, in the 1920s, Maritain could see the archetypical insider Jew behind modernity's ills, he now emphasized how Jews were rejected and persecuted in the modern world, for it is "the vocation of Israel that the world loathes."[103] Perhaps most importantly (and here one can identify a resounding refutation of at least one part of his 1921 position), he now saw it as logically impossible to be an antisemite and a Christian, for it is only "in obeying the spirit of the world, not the spirit of Christianity that Christians can be antisemites." The Christian antisemite betrays Christianity itself, not just in theory, but in practice, for in "demeaning the race from which God and the Immaculate Mother of God came forth . . . the bitter zeal of the antisemite always finally turns into a bitter zeal against Christianity itself."[104]

Maritain's theology largely remained consistent, but its application reflected a growing emphasis on Christian personalism and democratic pluralism and a degree of empirical perspective not typically associated with the modern revival of medieval Thomism. One of his most influential books, *L'Humanisme intégral* (*Integral Humanism*, 1936), evoked the hope of a new Christendom, animated by a humanism that "does not worship man but really and effectively respects human dignity and does justice to the integral demands of the person."[105] Such a "heroic humanism" would have to overcome "the extreme partisans of racism in Germany, those who wish to return to a national and racial (Nordic) religion anterior to Christianity," as well as a Soviet communism that unconsciously aped the Christian mission to redeem a fallen world.[106] Both ideological extremes could be seen as variants of the same antihuman totalitarianism resulting from a centuries-long "dialectic of anthropocentric humanism" — the materialization of man that also characterized a selfish "bourgeois" humanism. Maritain concludes, "Let things continue this way and it seems that earth will no longer be habitable, to use a phrase of the venerable Aristotle, except by beasts or gods."[107]

Maritain's predicating of this new humanism on "the preliminary liquidation of modern capitalism and of the regime of money-profit,"[108] along with his condemnation of the atrocities of Franco's "crusade" in Spain after 1936, led a number of Catholic critics on the right to call him a "Marxist Christian" tainted by his association with Jews, or in the revived terminology of the postwar period, Judeo-Bolshevism. Most notably, Maritain became embroiled in a very public quarrel with Claudel in the latter half of the 1930s, but such political tensions also managed to disturb the monthly Thomistic Study Circles and annual retreats convened by the Maritains since the early 1920s at their Meudon home. The 1937 retreat would prove to be the last one, and on 24 September, Jacques confided the following to his notebook concerning the longtime spiritual director at Meudon, Father Reginald Garrigou-Lagrange:

Father is very worked-up against me; goes so far as to reproach me, a convert, with wanting to give lessons in the Christian spirit to "us who have been Catholic for three hundred years." (And why not since the Crusades? He forgets that he also was a convert, through the reading of Ernest Hello.) It seems that Raïssa and Véra are being implicated as dragging me along by their influence. (Russian Jewesses, are they not? They who detest these political quarrels, and who would have been so glad if I could have remained isolated from them, if I had not seen there a testimony to be rendered to truth.) This puts me in a black rage, which I do not hide. The retreat begins under a very bad sign. Father Garrigou would like to prohibit me from speaking on the philosophy of history, and from judging events, and from acting on young people in these matters. He is not the only one in Rome to think like this, I know very well, and to be terrified of the "political Maritain." Metaphysics only! But he himself does not hesitate to pronounce in favor of Franco and to approve the civil war in Spain.[109]

Lest this might seem like oversensitivity on Maritain's part, it should be noted that Franco's Interior Minister — and son-in-law — Ramón Serrano Súñer would the following summer devote one of his radio broadcasts to excoriating "this converted Jew who spreads throughout the world the fable of Franco's massacres and the immense silliness of the legitimacy of the Barcelona government."[110] The Nationalists had from the beginning of the civil war justified their anti-Republican cause as a crusade against "Jewish-Masonic-Bolshevism."[111] Maritain's July 1937 article "*De la guerre sainte*," ("On the Holy War") published in *La Nouvelle revue française*,[112] had questioned that claim and thus rendered him an agent of that internationalist conglomerate enemy that ranged itself against "Christian and Catholic" Spain.

Novelist François Mauriac took up the defense of Maritain in *Figaro,* writing less a refutation of Súñer's raving than a warm tribute to both Maritains:

Jacques Maritain is not a "converted Jew" as the Minister of Salamanca assures us. If he were, he would not seem to me less worthy of being admired and loved, but after all he isn't. We believe, however, that she to whom God has joined him, has certainly helped him become the exemplary Christian who, like his Master, makes no distinction of persons, but venerates in each single person a redeemed soul, and on the faces of all races, rec-

ognizes the features of the same Father. . . . Jacques Maritain, in
taking his stand, with all the power of his logic and all the fire
of his charity, against the pretention of the Spanish Generals to
be waging a holy war, has rendered to the Catholic Church a
service whose importance is measured by the fury it un-
leashes.[113]

Maritain would wait until February of 1939, the year general war erupted,
to more pointedly reply, in an interview published in the American Catholic
periodical *Commonweal*, that although he was indeed a convert, "Alas no,
I am not a Jew. I regret that, because it is a great privilege to be of the race
of Jesus Christ and the Blessed Virgin."[114]

Toward the end of the 1930s, however, this "great privilege" entailed more than just a pride in pedigree, as Maritain knew full well. He
associated the looming specter of another European war with what he already feared would amount to a "passion of Israel" driven by race hatred.[115]
Accordingly, he saw it as imperative that Christians oppose the subjection
of the human person to racial categorization, drawing on both recent
Church teachings and his collaboration with other Catholic opponents of
racism. Writing in the American Jesuit John LaFarge's *Interracial Review*
in May 1937, Maritain insisted that "racialism to an unimaginable degree
degrades and humiliates reason, thought, science, and art, which are henceforth made subservient to flesh and blood and are stripped of their natural
'catholicity.'" Both Maritain and LaFarge, the latter an outspoken opponent
of racism in his native United States and the future editor of the major
Catholic magazine *America*, could cite a papal lead in this regard. The 31
December 1930 papal encyclical *Casti Connubii* had, in upholding the
sanctity of the marital bond, condemned the kind of anti-miscegenation
legislation found in numerous American states and which would be replicated in Nazi Germany in the mid 1930s.[116]

In a personal letter, LaFarge responded to Maritain that inculcating
"the principles of justice toward people of other races" depended vitally
upon fostering "a new mentality truly supernatural, in the light of the
catholicity of the universal Church."[117] But how to witness to this "new
mentality," already expounded upon by Maritain in *Integral Humanism*,
and broached by LaFarge the following year in his work on a never-to-be-
promulgated encyclical commissioned by Pius XI as a denunciation of
racist antisemitism?[118] After the pope died in February 1939, a passing
which caused Maritain a great deal of "sadness and anguish,"[119] his suc-
cessor indefinitely shelved the letter. *Humani Generis Unitas* thus lan-

guished in the subsequent pontificate of Pius XII. If it had been made public, the "Hidden Encyclical" no doubt would have "antagonized the Nazi regime"[120] as one historian points out. But it also would have replicated some of the same harsh language about Jews seen in Maritain's "Impossible Antisemitism," describing them as "this unhappy people, destroyers of their own nation, whose misguided leaders had called down upon their own heads a Divine malediction, doomed as it were, to perpetually wander over the face of the earth . . . nonetheless never allowed to perish."[121] In the years of atrocity soon to follow, this longstanding Christian teaching of a Jewish people "never allowed to perish" suddenly would be put into question.

CONCLUSION

Restoring the constant of a spiritual supernaturalism in Maritain's Jewish Question complicates an otherwise simple and direct causal linkage between his developing philosemitism and his changing politics. But it reveals much more than a Whig-historical "early Maritain"/"later Maritain" schema. A primarily theological framing of the Jewish Question, asserting a reality above and beyond the political, had always allowed Maritain to maintain a measurable, albeit philosophically fluctuating, distance from the antisemitism that formed a tangible component of Maurrasian integral nationalism.

One cannot tell whether his discomfort — accentuated by his love for Raïssa — with overtly antisemitic outbursts such as those emitted by the *Camelots du Roi* would have eventually led him to break with the Action Française, which subsequently became known as much for its quaint monarchism as its radical potential. Indeed, by the mid 1930s, a number of individuals such as the rising fascist writer Robert Brasillach would distance themselves from Maurras for not being *enough* of a right-wing extremist.[122] As it happened, in the 1920s Maritain resisted breaking with Maurras until Pope Pius XI effectively ordered him to do so, until he appreciated the potential discrediting of Thomism due to its association with the extreme right, and until he embraced a clarified vocation of admonishing a new generation of Catholic intellectuals to place their faith above all other considerations.

Yet this very "primacy of the spiritual" also made almost intractable some of the anti-Jewish stereotypes he held, that is, until the practical consequences of fascism and antisemitism in the 1930s forced him to try to reconcile his theological presuppositions with his burgeoning personalist and pluralist social and political philosophy. As a result, Maritain's ambivalent philosemitism, characterized by a preoccupation with the mystery of Israel and influenced by his ambiguous engagement with modernity, would remain a work in progress through the 1930s as well as into the Second World War and the Holocaust. Given his acknowledged influence on a "generation of Catholic intellectuals," what can be said of Maritain might prompt further inquiry into how French Catholics (and Catholics in general) dealt with the antisemitic temptation of their time, which like other temptations could present itself in changing forms — according to circumstance, if not opportunity.[123]

The Action Française crisis and subsequent estrangement notwithstanding, Maritain's relationship with Maurras had not completely ended with the controversies of the interwar era. After the 1940 fall of France to the *Wehrmacht*, the latter personage found himself invoked as the intellectual godfather of Vichy France. That authoritarian regime invoked a series of anti-Jewish laws that served as prelude, however unintentionally, to state cooperation with the Nazi Final Solution, and Maritain condemned that regime and its policies from exile in America.

Condemned to national degradation and life imprisonment after the Liberation in 1945, Maurras famously exclaimed, "This is the revenge of Dreyfus!" But we should not count these as his last words. Before expiring in 1952, the erstwhile *académicien* augmented his lonely narrative of betrayal and vengeance, concluding his last book, a posthumously published tribute to Pope Pius X, with a four-page profession of his hatred for Jacques Maritain. He painted the picture of a consummate opportunist, "an excellent professor of philosophy lacking the talent to be a philosopher himself," who had dropped Maurras for "two new masters of sacred sociology," the Abbé Gregoire and Harriet Beecher Stowe, receiving from them "the revelation of the Rights of Man and *Uncle Tom's Cabin*." Guilty of simony "in character and vocation," he could now enjoy a carefree life, this "happy husband of the Jewess." For Maritain, these words "literally struck me in the heart (my heart attack, in March 1954)."[124]

But Maritain had already survived Maurras. Both the scholarly Catholic philosemite on the one hand, and the most violently antisemitic French fascists on the other, had long since left the *vieux maître* behind. They, and the prejudice known as antisemitism, had by the end of the 1930s moved on to a new future.[125] In the 1920s, Maritain became embedded in an emergently antisemitic milieu nurtured by a widespread fear of Judeo-

Bolshevism and a distrust of liberal democracy. His significance for the history of antisemitism in modern France lies in how he divested himself of these tendencies as a violently racist prejudice against Jews took hold in interwar Europe. But just as a Catholic rejection of racism — as well as an empirical appreciation of incipient antisemitic violence — helped support this divestment, a fidelity to basic theological presuppositions bonded his philosemitism in fundamentally anti-Judaic stereotypes. Accordingly, Maritain's Jewish Question by no means resolved itself before 1939–1945, when the systematic murder of six million Jewish men, women, and children reframed the question yet again, this time from interwar anxiety to wartime horror.

CHAPTER TWO

THE EVIL FIRE THAT CONSUMES PEOPLES:
APOCALYPTIC ANTISEMITISM, 1938–1941

> In order to fan the evil fire that consumes peoples, there are, in the Europe of today, those who want extermination and death, and first and foremost the extermination of the Jews—because, after all, that is really what it comes down to does it not?—and who, under the idiotic apparatus of scientific racism and forged documents, conceal from others, and perhaps themselves, the insane hope for a general massacre of the race of Moses and Jesus.

> *Jacques Maritain, February 1938*

By the late 1930s, Maritain foresaw the unleashing of a war of extermination against European Jewry within a looming general conflict. He had written already in 1937 of the impossibility of antisemitism within the Christian conscience. Now, in the February 1938 public lecture quoted above, he offered a dire appraisal of the anti-Jewish hatred growing in power and murderous potential across Europe. If at an earlier stage in his life, he could take a somewhat dispassionate stance on the Jewish Question, Maritain now had committed himself to combating antisemitism, a commitment that established his permanent reputation as a Catholic philosemite. But even though a later era would witness an almost unanimously positive assessment of Maritain's philosemitism, in the late 1930s his public engagement on behalf of Europe's beleaguered Jews embroiled him in continued controversies which also affected his Jewish-born wife, Raïssa. In September 1939, war erupted as Germany invaded Poland, setting into motion a series of Nazi victories that confirmed Maritain's prewar lament at the "twilight of civilization."[1] The June 1940 fall of France, viewed from America, struck Maritain as ushering in an apocalyptic end of an age, characterized by the "liquidation of a world"[2] and a descent into darkness that imperiled Jews more than any other people.

Maritain's views on Jews and Judaism had continued to evolve as dire prewar prognostications materialized into escalating horrors. He became increasingly conscious of language shaping reality, having watched as reflexive words about Jews and Judaism influenced anti-Jewish actions throughout Europe. His own choice of words in turn became more critical, as his primarily theological framing of the Jewish-Question-as-Mystery-of-Israel elicited praise from Jews and Gentiles alike, but also drew criticism from other readers who saw his views as too pro-Jewish or even, conversely, ultimately anti-Jewish. In a world in which answers to the Jewish Question now took on a life-or-death importance, Maritain's eschatological response correlated with his assessment of the war as an essentially apocalyptic conflict. Within the apparently senseless destruction, he perceived an apocalyptic hope embracing both Christians and Jews.

Facing an increasingly post-Christian society and culture had allowed Maritain by now to disentangle Christianity from Christendom. Many years later, the American scholar of antisemitism Franklin Littell would encapsulate the countercultural import of this kind of post-Christendom Christian acknowledgment of Jewish identity:

> What is it if not presumption for us to assume that "the Jews," called by God to be carriers of history, would desire to blend into the Gentile world? Here again the modern humanitarian line of thought is deceptive. For a Christian to pursue such doctrine is not only unjust to the Jewish people; it also reveals a fundamental flaw in the doctrine of the church, for the church — where it in truth exists — is also called to be a counterculture. *Gleichschaltung* (homogenization) should be as repugnant to believing Christians as it is to practicing Jews. If our modern, enlightened "Christians" were more certain of their own calling, they would have less difficulty in comprehending God's call to the Jewish people.[3]

As will be seen in this chapter, Maritain could anticipate this kind of post-Holocaust, if not post-Vatican II thinking, not only because of a change in his appreciation of Judaism, but also because he feared the possibility of Christianity being forced back into "the catacombs."[4] This countercultural turn in a time of crisis and collapse opened his thinking to a common Jewish-Christian destiny to a degree unthinkable a decade or two earlier.

Hitler's war, in its military, political, humanitarian, and spiritual dimensions, understandably overshadowed all else for the scholar Maritain. Even as he contemplated anew the relationship between Jews and Christians in the economy of salvation, his immediate attention remained fixed on his native land defeated and debased under the military jackboot of the Nazis and the collaborationist aegis of the Vichy regime. During the war, Maritain sought from his American exile to foster hope in his countrymen as well as himself, offering his Thomistic prognosis of Nazi Machiavellianism's inevitable self-destruction. The Third Reich could in the meantime perpetrate unprecedented horrors, however, and news of such atrocities coincided with Maritain's hopeful reading of Saint Paul's eschatological promise that "all Israel shall be saved."

Maritain's resolve to fight what he saw as the Pagan Empire vied with the temptation of despair throughout the war years. He drew on the Christian virtue of hope for sustenance during this period, both in response to the submergence of France under the swastika and the growing evidence of the Nazi slaughter of countless innocents. That the Third Reich's war against the Jews took shape with French complicity only deepened his anguish and heightened his anger as he sought to understand and influence what was happening in his war-torn world. To his mind, grounded in metaphysics and oriented toward the sacred, even the most senseless of wars had to have a meaning, promising somehow a renewal of creation. "However terrible may be the ordeal," Maritain wrote at the beginning of the war, "it will not be a tragedy but a sacrifice. And the end of a tragedy is death; but the end of a sacrifice is salvation and resurrection."[5] This refusal of tragedy, and insistence upon the ultimate goodness of sacrifice, salvation, and resurrection, conditioned his response to a war that gave every indication of containing at its destructive heart what Maritain already described as the "passion of Israel."

COMBATING ANTISEMITISM

In *Integral Humanism* and other writings from the middle of the 1930s, Maritain had formulated a pluralist and personalist Christian response to what he saw as the breakdown of modern civilization. But the crisis of the late 1930s, including the rise of violent racial antisemitism, demanded more than simply waiting for a thoroughgoing transformation of modern western culture and the coming of a New Christendom. Maritain believed that the widespread hatred of Jews must be arrested before it could be allowed to lead to fratricidal war and mass murder. The agitation of the Jew-baiters needed a rebuttal. His 5 February 1938 public lecture at Paris's *Théâtre des Ambassadeurs*, "*Les Juifs parmi les nations*" (The Jews among the Nations), dealt with "this immense and sorrowful subject" of the "tragedy presently suffered by the Jews in some regions of Europe."[6] Maritain asked his listeners to reflect on the likely outcome of the antisemitic fervor gaining momentum in various parts of the continent, namely "the extermination of the Jews . . . a general massacre of the race of Moses and Jesus."[7]

Maritain's survey of antisemitism across Europe began with East Central European countries such as Poland in which significantly large and relatively unassimilated Jewish minorities often maintained distinctive traditions, schools, and the use of Yiddish over the majority language, and where the popular mind also associated them with an artisan or mercantile class in an overwhelmingly peasant population. Traditional resentments, aggravated by recent patterns of immigration across post-war borders and the economic stress of the Great Depression, fostered tensions that went beyond the scope of those typically associated with ethnic and religious minority relations in the region. The irresponsibility of political leaders helped make pressing social and economic issues into insoluble racial issues, fostering a political antisemitism in which passions replaced reason, mutual suspicions became mutually reinforcing, illusory solutions such as laws of exception and other discriminatory measures appeared, and these same politicians only revealed their weakness in the face of the persistence of a so-called Jewish problem.[8]

The increased tension and inevitable frustration, in turn, spawned a racial antisemitism targeting not only recent Jewish immigrants but also more assimilated, in some cases even baptized, Jews. "Lucrative professions" henceforth would be closed to the Jews, whose supposed collective ethos, pecuniary and predatory, marked them as antithetical to the more "disinterested, spiritual, and occidental" values of their Gentile neighbors, the latter alone truly belonging to western civilization. The inevitable conclusion found *any* number of Jews in a given country intolerably excessive: "Everywhere where there are Jews, there will be found to be too many of them. In reality what is denied them is quite simply the right to live."[9]

One could always support economic charges of Jewish usury and speculation with a few lurid examples, Maritain conceded, but generalizing thus about "seventeen million" Jewish people seemed "not very reasonable."[10] Societies should of course defend themselves against swindlers and exploiters, through "draconian legislation" if need be, but these kinds of laws should pertain to all individuals, not just Jews, for such crimes would still be committed by Gentiles, "even if all the Jews were exterminated."[11] As for identifying Jews with cultural decadence and the sowing of societal discord through lies and propaganda, Maritain marveled at how many non-Jews could fit this description, for "Streicher and his associates are not Jews, nor are Rosenberg, Goga and Cuza,[12] Lenin and Stalin," or even France's own preeminent sower of deranged and hateful falsehoods: "M. Céline is not himself Jewish, even though it appears that he only journeyed to the end of the night to find there waiting for him the *Protocols of the Elders of Zion*, left in the filthy shadows by the former Tsarist police." But rational consistency should not be expected of "such powerful brains" as the antisemites of the day, who simultaneously attributed to the eternal Jew both an "anarchic fever of liberty" and a predilection for "communist conformism."[13]

Finally, returning to the predominant identification of Jews with Mammon, Maritain lamented how Jews and Gentiles alike found themselves adversely affected by the same structural problems within capitalism, though antisemitism only obscured this fact, with tragic consequences: "Antisemitism distracts men from the real causes of their ills by inciting them against other men and against an innocent multitude, such a miserable crew who, rather than fighting against the tempest, would prefer to throw overboard some of their companions while waiting to slit each others throats and set fire to the boat on which a dreaming humanity has embarked."[14] For Maritain, Germany epitomized what he saw as the essential madness of antisemitism, as Nazi racism originated without having to draw upon the preliminary social and economic grievances seen in the peasant countries of East Central Europe. But the supposedly more advanced Germans could only be described as a "pathetic and unhappy people" seeking unanimity within its national self by attacking Jews and Christians alike.[15] This scathing indictment of a nation echoed Maritain's anti-German excursions of the two preceding decades, and even touched upon German Jews, directing an unmistakable annoyance at their undying love for a Fatherland that had all but disowned them.

In fact, Maritain's philosemitic indictment of German Jewry reiterated his past criticism of "carnal Jews," but now held them up to what he saw as a Jewish rather than explicitly Christian standard:

> I do not reproach German Jews for not, as certain of them have done in difficult times, having made the best of Nazi persecution by converting to Christianity. I am stating that they have not imitated their ancestors from the times of the prophets, not having understood the cry of their own sufferings to turn to *their God*, and not having remembered *their sources*, which lie in Abraham,

> Isaac, and Jacob. To the terrible scourge that has fallen upon the
> Jews, it does not appear that among them they have formulated
> any response, be it inside or outside of Germany, other than le-
> gitimate complaints and a justified indignation, accompanied by
> calls for an American boycott of German goods and appeals in
> international humanitarian literature. . . . Is it that Israel, aston-
> ished and paralyzed by its own rationalism, no longer knows or
> no longer dares to place its confidence in this force?[16]

Neglecting the strength to be found in their spiritual heritage, these German
Jews therefore had played a part, albeit a secondary, passive one, in the
tragedy of an apostate German nation's descent into paganism. Regarding
the German nation as a whole, Maritain added sarcastically that he hoped
he had not inadvertently insulted the pagans of the classical age, "who
never succumbed to such a brutal materialism."[17]

Maritain's diagnosis of Nazi German racism as essentially pagan
and brutally materialistic transposed a temporal problem to the spiritual
plane, and underlined the antithetical, indeed antagonistic, relationship between antisemitic prejudice and Christian faith. Accordingly, he revisited
and summarized the theological implications of the Diaspora addressed a
year earlier in "L'impossible antisémitisme."[18] Most importantly for a lecture audience that had just been treated to a somewhat confrontational exposition of current antisemitic manifestations in Europe, antisemitism itself
had to be recognized not as an understandable if not justifiable reaction to
a contemporary Jewish problem, but as the modern neo-pagan hatred of Israel's ageless vocation. At a time when the Third Reich's race theorists bi-
ologized the Jewish Question and Nazi theologians extolled a "Positive
Christianity" purged of its Jewish elements, Maritain spoke of a "mystery
of the sacred order," its "principal elements" provided by Saint Paul, which
pointed to Christianity itself as "the expansive plenitude and supernatural
accomplishment of Judaism."[19]

This consciously reverent statement by Maritain testifies to a continuing ambivalence regarding Jewish identity, in that it also implied the
fulfillment of Judaism by Christianity. But this latter consideration stands
out in sharper relief now than it would have at the time. What matters more
in a historical sense is that these words also marked a lasting change in a
thinker who had permanently rejected any articulation of a "Jewish problem," resolving instead to honor Jewish difference as something essentially
"of the sacred order." Maritain had already argued for Jewish-Gentile com-
petition in the temporal realm as healthier for a given country than laws of

exclusion: "Thus, emulation between Jews and non-Jews should provoke an elevation of the cultural level, whereas recourse to the brutal practice of the *numerus clausus* (if not to a *numerus nullus*), as humiliating to non-Jews as Jews, tends in and of itself to lower this level."[20]

Maritain argued something analogous from a spiritual perspective, to the extent that he extolled a creative tension between spiritual brethren:

> It is an illusion to think that this tension can completely disappear; it is a villainy — one of the natural villainies of animalized man . . . and from which Christianity alone can, when it is truly lived, deliver peoples from wishing to finish with the question through antisemitic violence, be it overtly persecutory or politically mitigated. The only way is to accept this state of tension, and to face up to it, in every particular circumstance, not hatefully, but in the concrete intelligence that love demands of each of us that we quickly come to an accord with an adversary, finding common ground, and being conscious that "all have sinned and have need of the glory of God," *omnes quidem peccaverunt, et egent gloria Dei.* "The history of the Jews," Léon Bloy said, "blocks the history of all humanity as a dam blocks a river, to raise its level."[21]

In short, only a pluralist and personalist attitude toward the Jewish Other could help the Christian avoid betraying his own — and at this time equally imperiled — faith.

Jews and Christians alike could see their spiritual heritages endangered in the two major countries where antisemitism manifested itself most clearly as state policy. The Soviet Union and Nazi Germany constituted ideologically different manifestations of a war against the Jews. But, for Maritain, each pursued antisemitic policies that logically stemmed from a statist pseudo-religion. The Soviet state had officially outlawed antisemitism as a reactionary prejudice, but increasingly rendered Jewish life untenable through economic dispossession and sanctions against the Jewish religion. Nazi racial laws and the closing of professions had likewise removed Jews from the Aryan German family and fostered growing impoverishment.[22] However much Maritain thought that Soviet communism stemmed from a perverted but reformable impulse, he could hardly restrain himself from detesting a German cult of race and blood that to his mind constituted a contagion for other European nations and the United States. His indictment of Nazi Germany as the epicenter of antisemitism showed

a certain straining of Christian charity, as he made a point of publicly re-
minding himself that the German people should not be viewed as entirely
irredeemable:

> I know that Germany is not racism. Even though this "goes with-
> out saying," I have to point out that hatred for a people would
> be a great madness, and despite the racism and anti-Christianity
> that ravage their hearts, the humane reserves of Germanic cul-
> ture are not exhausted. But if the moral cataclysms that sweep
> over a country cannot impede those who hope to thereby secure
> world peace by desiring international accords, then the same de-
> sires in turn cannot prevent the truth from being told. The ex-
> ample of German antisemitism, which the National Socialist
> leaders have aroused and continue to violently overexcite, and
> which simultaneously they try to some extent to *regularize*, all
> the while making of it a preferred weapon of foreign influence,
> the example of this antisemitism and its propaganda, which is
> being furthered everywhere, in America as in Europe, does not
> bode well for what is left of civilization.[23]

This is not to say that Germany had to export antisemitism itself, of which
virtually every western country had its own supply.

Among smaller countries, the cases of Romania and Poland
showed the complicity of political and religious figures in socially and economically based antisemitism. Romania's post-1918 expansion, mainly at
Hungary's expense, had led to a population increase including many Jews,
but political leaders, with the collaboration of the Orthodox Church, had
encouraged inflating the claims of "illegal" Jewish immigrants in an atmosphere of political discontent. Prime Minister Octavian Goga of the National Christian Party, supported by the fascist Iron Guard, had persuaded
King Carol II just two weeks earlier (21 January) to sign a decree "review-
ing" the citizenship of Romania's Jews.[24]

In Catholic Poland, antisemitism drew on traditional prejudices,
aggravated by peasant resentment and insecurity. While antagonism toward
Jews drew on grassroots agitation rather than legislative cues, popular boy-
cotts had been followed by universities segregating students. The Catholic
press had often been complicit in this escalation of antisemitism,[25] with
government indifference in turn violating international treaty obligations
regarding the protection of minorities. Even the least hostile element of the
Polish population played its part: "Without professing antisemitism, [the
bystander] considers the drama of the Jews with the indifference of the *rea-*

sonable and cold man who passes on his way . . . this wounded Jew stretched out half-dead on the road from Jerusalem to Jericho."[26] Maritain wondered thus, both about Poland and his own France, where the Good Samaritan might come from.

Romania and Poland's less extreme, more piecemeal patterns of oppressing their Jewish minorities differed from the Russian and German programs, but Maritain thought that all were equally doomed to failure as putative solutions to what most people mistakenly saw as a temporal problem. The very completeness of such "solutions" promised nothing save tragedy. Encouraging emigration ran up against the difficulty of closed frontiers and the poverty of the emigrants, even if some overseas territories, such as Madagascar, could benefit from European immigrants. Maritain conceded for the sake of argument that such emigration might be worth the effort if it actually promised to defuse antisemitism. But realistically speaking, the trickle of voluntary emigrants would be replaced by normal population growth, and forced emigration would amount to death by starvation for countless refugees.[27] For such refugees could hardly expect to have their rights protected by a now powerless League of Nations. And an insistence on tolerance, given current political rhetoric and economic difficulties, promised at best only an illusory respite from the rising hatred of the Jewish people. What then, could mitigate this antisemitic fervor? Maritain offered an evangelistic answer, insisting that only true Christian love and a rethinking of the temporal corruptions of Christian ideals could prevent the extermination of the Jews and secure "a bit of peace for the world."[28]

Not everyone in the audience took to heart Maritain's concluding exhortation that "a lot of love, the spirit of justice, and charity" would be needed to "purify the atmosphere" and forestall looming mass murder.[29] Some listeners doubtless found his application of Christian love as mistaken as his respect for the Jewish faith. Several agitators in the hall tried to shout the speaker down, booing and assaulting him with cries of "bought by the Jews" and "a Jew himself." The president of the Paris municipal council dealt with such unrest by judging it best that Maritain not give a second public lecture on this subject.[30] Maritain already had drawn fire from the right for his anti-fascism and his refusal to endorse Franco's "crusade" in Spain, and subsequently had become embroiled in a very public quarrel with poet and playwright Paul Claudel — a devout Catholic and supporter of Franco — over the question of a proper Christian response to social and economic inequality.[31] Now this "Marxist Christian" found himself characterized as a race traitor to boot.

Lucien Rebatet, writing in the consistently vicious pro-Nazi weekly *Je Suis Partout* on 1 April 1938, offered his diagnosis of Maritain, the lover of the Jews: "This is where these peculiar Catholics like M. Maritain become most dangerous. The Jew is off-limits for them on account of his 'spiritual mission.' They tend to take the Jew for a refractory witness, but an unimpeachable witness of their religious ideal just the same." But even ordinary "obtuse Aryans" like Rebatet could look right through this "frenetic spiritualism" to detect its more vulgar and banal source, at least in Maritain's case: "M. Maritain is married to a Jewess. He has Jew-ified his life, and his doctrine, his theology, are falsified like the passport of a Jewish spy. M. Maritain represents, body and soul, what the Germans so aptly call a '*Rassenschander*,' a polluter of the race."[32]

For her part, Raïssa found it "impossible to accept the insult that is directed at my blood. That is intolerable. Whatever race one comes from, an injury directed at blood is made to God Himself, the author of life. It is intolerable that the name 'Christian' is usurped by those indulging in such offenses." In a letter written a week after Rebatet's attack, to friends Pierre and Christine Van der Meer de Walcheren, she wondered if she and Jacques would ultimately "die in exile." And should that be the case, she thought the number of "true friends" they would leave behind "would not reach ten."[33] While her husband expected such attacks, even if he did not laugh them off, he expressed an open consternation at another rebuke, this one leveled at him by an icon of the literary left: "If the stupid insults of certain antisemitic sheets leave me indifferent, I at least would prefer that my thought not be misunderstood in a revue such as the *NRF*."[34]

Writing in the *Nouvelle revue française*, one of France's most eminent authors, André Gide, had chided Maritain for allegedly missing the obvious joke of his fellow novelist Céline's "cynicism and off-handedness." Going beyond Maritain's failure to read *Bagatelles pour un massacre* and *Voyage à la fin du nuit* in their appropriately playful context, Gide further excoriated the philosopher for removing all but a confessional perspective from the complex Jewish Question. As he saw it, Maritain would have Gentiles barely tolerate their Jewish neighbors, offering them but an obligatory Christian charity while viewing them as a people supernaturally apart.[35]

In his reply, published in the same journal a couple months later, Maritain found Gide's critique nonsensical,[36] the latter misreading a primacy of the supernatural in his analysis of antisemitism as an exclusively confessional framing of the issue. Had Gide read the rest of his lecture? Maritain had not in his mind raised the issue of the historical vocation of

Israel to advocate for minimal toleration for Jews — quite the contrary. As for Gide's own reading of Céline, he would be better advised not to take so lightly such "bagatelles" about Jewish "maggots" when played against a backdrop of "death and ignominy" for Jews across Europe.[37]

Maritain had taken the fateful step of joining Henri Massis, Charles Maurras, and other men of the right in the "Party of Intelligence" at the end of the Great War, in large part as a rejection of Gide and others proclaiming a return to art-for-art's-sake.[38] Even if the Maritain of 1938, whom a recent biographer terms "manifestly a man of the left,"[39] regretted some of his past associations, he still could chastise Gide for much the same failing of old, defending the irresponsibility of the artist. One might acknowledge a certain consistency on Maritain's part, even if, as Yves Floucat states, it could largely be chalked up to intransigence rather than ideology.[40]

Maritain's arguments in "The Jews Among the Nations" also managed to receive a reading on their specific theological and philosophical merits, though Georges Bernanos, once again a friend of sorts after they found a common foe in Franco, could still make light of them, complaining that "I am perfectly capable . . . of honoring M. Jacques Maritain at the same time that I deplore his effeminate daydreams about the Jews . . . which win for him public acclaim at the *Théâtre des Ambassadeurs*."[41] And Claudel had already made it clear what he thought of the idea of a continuing Jewish vocation: "It is surprising to see so much intelligence, such a spirit of generosity and sacrifice, such a vivid sense of spiritual matters, gathered around something dead and petrified."[42] But if Catholic literary luminaries such as Bernanos and Claudel could indulgently shrug off the idealistic Judeophilic excesses of a respected peer, a lesser-known professor at the University of Liège offered a frontal assault on Maritain, whom he branded a deluded, heretical defender of the Jewish enemy.

Marcel de Corte's 17 March 1939 article in the Belgian *Revue catholique des idées et faits* began with a disclaimer ostentatiously separating its author from any personal attacks on Maritain that might currently have been in circulation, for such embarrassing slurs entirely missed the point. An "objective" critique must concentrate instead on Maritain's philosophical and theological errors in "*L'impossible antisémitisme*," which were lamentably legion. In that 1937 work, Maritain had confused the spiritual and the temporal, neglecting concrete historical realities at the expense of misguided spiritual exegesis. His notion of historical progression outlined in *Integral Humanism* smacked of Comtean positivism as much as of Christianity, and his positive account of Jews in past, present, and future history completely ignored their possession of a "second nature" that has always led them to deny grace. Like the German religious thinker Erik Peterson,[43] Maritain ascribed a continued election to Israel, where a more accurate reading of Paul would yield a verdict of continued reprobation, and Corte sealed this conclusion with an awkward but tellingly worded sentence: "The Jew is not 'an always chosen people.'"[44]

Withdrawing his attention momentarily from the notion of "the Jew" as accursed denier of God's grace, Corte then waxed alarmist: Maritain's representation of Jews as a sacred irritant might inflame more than assuage antisemitic passions in Europe. Or worse yet, rather than rendering Jews victims, it might make them into masters. For elevating Jews to the status of God's moral instigators would segregate them once again, but this time in an "ennobled ghetto" from which they could dominate Christians without fear of reprisal.

But Corte did not think Maritain had gotten everything wrong. If not for his more or less "Protestant determinism of Grace," he would have realized the true significance of the anti-assimilation impulse that comprised the only correct element of his reading of the Jewish problem, for Jews indeed should be considered inassimilable given their undying drive to dominate Gentiles. Drawing a neat distinction between an inadmissible hatred of Jews and the obvious need for legal statutes "isolating them," Corte then fashioned a maxim of Christian love for Jews that amounted to an impossible *philosemitism*: "The Christian must force himself to love the Jew, even if he is his enemy."[45] In the concluding juxtaposition of "individual charity" and "collective severity," Maritain might have spied the shadow of his own earlier position on the Jewish Question, but his angry riposte to Professor Corte did not pause to reflect upon the past, at least not directly.

In a response article appearing on the first of July in *La Question d'Israël,* a publication of the missionary priests of Notre Dame de Sion, Maritain branded Corte's "exclusively supernatural interpretation" of his thesis as "completely baseless" but quite understandable. For the Belgian professor's attempt to articulate a politics separated from Christian virtues fed on "fundamental prejudices" with which Maritain had once been all too well acquainted: "This then is a Maurrassian formula, my dear friend, not a Catholic formula."[46] He could not help but feel annoyed with such "clever antisemites who vituperate against 'Jewish racism' while forgetting that the one who is first and foremost responsible for this concept of a chosen race, taken in its purest sources, is the God of Abraham, of Isaac and of Jacob, the God of Israel, *your God*, dear Christians who want to turn against the chosen olive tree to which you were grafted."[47] Showing himself incapable of analogical thinking, Corte had also mistakenly charged Maritain with equating Israel and the Church simply because they serve the same God. Maritain rejected this as utter nonsense.[48]

But Maritain saw Corte's misreading of "*L'impossible anti-sémitisme*" paling before other more intrinsic errors such as an extremely selective and negative reading of Saint Paul's eschatology of Israel, an unwillingness to allow a theological construction of group identity the same dignity as the sociological theses of Max Weber or Werner Sombart, and the simultaneous presumption to posit one's own theory of Jewish "second nature" such as to "give pleasure to Julius Streicher and encourage him in his paths."[49]

Drawing back a moment from attacking his attacker, whom he had left in the ignominious company of Maurras and Streicher, Maritain reminded his readers that acknowledging the historical problems of Jewish-Christian relations since the beginning of the Diaspora did not itself necessitate or constitute any contemporary recourse to antisemitism. In fact, Christians needed to act preemptively, taking ever greater care with their language and their reasoning, guarding against the natural inclination to view the victim in almost as negative a light as the executioner, lest a burgeoning tragedy be made even worse:

> We are saying that in a time when antisemitic persecutions have assumed unheard-of proportions, when thousands upon thousands of unfortunates are outside the law, exposed to nameless brutalities and humiliations, to slow death, to outbreaks of "spontaneous" popular violence or the horrors of concentration camps, when one learns daily of the continual suicides of the Jews of Vienna and elsewhere, or that, like last winter, cold and hunger are decimating entire trains of Jews stopped at closed frontiers, or that, at the hour in which I write these lines, ships filled with Jews dying of distress wander the Mediterranean from one port to another, turned back everywhere, the only suitable *realism*, and I am not speaking only as a Christian but to any man still possessed of a natural sentiment of *caritas humani generis*, is not to give utterance to or write a word which risks serving as an excuse for degrading hatreds, and to find oneself someday charged with the blood and the despair of creatures of God.[50]

In between written ripostes, Maritain could also count some positive reviews from Jewish readers. Writing in *Paix et Droit,* a review published by the *Alliance Israélite Universelle,* in May 1938, the budding moral philosopher Emmanuel Lévinas urged his fellow French Jews (though born in Lithuania, he had adopted French citizenship) to look closely at Maritain's exposition of the spiritual essence of antisemitic hatred, something that "the rest of the Jewish press has neglected a bit . . . the metaphysics of antisemitism."[51] The young philosopher accepted Maritain's characterization of a providentially necessary tension between Jews and Christians, while also appreciating the primal identification of antisemitism with an anti-Christian impulse: "No one doubts that racist antisemitism menaces Christianity as much as it does Judaism. But that this is a merciless hostility, that it is not purely doctrinal, that it comes from the depths of Nature, even from an instinct of Nature, that is the point on which M. Maritain sheds new light."[52]

In a personal letter, Maritain's friend the Romanian-born poet Benjamin Fondane agreed that he captured the supernatural essence of the Jewish Question, but the poet also offered frank criticism. Given the long history of Jewish woes and wanderings before the time of Jesus, he failed to see how Maritain could find the answer in Christian faith, something Fondane regretfully saw as a worldly expedient: "It is not that I reject the Christian solution out of hand, but taking it as it is means admitting *that there is a solution* to the question of Israel, and that this solution *is in our hands.* It is this that I find doubtful.[53] One can assume Fondane did not change his mind in this regard before his death at Auschwitz in 1944.[54]

In the United States, Father John LaFarge read the text of the *Théâtre des Ambassadeurs* lecture and wrote Maritain that his warning about the antisemitic contagion was "unfortunately well-founded, even in the United States. It seems to me that there is a sort of antisemitic mystique, similar to the socialist or communist mystique, and as the Sioux would put it, it is a very strong medicine."[55] Maritain therefore would rejoice at the translated lecture's publication in the United States the following year, writing to the University of Chicago philosophy professor Mortimer Adler: "It is a great joy for me that you loved the little book on the Jewish Question. I saw the review in Sunday's New York Times. . . . Because of the miserable *Father Coughlin* I am particularly happy that this little book has appeared in America."[56]

Unfortunately, we do not know whether or not Maritain managed to discomfit the antisemitic "Radio Priest" Charles Coughlin with his book, but he did earn the admiration of the leading spokesman for American Jewry. Speaking in Carnegie Hall on 23 October 1939, Rabbi Stephen S. Wise told his audience that his words that day were drawn from the latest book by a man described by *The New York Times* as "one of the most eminent Catholic mystics": "Professor Maritain has made it crystal clear that 'while it is certainly possible for Christians to be anti-Semite,' [*sic*] it is possible for them only when they obey the spirit of the world rather than the spirit of Christianity."[57] But by this time of course, war had begun.

THE END OF AN AGE

Maritain viewed the coming of the Second World War, the German domination of Europe, and the Nazi murder of Jews and others from an explicitly apocalyptic perspective, reflecting the familiar influence of Bloy, but exhibiting a new urgency. For example, the 1939 English translation of his 1938 lecture, "*Les Juifs parmi les nations,*" published in English translation in the United States as *A Christian Looks at the Jewish Question*, concluded with the following appraisal, not present in the 1938 original:

> Never before in the history of the world were the Jews persecuted so universally; and never has persecution attacked, as today, both Jews and Christians. We can see here a sign that we have entered upon an apocalyptic period in history; this is also a sign that we must shape our means to the conditions of such a period. For a long time an all too human civilization put its trust in material forces, while invoking — and not always hypocritically — equity and the spirit. Today these material forces have been brought to the state of barbarism, and this is only the natural result of the perverted mentality which, in its desultory belief that through them it could reign supreme, put everything in their power. In order to face the violence let loose in this way, men of freedom must not renounce the means which lie at their disposal in material energies, provided that these are subordinated to the spirit of justice. But they can no longer put their confidence in them, since the world itself summons them finally to put their trust in love and truth alone.[58]

This diagnosis of an apocalyptic crisis in western civilization built upon his interwar call for an integral humanism to confront the ascendancy of what he called in early 1939 a "demonic pseudotheism" and the approach of a "biological inferno."[59] With a continual eye on the agony of the Jews,

Maritain compared the sufferings of his own France and other countries such as Poland, concluding that the sustaining of human hope would demand not only heroes, but also prophets and martyrs.

These uncertain times truly began in late September 1938, as the threat of war over the Sudetenland flared and the Maritains simultaneously packed for either a lecture trip to America or evacuation to the countryside. Jacques related the following to his diary: *"End of September 1938 —* The Czechoslovakian tragedy and the threat of war. We pack our trunks for America (Raïssa and Véra are to accompany me if we make the trip), and at the same time as other trunks for Avoise (papers and letters sent to Abbé Gouin's house to be preserved from eventual bombings and fires), thinking all the while that war is going to break out and we will not be able to leave."

On the twenty-ninth, however, the Munich Conference achieved "peace in our time," and on the first of October the trio left for two months in the United States.[60] They therefore missed the first outbreak of widespread and concerted violence against the Jews of Nazi Germany, the Night of Broken Glass on 9–10 November. They had been several weeks back in France, however, when, on the tenth of February 1939, Pope Pius XI, who had recently declared, "Spiritually, we are Semites,"[61] died, and Maritain paid tribute to the deceased pontiff — "without a doubt the greatest figure of these times" — on Radio-Paris.[62] Two days earlier, Maritain had presented another public lecture in Paris, the title of which bespoke a western world facing encroaching darkness.

This 8 February 1939 presentation at the *Théâtre Marigny*, later published as *Le crépuscule de la civilisation* (*The Twilight of Civilization*), explored the connection between humanism and Western Civilization in an age of ascendant totalitarianism and democratic retreat. Maritain commenced his analysis by affirming that something positive lay at the heart of humanism, as it "tends essentially to render man more truly human and to manifest his original greatness by enabling him to partake of everything in nature and in history capable of enriching him."[63] But in its anthropocentric turn since the Renaissance, a deformed humanism had closed off human nature to its supernatural fullness in the name of human autonomy: "After having put aside God in order to become self-sufficient, man loses his soul; he seeks himself in vain, turning the universe upside down in his effort to find himself again. He finds only masks, and behind those masks, death."[64] Cut off from its divine origins and destiny, lost humanity lunges toward the irrational in its aspiration to regain a sense of freedom, as in the case of Nietzsche, only to succumb to the Nazi "cult of race and blood . . . the gospel of the hatred of reason."[65] Nazism's reaction to anthropocentric humanism has as its polar counterpart the communistic completion of this closed humanism in which it is "reason itself which decapitates reason."[66]

Distinguishing in order to unite, Maritain then outlined the essential features of the Nazi and Soviet attempts at totalitarianism.[67] Nazism like fascism "makes of God Himself an idol, since it denies, if not in words at least in deed, the nature and transcendence of God; it invokes God, but as a protective genius attached to the glory of a people or of a state, or as the daemon of the race."[68]

Communism of course denies God altogether. But both are more "anti-Christic," Maritain argued, than anti-Christian, as they constitute less an opposition to religion per se than an "existential opposition to the action of Christ in the bosom of human history."[69] Making of blood or race a god "defies the God of Sinai and the God of Calvary," while communism replaces divine truth with temporal dogma.[70] Nazism hates truth itself, offering only a "mad religiosity linked with utter nihilism," so that whereas communism may perhaps have the potential for eventual internal reform, the German national ideology cannot be defeated merely by reason.[71]

Civilization's hope lies in a personalistic integral humanism that might recast human potential in the light of the Incarnation, and which could not rest as a philosophical proposition but also has to entail transforming the life of the masses and ending "the dissociations of the things of God from the things of the world . . . divorced from the exigencies of the Gospel."[72] The dissociation of the spiritual and the temporal therefore goes against the letter and the spirit of the Gospel, and repairing this rupture will constitute both a "spiritual and social resurrection" unattainable without great suffering, even unto death: "Whence it follows that in order to prepare a new age for the world, it is possible that at the outset martyrs be necessary to the cause of the love of neighbor."[73]

Christians must pursue this risky work in real life, not simply contemplatively—for even if the Gospel opposes itself to the world as it is, it does not set itself apart from or in opposition to nature itself, which is perfected by grace. Christ stands in necessary opposition to what Maritain called the Pagan Empire, animating resistance to new Neros. Carl Schmitt's influential political philosophy had provided "the essence of *pagan* politics" in constructing political unity through hatred of an external enemy. But this kind of racist nationalism, in addition to directing its animosity "*against the other*," pits itself against God.[74]

More than had been the case in earlier lectures, Maritain's prescriptive solutions went beyond evangelical exhortations to draw together Christian faith and democratic practice in a manner that only would become more explicit, and convincing, during the war years. Democratic pluralism constituted the temporal vehicle for combating the neo-paganism he saw as ascendant in Europe, and for Maritain, the United States offered the very model of a coexistence of Christian values and democratic faith.

He cited his recent autumn 1938 visit to the United States — he had already lectured there in 1933 and 1934 — as inspirational. President Franklin Delano Roosevelt's equating of democracy with human dignity contained a welcome and necessary religious element not seen in countries such as laic France. For their part, Europeans would doubtless open themselves up to true democratic renewal as they divest themselves of a pervading Rousseauian influence and "the homicidal errors of bourgeois individualism, which might be called miscarried democracy."

By contrast, an "integral humanism and an organic democracy . . . proceed from a theocentric inspiration." Christianity does not inherently tie itself to any given ideology or particular regime, but the challenges and dangers of the present age had shown how religion, conscience, and civilization itself all depend vitally on the survival and flourishing of liberty. In the political realm, only democracy — inspired in its hidden sources and hopeful renewal by Christianity—could save the human person from a fate of totalitarian slavery.[75]

On 3 September 1939, the French government joined its British ally in reluctantly declaring war on Germany after the Reich's invasion of Poland. Four months and a day later, the Maritains — Jacques, along with Raïssa and Véra — left for North America for a lecture tour of several months that would be extended by over four years of exile. For Maritain, now living in New York,[76] the fall of France underscored the ascendancy of what he called "the sovereignty of hate."[77] On the twenty-first of June 1940, seven days after the *Wehrmacht* entered an undefended Paris, *Commonweal* published this Frenchman's bleak appraisal: "We have entered into the country of the Apocalypse and of great sufferings."[78]

Lest this dire reading of the Nazi ascendancy appear but a moment of pathos on Maritain's part, he would sustain this tone throughout the high tide of Axis victories, proclaiming two years later the veritable end of an age: "If we want to take the measure of the horrible war that the Pagan Empire has unleashed on the world and which kills not only men but consciences as well and wears nations threadbare, starves the children, and destroys throughout Europe and the world the vital resources of the generations to come, we must understand that it is a moment of paroxysm in the liquidation of a world. The end of the Roman Empire was a minor event compared with what we behold."[79]

Maritain worked to foster an apocalyptic hope by working from abroad to animate French resistance to both the Nazi occupiers and the collaborationists at Vichy. In late 1940, he wrote *À travers le désastre* (published in English as *France, My Country, Through the Disaster*), a book mimeographed and distributed by underground publishers in France, and described by one historian as the "breviary" of the Catholic Resistance.[80] Like *Annales* historian and future resistance martyr Marc Bloch's *Etrange Défaite*,[81] Maritain's book, written in the immediate wake of catastrophe and without recourse to archival documents, sought to both account for the defeat and counter the facile and manipulative diagnoses emanating from the collaborationists in occupied Paris and Pétainist Vichy.

As the secular Jewish historian wrote *Strange Defeat* in what he called a "white heat of rage,"[82] the devout Catholic philosopher began *Through the Disaster* in a state of deepening sorrow, confiding to Adler that "I hardly see any more human hope, because for me a free France was the hope of the world. The idea of a France that could be subjected to Hitlerian influences casts me into horror. But perhaps we are entering into a period comparable to that of the Hundred Years War, with such a time of chaos calling forth the miracle of Joan of Arc. But if it is the great Pagan Empire that is installing itself throughout the world, only the catacombs will remain."[83]

Through the Disaster begins with the author drawing a sympathetic yet irritated analogy between the defeated French and persecuted Jews, insisting that both groups lacked the spiritual insight to awaken prophetically to the deepest danger at hand, that of the loss of the soul: "Yet is it not the darkest sign of all that, though crushed by apocalyptic evils, the French see no prophet arise among them to voice the horror of what has occurred and stir the spirit to its depths? This same absence strikes us among the Jews in whom, though they are persecuted throughout the world, the spirit of prophecy remains lifeless."

Maritain then turns to historical explanation of the defeat, anticipating future historians in adopting a multi-causal sophistication, even if, lacking documentary evidence, he adds that France's "military breakdown undoubtedly was due to the crushing technical superiority of German armament and to numbers."[84] Almost seventy years hence, historians know that France and its allies actually had a slight advantage in these respects.[85]

But this interpretive misstep — Maritain himself concedes that he and his contemporaries "lack essential documents"[86] — probably derived less from a mistaken attempt at historical precision than political prudence. As Pétain and Pierre Laval had only begun to take their authoritarian revenge against the democratic Third Republic, Maritain took care to distance his explanatory framework from any notion of decadence or betrayal. The latter term might have use, "provided only that in the word *betrayal* we see something much broader, complex, something less suggestive of criminal intent than is usually meant by the word."[87]

What caused the defeat as far as Maritain was concerned — that is, what elements in a broad and complex sense accounted for the betrayal of France? No one factor suffices, and an interrogation of tragedy rather than a criminal investigation such as one sees for example in "Pertinax's" *The Gravediggers of France*,[88] predominates in his book. Interwar politics pitted class against class, while political leaders lacked creativity and insight — "bourgeois leaders who, whether radical or reactionary, profoundly feared and despised the people . . . frittering away the vitality of the nation and aggravating its divisions."[89]

Foreign governments exploited these weaknesses and fissures by exporting poisonous ideologies, sometimes manipulating a venal press, sometimes through parliamentary parties. The charge applied to both sides in an increasingly polarized body politic, for "the promptings of Rome, and even at a certain point, Berlin, played as strong a rôle in the extreme right as did those of Moscow in the extreme left."[90] Despite his association with the antifascist left and his designation by some as a Marxist Christian, even the Popular Front figured in this indictment as a "product of Russian Machiavellianism and built upon a lie." And the sordid business of the Spanish Civil War, which further polarized France, helped set the stage for the general war in which France would meet disaster.[91]

But French society itself should not be characterized as decadent and doomed to defeat, even if it undoubtedly lacked a strong sense of spiritual unity. Paradoxically, the very maturity and solidity of French democratic culture constituted a particular vulnerability given the political perils of the time: "The French people, precisely, I dare say, because of its longer experience with political life and self-government, was in the thick of a wave of self-criticism at the very moment when, on the other side of the frontier, the totalitarian chieftains were labouring with all their might and means to rouse the masses to the highest pitch of unquestioning fanaticism."[92]

This badly timed hyper-rationalism extended to the high command, and played a fatal role on the battlefield. The general staff and the government pushed the absurdity of what one cabinet member had called a "Cartesian war"[93] against Nazi Germany to its logical, tragic conclusion, betraying the complacent trust of a French people who had provided such military and political leaders in the first place. That said, the French nation had also furnished the soldiers who maintained their morale through nine months of phony war and held up under the terrible onslaught of the Blitzkrieg, until the high command and the government lost the will to continue: "The dispersion never became a general panic; it was not the cause of the defeat but its sequel."[94]

For Maritain, the criminal folly of the Armistice, not the tragedy of the military defeat itself, is what made of France a defeated nation. Rather than delivering France from overwhelming defeat, the Vichy regime had rendered France finally bankrupt and prostrate before the German conqueror. The Marshal and other capitulationists justified the ceasefire to the French people under false pretenses and without foresight as to its future implications. Maritain's judgment might have assumed an even more bitter tone of reproach but for his erroneous assumption (today's historians know differently)[95] that Vichy's "racist laws [beginning with the 3 October 1940 *Statut des Juifs*], which are a denial of the traditions and the spirit of France, were adopted under German orders."[96]

Despite the alleged pro-Catholic stance of the Marshal's New Order, Maritain dismisses its authoritarian ideology as neither innovative nor traditionalist, but a "bizarre mix of commonplaces, where theses borrowed from Catholic social teachings are imbedded in the teachings of the political school of total nationalism."[97] Viewing the moral bankruptcy of collaboration with the Nazis and persecution of the Jews, Maritain offers what might constitute both an appraisal of the Catholic Church in France and a warning, insisting that the "Church of France is not eager to chain herself to a state clericalism which would ruin in the long run the spiritual revival of which she is proud."[98]

Looking to the future, Maritain offers a simultaneously apocalyptic and hopeful prognosis for France emerging from the disaster as a happier and more cohesive polity. And even as he rejects the National Revolution as proclaimed by Vichy he proffers his own variant of national regeneration, one that takes pains to antedate France's ills to an epoch long preceding 1789. The defeat and the occupation have begun a necessary process of sweeping away Cartesian and Machiavellian errors, philosophical precepts foolishly and fatally wielded by the French bourgeoisie, "those unfortunates that toyed with Machiavellian thought but lacked Machiavellianism in their blood. They missed the rise of the terrible countenance of total Machiavellianism, of Machiavellianism gone mad, triumphant over their reasonable Machiavellianism, and, for the advantage of the most inhuman and pitiless of revolutions, making game of their worship of an order without justice."[99] Such a combination of cynicism and naïveté among the elite must no longer be accepted by the people at large.

Whatever the venerable Pétain has told them, the French people have become increasingly aware that in a long war, defeat would lead not to peace and prosperity, but to degradation and slavery. The survival of Great Britain and the appearance of the Gaullist movement will help ensure the continuation of the war, but even after victory, both France and its nemesis Germany would have to undergo something of a cultural revolution for a true resolution of the conflict to ensue: "The problem of Franco-German cooperation is indeed a crucial European problem. If it is ever to be solved, it can be solved only between a Germany liberated from Nazism, Prussianism, and imperialistic dreams, and a France cleansed of the moral defeatism of its skeptics and the conservatism of its pseudo-Cartesians."[100]

But this cleansing must involve further apocalyptic outpourings of evil and suffering that amount to an unfolding of divine justice perhaps imperceptible to an extent that only hope would remain to guide consciences toward the future: "The justice of God must indeed come to pass; the Apocalypse is only just beginning. We may foresee that the liquidation of which the present war is but an episode will proceed by steps, perhaps with lulls wonderful to be had but short-lived, until the time marked by Paul the Apostle for what he calls a resurrection from the dead. Meanwhile those who refuse to worship the beast will have to huddle in the catacombs of history and to devise hitherto untried ways of holding their own against evil."[101] To make concrete sense of these apocalyptic pronouncements, Maritain explains that the experiences of others could give the French an idea of what further sufferings lay in store, for however forlorn his compatriots felt at the moment, the Poles, their country occupied in its entirety by the Germans, are "tortured incredibly by a sadism both fiendish and disciplined," and if anything, "the Jews are more forsaken" still.[102]

Establishing this wider human perspective had as its aim the forestalling of moral compromise in a France whose citizenry lay vulnerable to the blandishments, nostrums, and rationales of Vichy. The Jesuit theologian and future cardinal Henri de Lubac, who worked in Lyon with the

Catholic resistance publication *Cahiers du Témoignage Chrétien*, reflected after the war that Maritain's book "might be considered a preview *Cahier du T.C.*"[103] The first issue of *Témoignage Chrétien* appeared in November 1941 and addressed itself to the Vichy regime's anti-Jewish policies with the title page admonition: "France, Be Careful Not to Lose Your Soul."[104]

By this time, the first *Statut des juifs*, which had defined "Jewishness" even more rigorously than had the 1935 Nuremberg Laws, and immediately preceded the internment of 40,000 foreign Jews, had been followed by the establishment of the Commissariat-General of Jewish Affairs (*Commissariat Général aux Questions Juives*), under the antisemite Xavier Vallat in March 1941, and the imposition of a second Jewish Statute in June.[105]

The Aryanization of all Jewish businesses in the Unoccupied Zone, this time following the German lead in the Occupied Zone, ensued a month later. The exiled philosopher, whose writings were frequently reproduced in this and other Resistance publications, saw himself as participating in France's spiritual resistance against Nazism, collaboration, and the war against the Jews, for "by saying here what they are forbidden to say in France, I uphold the very rights of this people which is my own, and in so doing our communion is strengthened."[106]

After the war, *Time* magazine reported on Maritain's years of exile in rather quaint terms: "He settled down to a Greenwich Village exile, walked daily to Mass at old St. Joseph's, consumed quantities of peanuts and ginger ale, and held a Sunday salon frequented by savants and celebrities."[107] Perhaps this casual impression of his New York years originated with Maritain himself, given his self-effacing, disarming manner.[108] But in truth, his stay in the United States hardly amounted to such a relaxed time of spirituality, snacks, and discussion, and René Mougel aptly stresses the "abyss from which [Maritain's] hope rose up again."[109]

The exiled scholar embraced a wide range of activities and commitments. While he taught at Columbia and Princeton in order to make ends meet,[110] he also helped form the francophone university-in-exile, the *Ecole Libre des Hautes Études* (of which he assumed the presidency in 1943), based at New York's New School for Social Research.[111] Maritain, working with other activist exiles, relied on the assistance of the New School's president, Dr. Alvin Johnson, among others, to lobby the State Department for exit visas for imperiled scholars and their families and to find them posts at universities around the country.[112]

He also became involved in the work of the Emergency Rescue Committee, associated with Varian Fry's mission in southern France locating, sheltering, and spiriting out of the country endangered artists and intellectuals such as Hannah Arendt and Marc Chagall. Contributing to the lists of those to be rescued, Maritain apparently became involved in an international tension. As one of Fry's recent biographers explains, "Maritain accused Thomas Mann of favoritism to German writers. Max Ascoli told Maritain he was ignoring Italians and pushing too many French names." And so on.[113]

Maritain also wrote subsequent books and delivered lectures for the Allied war effort, working closely with the U.S. Office of War Information, while giving radio addresses to his compatriots in occupied France over the airwaves of the Voice of America on a weekly basis, and periodically for the Gaullist Free French on the BBC.[114] Through all these media, he equated democracy's cause with that of Christian civilization, extolling French patriotism and denouncing German atrocities. In *Through the Disaster* and subsequent writings, Maritain sought to strike a note of Christian democratic hope, seeing in democracy the "temporal manifestation of the Gospel."[115]

Writing to Adler, he waxed enthusiastic about his writings as weapons of war: "I also just received a short letter from the unknown man who reprinted and diffused in France, in a clandestine way, my book, *A Travers le Désastre*. He tells me the book was read by everybody in France and he asks for new texts. One of these could be a manuscript on "Christianity and Democracy" which I wrote in July for the Office of War Information. The plan is to diffuse this book in France by dropping it from planes. You can imagine my philosophy falling thus from heaven! The customary red tape makes this hope precarious."[116]

By 1941, hope had become increasingly precarious for all those caught within the Nazi orbit, and as Maritain had rightly stated in *Through the Disaster*, for none more so than the Jews. The year began with the death of one of the Maritains' early mentors, whose end had been hastened by waiting for hours in the freezing cold in a long line on a Parisian street. At the age of eighty-one, and crippled with rheumatism, "the dying Henri Bergson had shuffled through the streets of Paris in his carpet slippers to declare himself 'Academic. Philosopher. Nobel Prize winner. Jew.'"[117] On behalf of Vichy and the Nazi occupiers, the French police had begun to register all Jews; the famous philosopher declined Vichy's offer of an exemption and denied himself the consolation of the Catholic baptism to which he had inclined in his later years, in order to remain with, as he stated in his last will and testament, "the persecuted ones."[118]

APOCALYPTIC HOPE

Maritain's apocalyptic vision of the war[119] brought horror and hope together in a cosmic drama of a world convulsing in the throes of triumphant evil: "Our age is such to call all causes from all points of the globe to be delivered pitilessly of their effects; everything that is hidden will be dragged into the open, the principles of death will unleash their energy and open into monstrous sores. Such a total outpour of evil has its hope, for evil is after all finite. That very fact may be our last hope, and the last hope is rock strong."[120]

How could Maritain draw what he called a "rock strong hope" from such a grotesque and terrible prophetic vision? Even before the outbreak of war, he had understood that a general war would likely include a drive to destroy the Jews of Europe. This would signify the end of civilization itself, with a remnant of Christians like himself driven underground. Therefore, one might ask what philosophical and theological sources Maritain drew upon to justify such apocalyptic hope in the future of humankind in general and the Jews in particular.

His philosophical allegiance to the Aristotelian-Thomistic tradition of natural law influenced his moral and political judgment that so-called total Machiavellianism would soon destroy itself and the Christian roots of democracy would become ever more apparent. His 26 September 1941 lecture given at the University of Chicago, "The End of Machiavellianism," offered a philosophical rationale for having confidence in an inevitable victory over Nazi Germany and its allies. Maritain painted an unsympathetic portrait of Machiavelli's life and motives, perhaps ignoring the fact that the Florentine, too, wrote from a position of political exile and love of homeland. He questioned even Machiavelli's vaunted shrewdness as a political observer, charging him with a "radical pessimism" and a "crude empiricism" that led him to separate politics from ethics after discovering the supposed relativity of good and evil. Maritain saw this as naïve and superficial, asserting that "human nature remains good in its very essence and root-tendencies and that such a goodness joined to a swarming multiplication of evils is the very mystery and the very motive of struggle and progression in mankind."[121] He also questioned the fatal illogic of constructing a political theory that transforms politics from an ethical consideration of the common good to the art of gaining and maintaining power. For this transformation still presupposes a moral consensus in a society ruled by an amoral, manipulative leader without accounting for the long-term "immersion of the rulers as well as the ruled in a rotted ethics, calling good evil and evil good."[122]

No wonder, Maritain argued, that one could see how the harmful ramifications of Machiavellianism inexorably went far beyond its founder's limited imagination. Ungrounded in any metaphysics in the traditional sense, Machiavelli has destroyed the "image of God in man," leaving a negation that constitutes "the metaphysical root of every power politics and every totalitarianism."[123] Without a guiding and restraining vision of the common good, itself subservient to the dignity of the human person, politics becomes a game of obtaining, maintaining, and increasing power, with no articulated end except the essentially meaningless and practically dangerous "health of the state." Early practitioners of *raison d'état* such as Richelieu had used Machiavellianism as a means to secure a still-recognizable common good. But in the nineteenth century, the ascendancy of positivism, as well as a peculiarly German exaltation of romanticism, idealism, and statism, had fostered Machiavellianism's transmutation from a practical art into a progressive science characterized by a "prophetical and mystical enthusiasm" in a world of allegedly inevitable progress through struggle.[124]

For Maritain, Machiavelli's premises and implications found themselves implicitly refuted by natural law and explicitly rebuked by the revealed Gospel. Consequentialism makes of politics something autonomous unto itself, no longer concerned with finding and fostering the good, and thus analogous with the self-deification at the heart of anthropocentric humanism. Banishing human dignity from policy considerations, the artist of power forswears any moderating scruples, embracing "that impetuous, revolutionary, wild, and demoniacal Machiavellianism, for which *boundless* injustice, *boundless* violence, and *boundless* lying and immorality are normal political means, and which draws from this very boundlessness of evil an abominable strength."[125] The wielder of political power, like Jesus, has faced Satan's tempting offer of all the "kingdoms of the world," but has accepted with alacrity the world's invitation to establish the "Empire of Man making himself God, the diametrical opposite of the kingdom of Redemptive Incarnation."[126] This exaltation of the all-powerful state and the nullification of the vulnerable person finally destroy politics itself, leaving but "an entanglement and commixture of the life of the animals and the slaves, and of the lives of the saints."[127]

Entangled lives of animals, slaves, and saints: the months that passed between this September 1941 lecture and its January 1942 publication corresponded with the emergence of the policy of the Final Solution. On 18 September 1941, Heinrich Himmler sent a letter conveying to three subordinates the Fuhrer's wish that the area within the Reich's prewar frontiers be cleared of all Jews; on 20 January 1942, Himmler's deputy Reinhard Heydrich presided over the Wannsee Conference, at which fourteen officials set the details of the deportation to Poland and extermination of all Europe's Jews.[128] What future if any might lie beyond such a Final Solution? Maritain's logic of absolute Machiavellianism achieving the destruction of politics, and therefore the destruction of people, leads to the further projection, however terrifying in its intermediate implications, of Machiavellianism's own unavoidable collapse.

But how could such sweeping success in and of itself guarantee failure? One must consider the question of temporality and duration, and ask what Machiavellianism actually achieves except for "the illusion of immediate success."[129] Maritain enigmatically insisted that "justice works through its own causality," and that our own human sense of time cannot comprehend even temporal history's *longue durée* let alone a Providence that transcends time: "We do not understand the fair play of God, who gives those who have freely chosen injustice the time to exhaust the benefits of it and the fullness of its energies. When disaster comes to those victors, the eyes of the righteous who cried against them to God will have long putrefied under the earth, and men will not know the distant source of the catastrophe."[130] Maritain placed this "dimension of time . . . at the very core of the question," for the work of justice typically involves "picking . . . fruits of bitterness, sorrow, and defeat," not tangible success. The pursuit of justice in a world dominated by the lure of immediate results therefore requires hope, and hope cannot sustain itself, often against all apparent odds, without faith. Faith in God, and a consequent restoration to politics of a love for the human person as *imago Dei*, must follow Nazi Machiavellianism's transient reign.[131]

Rejoining politics with morality could reanimate a true democratic politics, but Maritain insisted that there are no guarantees in earthly life, only in the life to come. He deemed the recognition and practice of virtue as necessary but not sufficient for the flourishing of states and societies — that is, they cannot necessarily "prevent the natural laws of senescence" or "physical catastrophes" from dealing their destructive effects. Nonetheless, "justice and righteousness *tend by themselves* to the preservation of states. . . . Injustice and evil *tend by themselves* to the destruction of states," something Maritain called "the law of the fructification of human actions which is inscribed in the nature of things and is but the natural justice of God in human history."

In short, while God's justice presents itself in temporal history, "it reigns only in heaven and hell." Maritain thus demanded of those who combated Nazism an armed strength guided by moral purity, and this insistence on what one might call "clean hands" drew criticism from political realists such as Raymond Aron and Hans Morgenthau. Whereas Aron debated Maritain at length on the question of the purity of means,[132] Morgenthau offered a dismissive aside: "The end of Machiavellianism, which Jacques Maritain's too orderly and too progressive mind sees already in our grasp, is not just around the corner. It is not of this world at all. If it were, salvation from evil itself would be of this world."[133] But Morgenthau's retort was published almost six months after the war in Europe ended, by which time one could more easily extend humor to the subject. That said, could one not argue that the utter collapse of Nazi Germany tended to bear out Maritain's thesis that at least the Hitlerian species of Machiavellianism could only end in destroying itself? And far from seeing salvation at hand immediately afterward, as Maritain had acknowledged, what would be left of civilization afterward remained to be seen.[134]

Looking at the question again, we can see that Maritain's analysis of the contemporary crisis in "The End of Machiavellianism" — as much a political theodicy as an exposé of Machiavelli — simultaneously made reference to the temporal and the spiritual, to the historical and the eschatological. Michel Fourcade observes that for Maritain the Second World War constituted "a sort of *lieu théologique*."[135] Therefore, his analysis inevitably transcended — or violated — the canons of political science.

In another contemporaneous work, Maritain emphasized this coexistence of the finite and the infinite in returning to the exemplar of his apocalyptic hope, the Apostle Paul. His 1941 book *The Living Thoughts of Saint Paul* begins by addressing the Jewish roots of Christianity and the analogous historical circumstances of the Holy Family of Jesus, Mary, and Joseph almost twenty centuries earlier and the Jews of his own day:

> It is from Israel that came forth the Saviour of the world; it is in the womb of a young Jewish girl — the only absolutely pure creature among all purely human creatures — that the Word through Whom all has been made took on human flesh — only to be greeted by the first pogrom of the Christian era, the massacre of the little Jewish innocents, among whom King Herod sought gropingly to strike down their King; and no sooner was

He born than He was carried off along the highways by Joseph and Mary. Who are these but an indigent family of minor artisans, penniless, without affidavits, without visas, the first Jewish refuges of the Christian era, with their poor, tired donkey.[136]

On the very first page of this book, therefore, Maritain demands that his reader reflect upon the following propositions: that true purity is spiritual not racial; that the mass murder of Jewish children is an attempt to kill the Christ Child; and that the dispossessed, displaced, and stateless Jews of his time suffer for the sake of all mankind.

Having begun his book with an evocation of the Nazi war against the Jews, Maritain proceeds to mine the richness of Jewish tradition and expound upon Christianity's spiritual debt to Israel. Designating Moses and Paul as the "two greatest leaders of souls that humanity has ever known," he emphasizes their Jewishness, their having spoken with God, and their simultaneous aura of "awful majesty" and status as "vagabonds along the roadsides."[137] The latter of these majestic vagabonds forms the focus of the book, and the author credits Paul with three main "intuitions" through which the message of the Messiah made itself known to the Gentiles. First, and most obviously, Paul has drawn the world's attention to "the universality of the Kingdom of God." Second, he has demonstrated the "primacy of the internal over the external, of the spirit over the letter, of the life of grace over exterior observances," in short, the implications of Jesus' "spiritual revolution" and the establishment of a New Law. Third, Paul testifies experientially that Christ crucified and risen illuminates the one true path to human fulfillment and freedom. Those who follow these intuitions, "by the Spirit and by love," participate in the eternal life of God, for "the faithful compose one body, which is the mysterious body of Jesus."[138]

The universality of the kingdom of God entails preaching Christ to all people, Gentiles and Jews alike. According to Maritain, Paul, exhibiting the wisdom not of the philosophers but of the saints, preaches salvation to all humanity, even as all imperfect persons stand condemned in the face of God's perfect justice. The juxtaposition of salvation and condemnation presents itself from the historical beginning as a countercultural proposition, scandalizing Jewish expectations of a triumphant, not humiliated, messiah, and contradicting Greek rationalism with the unexpected primacy of supernatural resurrection over the natural fact of death. But Paul's inspired genius involves his argument against the scandal and folly of how Jews and Gentiles alike stand condemned by their own standards — be it Jewish Law or Greek Reason — each having found a compelling path toward the "double illusion" of having saved ourselves and being assured we have done so.[139]

Whereas Maritain's exposition of Paul's gospel of universal salvation devotes equal attention to the Apostle's Gentile and Jewish interlocutors, his discussion of the primacy of the spiritual, and the triumph of the New Law, focuses almost entirely on Jews, for "Saint Paul's teaching on Israel and his teaching on the Law make up one and the same doctrine."[140] The Mosaic Law has served as a "pedagogue" for all, but with the coming of Christ, a new light has come into the world, offering salvation through "Christian hope." Those Jews who fail to grasp this revolutionary development find themselves trapped not only by the strictures of petty legalism and distorted tradition, but also the temporalization of eschatological hopes against which Maritain had railed for so long.

Summarizing Paul's verdict, he writes in effect of "carnal" Jews trapped by *politique d'abord*: "A people elect and a people victim — they are bound up in their Law as though in God's trap — as long as they rely upon the Law, not living faith in Him Whose death, wrought by their Priesthood in the name of the Law, now brings their deliverance."[141] This expression of Jews caught "in God's trap," written at the very time of the commencement of the Shoah, raises the question of Jewish responsibility for their own history of suffering. But Maritain takes care to emphasize Paul's essential statement of the mystery of Israel, which in effect asks whether the Jewish "misstep" itself allowed Jesus Christ to be preached as something more than a simply Jewish messiah. Paul's admonition to Gentile converts not to forget or disdain the fact that they have been grafted as a young branch onto an older, still vital olive tree points to the realization that God's promises are not repudiated, even if the mysterious redemption of Israel, for Maritain, still amounts to eventual conversion.[142]

The implicit emphasis on conversion — we should remember here that Maritain's adult life had been shaped by his own conversion — today leaves the author open to charges of denigrating Jews and Judaism by preaching and practicing "triumphalism." Rabbi Leon Klenicki articulates this unease if not resentment at reading Maritain and reflecting on his Pauline theology of Israel: "There is a paradox in his approach. Maritain defended the Jew as a citizen, his rights and equality in society, and denounced anti-Semitism passionately. His theology, however, and especially his reading of Saint Paul, projected a sense of contempt for Judaism, for the Sinai God-Israel commitment and its development through the centuries. He fought for the civil rights of Jews, but denied meaning to Jews in their spirituality and covenantal vocation. In many respects, and I tremble in pointing this out, he was a metaphysical anti-Semite."[143]

But Klenicki's critique falls short in two respects here. First, what he takes for a standing paradox can better be appreciated as a dynamic tension that continually challenged Maritain to rethink his approach to the mystery of Israel, albeit from a Christian viewpoint. As he wrote to his friend, Father John Oesterreicher, writing his book about Saint Paul made him realize the importance of distinguishing between the inspired language of biblical scripture and "human and historic narration" in the present, and made him conscious of the need to avoid blanket references to "the Jews."[144] Second, he saw in Paul's teachings something more significant than the law/love dichotomy through which Christian theology traditionally relegated Judaism to a dead legalistic religion: "Paul is not here thinking of a hardening, with regard to eternal life, of Jews taken individually who remain bound to the Mosaic Law (like other non-Christians, they can be in a state of grace if they are in good faith: that is God's secret). He is thinking of the hardening of the people, with regard to its vocation."[145] Such a hardening, moreover, he ascribes to God's initiative in the final analysis, not that of supposedly faithless Jews, for "it remains that if God has permitted this *faux-pas*, it is according to a design of love not only for the pagans but for Israel itself, which remains the chosen people, and who will be reintegrated at the end, and in such splendor."[146]

Paul's teaching about Israel's "misstep" or "lapse" and its enduring consequences aside, Maritain takes pains to emphasize that the unity of Christians and Jews — finding true freedom through Christ — can be grasped by looking at the past, not simply at an eschatological future. For if love fulfills the Jewish Law, it requires a faith and hope prefigured and sustained by Israel, whose great spiritual leaders, Moses and Abraham in particular, demonstrated their understanding of faith as "the substance of things hoped for," with hope itself constituting promise — not possession.[147] Therefore, Jewish sources can be drawn upon to justify and deepen Christian hope as essentially supratemporal and spiritualized by grace.

Maritain's reading of Paul also inverts the progression of externally imposed law to internally felt law to describe the Christian as someone who has gone from the inside to the outside of the earthly city: "The Jewish altar was inside the Tabernacle of the Temple of Jerusalem — enclosed within a people and bound to its temporal destiny. The Christian altar is without, because the depth of Christ, being the perfect sacrifice and the perfect reparation, has abrogated the ancient sacrifices and carried salvation to the whole world. He suffered without the city. Let us leave behind the Judaic worship and the ceremonial observances of the Old Testament, which were figures of reality. And let us follow Jesus without the city, to suffer with Him, in the hope of the abiding city to come."[148] If one concentrates only on the supersessionist intimations of this passage, one misses the more essential point Maritain makes: the continued stress on the "city," when taken into the context of Maritain's other writings at this time, applies not only to Jerusalem but also to Athens, wherein the considerations of the *polis* became all. Both "cities," for Maritain, still have their figurative "temples," each of which offers an inadequate, temporal promise of realizing true human freedom.

Nor is Maritain's reading of Paul's mystery of Israel a self-consciously and complacently triumphalist statement of Christian superiority over a supposedly moribund religion. Christ is indeed destined to "subdue all things . . . until at the very end death itself is subdued," but this should be seen as the culmination of God's self-giving, not a work of destruction. According to Maritain, Antichrist, not Christ, will destroy both the Law and the City, for the Antichrist is lawlessness itself: "No law will exist for him except his will to power." The equation with Nazism in its Nietzschean genealogy appears clearly here, although Maritain takes care to draw no assumptions about the identity or nature of this ultimate but all too human antagonist: "The antagonist of Antichrist might be the truly human heritage of human civilization and the truly human pattern of human civilization . . . which long since has little by little been crumbling, and which, moreover, according to Paul's teaching on the mystery of Israel, will flower again some day, under new forms, like a resurrection for the world."

Thus the redemption of Israel and humanity are one and the same resurrection, one and the same final victory over death and despair. In looking for an answer to the mystery of Israel, and the apparent culmination of evil before the redemption of a broken world, Maritain cites not only the Pauline scripture but the Jewish scriptures — for example, Job — to emphasize that God does not have to explain Himself.[149] Yet as the evidence materialized that the Nazi regime had perpetrated an unprecedented crime against the Jewish people, Maritain, like Job, would still ask for answers.

CONCLUSION

Maritain's outspoken response to the increasingly open secret of the Nazi war against the Jews drew on his prewar denunciations of antisemitism, which in turn had been provoked by his prediction that unchecked anti-Jewish hatred would lead to the mass murder of European Jewry. He believed that a "general massacre of the race of Moses and Jesus," an unleashing of "extermination and death," would materialize in the midst of a general war begun by an irreconcilably racist Third Reich. When the war came in September 1939, it confirmed Maritain's apocalyptic expectations, and his sense that western civilization had entered its twilight deepened when France itself fell to the Germans in June 1940.

Yet Maritain's apocalyptic conception of the Second World War, even if it evoked the "liquidation of a world," did not amount to the end of the world itself. As he would write later in the war, an apocalyptic age by its very nature entailed a measure of hope: "In other words, the age in which we are already engaged is an apocalyptic age. Here I must point out that in my opinion the data of the Judeo-Christian eschatological literature must be interpreted as announcing not the end of the world but, on the contrary, a splendid renewal of the world for the time which is described as following the annihilation of the 'lawless' man."[150] While Hitler obviously personified lawlessness to Maritain as he did to countless others, Machiavelli, even more than Nietzsche, served as the lawless man's intellectual godfather.

Maritain added Machiavelli to his list of the founding fathers of deformed modernity — those "three reformers," Luther, Descartes, and Rousseau. But Machiavelli further served as a worldly foil for Maritain's wartime theodicy, with the Renaissance political strategist offering subsequent generations a cynical pathway to obtaining the kingdoms of this earth, only to be thwarted in the end by the promise, however distant, of divine justice. Maritain's Thomistic emphasis on natural law guided his conclusion that destructive evil's very lack of creativity deprived it of the ability to create anything lasting. Therefore, even if Maritain confronted an apocalyptic war — and at the very heart of that conflict the "extermination" of the Jews — with real anguish, he also held to the belief that, beyond the "outpour" of evil, a redemptive outcome, involving both Gentiles and Jews, lay in store.

Maritain's reading of Saint Paul, particularly his Letter to the Romans, helped him to affirm the enduring chosenness of "Israel," and underlined his absolute rejection of antisemitism as a contradiction of Christian faith. In the context of his times, Maritain further associated the eschatological promise of Jewish salvation with the rescuing of a once-Christian civilization from its own incipient apostasy, further granting Jews and even Judaism itself an unprecedented dignity. But the violent events that spurred Maritain's indictment of antisemitism at this time could also serve to reiterate a historical narrative of Jews being cursed for their rejection of Christ, and the very scriptural sources cited by Maritain testified to their supposedly unending blindness and obstinacy. And so, the terrible confirmation in 1942 of what Maritain called the "passion of Israel" would present the philosopher with an agonizing problem: how to reconcile an apocalyptic hope for Jewish redemption with a program of mass murder, aided and abetted by so many putatively Christian perpetrators and bystanders, the nature and scale of which defied even his most dire prewar predictions. How then would what Maritain called "the fair play of God" unfold — and to what end?

CHAPTER THREE

THE PASSION OF ISRAEL:
FINAL SOLUTION AND MASS CRUCIFIXION, 1942–1944

St. Paul tells Christians that they have been grafted upon the olive tree of Israel and have become partakers with them of the roots in the fatness of the olive tree. "Spiritually we are Semites," Pope Pius XI stated. It is our own roots, the carnal race of our God, which are now lacerated and crushed throughout the world. As a Christian, I know that my God is being slapped in the face by this anti-Semitic rage, and that in these abandoned and helpless, starving and murdered crowds, Christ, who is persecuted in every persecuted, is now suffering a new kind of passion. The central fact, which has the deepest meaning for human destiny, is that the passion of Israel today is taking on more and more distinctly the form of the cross and is that henceforth Christ should not separate, but unite Jews and Christians. Such is, from a Christian perspective, the significance of the "greatest mass crucifixion in history."

Jacques Maritain, April 1943

This passage encapsulates Maritain's conviction that the "passion of Israel" then underway in Hitler's Europe embodied both horrific and redemptive aspects, and that these aspects could best be understood as Christologically integrated. Despite the fact that these words came from the pen of a Catholic philosopher of an increasingly theological bent, they are not to be found in a scholarly tome intended for a learned circle's perusal or in a devotional tract meant to be read and meditated upon within the Church. Instead he made these remarks to a primarily Jewish audience in New York.

   In offering a Christian theological framing of the ongoing slaughter of European Jews as, among other things, a mass crucifixion, Maritain must have caused at least some of his listeners a certain discomfort. Given the long tradition of many Christians branding Jews "Christ killers," this association of countless murdered Jews with the Christian God Incarnate, with the Crucifixion, and with the Church could not help but induce mixed feelings. Nonetheless, his sorrowful empathy for Jewish suffering made itself felt and received acknowledgment at a time when the terrible secret of the Nazi program of mass murder had been publicly exposed, even if the scale of the programmatic slaughter still defied belief.[1]

The *Endlösung*, or Final Solution of the so-called Jewish Problem, took shape within Nazi-dominated Europe as a systematic and comprehensive policy of extermination forged between the summer of 1941 (Operation Barbarossa, 22 June 1941) and the beginning of 1942 (the Wannsee Conference, 20 January 1942).[2] The Nazi regime had already perpetrated widespread massacres and had established ghettoes in the East. At some point, probably late in the summer of 1941, Hitler decided on a decisive policy of deportation of Jews throughout Europe to death camps in Poland, a decision implemented under the aegis of the SS with all due fanaticism, secrecy, and haste. In fact, the perpetrators carried out the killing process with such speed that by the time Maritain and others in the Allied nations began publicly talking about these atrocities, most of the Final Solution's victims had already been murdered — something clear, of course, only in retrospect. Historian Christopher R. Browning succinctly narrates the horrendous sweep of death by decree through these simple statistics: "In mid-March 1942 some 75 to 80 percent of all victims of the Holocaust were still alive, while 20 to 25 percent had perished. A mere eleven months later, in mid-February 1943, the percentages were exactly the reverse."[3]

For Maritain, the sudden liquidation of European Jewry materialized in the context of an apocalyptic war waged by neo-pagan forces against a Christian — or as he now allowed, a Judeo-Christian — civilization in decline. At the very center of the larger conflict, he considered the Nazi war against the Jews a threat both to the Jewish people and the Christian faith, insisting upon the reasonableness of hope while acknowledging the temptation of despair as evidence mounted of the scale of the atrocities in East Central Europe:

> The Christian spirit is threatened today in its very existence by implacable enemies, fanatics of race and blood, of pride, domination and hate. In the midst of the terrible ordeal, everything indicates that in the depths of human conscience a powerful religious renewal is in preparation which concerns and which will draw back all the believers of the great Judeo-Christian family, not only the faithful of the Catholic church and those of the Protestant churches, but also those of Judaism whose abandonment to suffering and nameless iniquity, and to the sword of vile executioners, would be an unbearable horror for the soul if we

did not see therein a terrible reminder of the promises of their God. And it is by working in the depths of earthly life, so as to transform temporal existence, that this spiritual renewal, whatever irreducible dimension it may imply on the dogmatic and religious plane, will exert a common action and produce common fruit.[4]

This reference to a "great Judeo-Christian family" reflected an increasing emphasis on the interdependence of Jews and Christians both in the temporal defense of western civilization and, even more significantly, in the economy of salvation. In this time of war and extermination, the common spiritual destiny of Jews and Christians appeared ever more obvious to a Catholic thinker tormented and intrigued by the cumulative effect of centuries of estrangement.

Maritain had assumed an increasingly uncompromising public opposition to antisemitism in the interwar period, even though his ambivalent philosemitism centered on a primarily theologically based veneration of Israel freighted with persistent anti-Jewish stereotypes — including stubbornness and carnality. But the increasing tendency of racist antisemitism toward hateful rhetoric and violent deeds forced him to confront the language used by Christians in referring to the "elder race." It became clear to Maritain before 1939 that the brutal manifestations of anti-Jewish sentiment promised an "extermination of the race of Moses and Jesus," a veritable "passion of Israel." In the midst of an ensuing apocalyptic war, this passion of the Jews assumed a pointedly eschatological significance and prompted intense questioning on his part. These questions centered on the meanings of moral evil, racist antisemitism, and what Maritain called the "passion of Israel."

A Thomistic, natural law diagnosis of otherwise "unbearable" evil led Maritain to conclude that a "consummation" of a redemptive work of love presented itself, even within the context of *Einsatzgruppen* massacres, squalid ghettoes, and death camps. His theory of modern antisemitism as an essentially Christophobic phenomenon paradoxically drew heavily on Jewish influences, including the writer Maurice Samuel and the painter Marc Chagall. This understanding of antisemitism as Christophobia correlated with his appreciation, reinforced by Saint Paul and Léon Bloy, of salvation coming, in Jesus' words, "from the Jews."[5] Maritain became conscious at a deeper level of the positive power of words and images to denote Judeo-Christian communion in suffering. This consciousness coincided with a heightened awareness of the denigrating import of some traditional Christian representations of Jews. Such increased sensitivities showed themselves in Maritain's attempt to navigate and negotiate the most problematic aspects of his own identification of the Final Solution as a sign of Israel's continued election as the people of God and as a crucial step toward their perhaps imminent integration into the body of Christ.

"THE HORRORS THAT GOD ALLOWS TO HAPPEN"

How did Maritain's Thomistic understanding of the problem of evil apply itself to the mounting evidence of mass murder, particularly the systematic killings of millions of Jews? During World War II, both Christians and Jews were being slaughtered, but he granted the agony of the Jews a theological-historical specificity, if not a certain primacy within the larger tragedy. For Maritain, antisemitism was essentially the modern world's attack on Christ. Therefore, persecuted Jews unwittingly suffered on Jesus' behalf. As Jesus in turn suffered with them, they consequently drew closer to recognizing their true Messiah. Seeing that the perpetration of such a horror could lead to the messianic redemption of Israel required a fuller understanding of God's permission of evil. Maritain drew on Thomistic thought to approach the problem of theodicy in the face of unprecedented horror. He explained in the 1942 Aquinas Lecture at Marquette University that "sin and the suffering and sorrow that form its retinue are not permitted for the greater perfection of the machine of the world, but for the consummation of a work of love which transcends the whole order of the world."[6]

In his lecture, "Saint Thomas and the Problem of Evil," delivered on the sixth of March, Maritain asked two essential questions about the evil perpetrated by and experienced by human beings: Why is there evil in the world? And what responsibility, if any, does God bear for its manifestations? Following Saints Thomas and Augustine, Maritain declared, "Evil is neither an essence nor a nature nor a form nor an act of being," but rather a *"privation* . . . like a wound or mutilation of the being," its power coming from "the very power of the good that evil wounds and preys upon."[7] For Maritain, evil was parasitical, predatory, and corrupting. Rejecting the Enlightenment caricature of God's permission of evil, he argued that Saint Thomas's view of evil differed utterly from Gottfried Wilhelm Leibniz's later "best of all possible worlds" rationalization.

Leibniz's theodicy sought to explain evil and justify God using the language of an emerging Enlightenment. The result was the notion of a bloodless, mechanistic deity bearing little resemblance to the suffering God-in-man of Christ:

> This philosopher, then, will tell us that it is a good thing for a
> mother to bewail the death of her child, because the machine of
> the world required it in order to be more perfect. . . . Explain
> this Leibnitzian position to the mother in question . . . and she
> will answer that she cares not one whit for the machine of the
> world — let them give back her child! And she will be ab-
> solutely right; for such questions are not resolved by the machine
> of the world but in the darkness of faith, and by the cross of
> Jesus.[8]

A merely natural explanation of evil and its effect on human beings cannot suffice. In Maritain's anthropology, the person embodies an intrinsic relationship not only with nature but also with God. Because of the human relationship to God, moral evil is the tragic "sin of a person, the disaster of the universe and a wounding of God."[9]

Because God created humankind not simply "in a state of pure nature . . . but in actual fact . . . in a state of grace,"[10] mutual love between God and the human person requires freedom, including a freedom to err, even to err monstrously. In these terms, evil becomes less a philosophical problem than a theological mystery. Maritain applied this spiritually existential perspective to the horrors of his time: "I do not say, moreover, that he who is at this moment prey to evil can find satisfaction in any answer no matter how true it may be. The experience of that which is in itself without any consolation, the experience of death can be surmounted or, rather, absorbed, only by another experience, of a divine order — by the experience of paschal love."[11] The paschal mystery, centering on the redemptive death of Jesus Christ, provides the only real opportunity for a "supernatural transformation of the creature into God." With Aquinas, Maritain concludes that sin, including the evil at its core, "is the price of glory."[12]

If sin and evil are indispensable to redemption and glory, is the Creator responsible for what appears as the inevitable sins of His creatures? In the midst of the bloodiest conflict in history, the question of evil in the light of divine power and goodness and human agency and fallibility could not help but assert itself. Maritain's Thomism asserted a defect of the will of the individual person as an originating — though not in and of itself evil — cause of an evil act. When the person "acts with that voluntary non-consideration [of "the rule," that is, of the natural law available to even a limited intellect], such an act will bear in itself the teeth-marks of nothingness."[13]

Maritain turns to both the exhortation of the Gospel and the nihilistic "will to power" in his own time to support the point that moral evil draws on the human person's unnatural and therefore sinful assertion of *nothingness*: "Here we have traced evil to its innermost hiding-place; here the creature is the primary cause, but negatively; I think we might summarize that doctrine in the words of the Gospel: 'Without Me you can do nothing.' [John 15:5] . . . but if it concerns evil, then the text should be otherwise interpreted. . . . Without Me you do nothingness, without Me you can introduce into action and being the nothingness which wounds them and which constitutes evil."[14] For Maritain, this opting for nothingness epitomizes an age in which centuries of anthropocentric humanism have now reached bloody fruition.

These fruits could be seen in "the social divinization of the State and of the anonymous mass incarnate in a Leader who is no longer a normal ruler but a sort of inhuman monster whose omnipotence is based on myths and lies."[15] As far back as the 1920s he had observed this deformative history, but he now emphasizes that God has not laid out a scripted plan for human history. People are not pawns being played for a higher purpose. Nor is "the divine scheme . . . a scenario written at a previous time, which is later to be performed by creatures."[16] In the perspective of eternity, mysterious to the human eye, neither fatalism nor determinism can supersede the imperative of trying to grasp the significance of evil: "As a matter of fact, we are surely called upon to build up a theory of evil if we are to interpret philosophically our time."[17] The regnant crisis of civilization demands such an understanding.

Could Maritain's Thomistic excursus, seeing within God's permission of evil an undying and transcendent love, apply itself directly to the incomparable sin of what would soon be called genocide?[18] He answered this question in another essay devoted specifically to antisemitic hatred and the evil of mass murder:

> Jesus Christ suffers in the passion of Israel. In striking Israel, the Anti-Semites strike Him, insult Him, and spit on Him. To persecute the house of Israel is to persecute Christ, not in His mystical body as when the Church is persecuted, but in His fleshly lineage and in His forgetful people whom He ceaselessly loves and calls. In the passion of Israel, Christ suffers and acts as the shepherd of Zion and the Messiah of Israel, in order gradually to conform His people to Him.[19]

The close, painful involvement of Christ alongside the victims of the evil of Nazism, even among those "forgetful people" of the original covenant, points to a love greater than any other. It also points to the identification of the Jewish people as a scapegoat or sacrificial lamb, on the one hand, with an attendant sense of blamelessness, and on the other, a reminder of Jewish forgetfulness, evoking what Paul called "blind eyes and deaf ears."[20]

These words, reiterated in various forms during the war years, originated in an article "On Anti-Semitism" published 6 October 1941 in *Christianity and Crisis* — a journal published by Reinhold Niebuhr, an American Protestant and Maritain's friend. The article summarized Maritain's overall appraisal of the emerging horrors experienced by Jews in wartime Europe and the corrosive power of antisemitic evil on the human conscience. Having asserted the utter incompatibility of antisemitism and Christianity, and having drawn the ire of those Catholics who disagreed with his conclusions, Maritain took stock of the moral destruction waged by antisemitism, both within his own France, and in the rest of the Christian world. In another context, the philosopher could emphasize how, in terms of ultimate significance, evil always harmed the perpetrator more than the victim: "It is better to be punished than to be guilty."[21] He saw the Vichy regime's antisemitic laws as both a contradiction of "the traditions and the spirit of my country," and (not entirely accurately, as historians would later ascertain) an imposition by the foreign occupier aided and abetted by opportunists such as Premier Pierre Laval.[22]

What Maritain saw as a base display of German racist hegemony and craven collaborationism by traitorous Frenchmen he could understand as a passing, however terribly shameful, episode within the larger context of a war only temporarily lost by France. He worried more, however, about the long-term danger of "psychic poisons" on the populace as a whole, fearing that "many weak people will resign themselves to the worst. . . . Finally they will find themselves perfectly able to look at or contribute to the destruction of their friends, with the smile of a clear conscience (life must go on!)." In short, Maritain saw the unfree French as particularly vulnerable to the threats and blandishments of their so-called leaders.

He obliquely acknowledged that these chief collaborators simply might be telling the general population what it wanted to hear, offering citizens of the True France a moral alibi for disengaging themselves from the fate of a few Jewish neighbors: "I feel horrified by the anti-Semitic corruption of souls that is being furthered in France by a leadership which still dares speak of honor." He continued, in speaking of the rest of the West, to describe Nazi German antisemitism as if it were a virus to which neighboring peoples had little or no immunity: "It is impossible to compromise with anti-Semitism; it carries in itself, as in a living germ, all the evil of Nazism. Anti-Semitism is the moral Fifth Column within the Christian conscience."[23] Without answering the question, Maritain certainly posed it. What made the French and Christian conscience susceptible to the pagan antisemitism emanating from the Third Reich?

During *les années noires*, Maritain never ceased defending the honor of the French people, or the integrity of the Catholic Church. In September 1942, he wrote to Hannah Arendt, who had escaped Vichy France along with Chagall and other targeted Jewish artists and intellectuals. He cautioned her not to identify the outburst of antisemitism by a "reactionary press" during the turn-of-the-century Dreyfus Affair with French Catholicism as a whole.[24] On the contrary, Maritain could cite a papal admonition to French Catholics not to involve themselves in that *fin-de-siècle* controversy. Nevertheless, the slowness with which French Catholics were now awakening to the persecution of Jews across Hitler's Europe, and in France itself, gave rise to a certain defensiveness on his part.[25] He continued to feel the need to explain away his past affiliation with the Action Française,[26] as his nuanced Christian anthropology and sense of history wrestled with a persistent set of essential types, be they Jewish or Christian, German or French.

Whatever the limitations of Maritain's analysis of the crisis of violent eliminationist antisemitism *in the very midst of its rapid unfolding*, one should recognize that, as an exiled intellectual, he primarily concerned himself with winning a global war against corrupted notions of person, family, and community. In *The Rights of Man and Natural Law*, written in 1942, he made explicit the nature of this evil: the reduction of the human person to an atomized, and merely physical, individual, first via bourgeois self-deification and then through totalitarian enslavement. He reiterated his attack on anthropocentric humanism, contrasting a hell-on-earth of Machiavellianism run amuck with a truly free world inhabited by the citizens of "personalist," "communalist," "pluralist," and "theist" societies.[27] Rather than prescribing the details of how to establish such free polities, Maritain pointed to the destructive power of the war itself as a clarifying force: "The present war gives us notice that the world has done with neutrality.[28] Willingly or unwillingly, States will be obliged to make a choice for or against the Gospel. They will be shaped either by the totalitarian spirit or by the Christian spirit."[29]

The Rights of Man and Maritain's other wartime works show that he did not believe that the Second World War embodied a Manichean struggle between good and evil. Instead, he insisted on the basic asymmetry of created good and corrupting evil. Nonetheless, his writings portray a dialectic at work within the war and throughout history. He summed up this dialectic in an axiomatic "double law of the degradation and revitalization of the energy of history. . . . Thus the life of human societies advances and progresses at the price of many losses."[30]

This juxtaposition of staggering casualty lists with advancement and progression in the *longue durée* of history appears for a reason, namely, to animate resistance to the antihuman enemy and explain what things were still worth fighting for: "In contrast to the myth of the twentieth century as the Nazis conceive it, in contrast to the millennium of brutal domination which the prophets of Germanic racism promise their people, a vaster and greater hope must surge up, a more fearless promise must be made to the human race. The truth of God's image naturally imprinted on us, liberty and fraternity — all these are not dead."[31] The human person as *imago Dei* encapsulated Maritain's Christian hope for humanity as well as his insistence on the redemptive necessity of struggle and suffering as participation in the divine.

Hence Maritain saw the dignity of the human person not as an abstract philosophical principle insulating the individual from the travails of the world. His conception of human dignity entailed a more than merely natural reality that had been increasingly and tragically obscured to the point where its uncovering and restoration could only come to pass in otherwise senseless bloodshed: "In the terrible confusion of our day, it is for those truths which are inseparable from the authentic principle of human emancipation that the free peoples are willy-nilly engaged in a merciless struggle. And it is through the distorting lens of the false philosophy of Emancipation for which they are shedding their blood; and it is only by dint of suffering that their eyes are little by little being opened."[32]

Maritain saw this war as awakening all humanity. An understanding of the natural law not only held the indispensable key to opening up a true and lasting conception of human rights, but also pointed to the unavoidable necessity of fighting to the finish in order to secure them: "Some have turned against these rights with an enslaver's fury; some have continued to invoke them, while in their inmost conscience they are weighed down by a temptation to skepticism which is one of the most alarming symptoms of the present crisis. A kind of intellectual and moral revolution is required of us."[33]

Writing at the behest of the United States Office of War Information, Maritain ended his work of political philosophy on a stirring note. Privately, however, he had been confronting the fullness of despair, as growing evidence of the magnitude of the relentless killings reached America. Through contacts in the American Jewish Congress as well as his connections with the Office of Strategic Services (OSS), the precursor of the Central Intelligence Agency, he learned more and more about the Final Solution in 1942. His *École Libre des Hautes Études* colleague Professor Paul Vignaux worked in the OSS New York office. The OSS "Bern channel" relayed Maritain's 9 August 1943 message of encouragement to the French Catholic Resistance, a message which included his desire to "salute our persecuted Jewish brothers."[34] But Maritain himself desperately needed encouragement during this period.

His 9 December 1942 letter to friend and former student Yves Simon illustrated his emerging awareness of the genocide he had foreseen during the previous decade, an anticipation which must have seemed to him like a mere abstraction compared to the unyielding reality:

> Thank you again my dear Yves. Know that you have given me a great consolation in a moment of sorrow that threatened to overwhelm me. How can one go on living while thinking of the horrors that God allows to happen, of the two million Jews massacred in Poland, of all that has been done in France to the refugees? The details that are coming in are atrocious. If I did not have these souls [Raïssa and Véra] in my charge, I would prefer to return there to be put to death.[35]

Maritain evidently viewed his own spiritual suffering as woefully inadequate in the face of these horrors, but reconciled himself to his relative helplessness in caring for two Jewish women — converts to Christianity to be sure, but such fine distinctions no longer mattered in the European slaughterhouse. These Russian-born refugees from France likely would have been deported to their deaths had they not accompanied him on a lecture tour in early 1940. That two exiled daughters of Israel helped save a Gentile from despair and death during this time, by presenting him with the burden of their care, makes for something of a post-biblical parable.

For Raïssa, these times of terror and misery constituted not a parable related but a prophecy fulfilled. As with her husband, Bloy's words and images about earthly suffering, apocalyptic horror, and the Jewish and Christian roles in the drama of salvation remained ever on her mind. She perceived within the maelstrom of the war a foretold meeting of Church and Israel through tortured love and shared suffering:

> But it is only today, confronted with the unspeakable Passion, that of Love, afflicted in the hearts of men and among nations, and in the light of present events, that we can really take stock of the prodigiously exact vision Léon Bloy had of the misery of his time and our own. Christendom, founded at the cost of the blood of martyrs, is falling into dust. The Church which is encharged with all the human race is like an abandoned mother who no longer has the power to protect her children. And who among the leaders of nations, still thinks of the rights of truth and justice, of mercy or of pity. . . . The Passion of Israel will be the reflected image of this agony of Love. And in this unspeakable community of suffering, Israel will recognize Him of Whom it is the symbol.[36]

Depicting the murder of millions as an "agony of Love" makes little sense when looking at the bare historical facts concerning the Final Solution and its implementation. But for Catholic consciences, such as Raïssa Maritain's and her husband's, merely designating the unthinkable as a senseless crime or a horrific tragedy would be rationally inadequate as well as incompatible with their spirituality animated by faith, hope, and love. Accounting for a God of Love permitting evil of this magnitude demanded that proportionate meaning be found. For the Maritains, this otherwise elusive meaning would be nothing if not Christological.

CHRISTOPHOBIA

In this spectacle of unprecedented evil, with war, occupation, and genocide degrading souls and destroying lives, Maritain saw Nazism as the greatest corruption of the human potential to control nature and forge a common destiny.[37] He saw Jesus suffering alongside the Jewish targets of the Third Reich's "most perfect machinery of murder and of death."[38] The Jews caught on this merciless wheel of fire could be described most fully in terms of their relationship with Christ as "His forgetful people whom He ceaselessly loves and calls," their messiah suffering all the while alongside them.[39] But Maritain avoided drawing further conclusions about Jewish "forgetfulness," lest he take the decisive turn toward blaming the victims.

Instead, and in keeping with a theology of love as mutual giving between Creator and creature, he argued that, in the hands of the Nazis and their collaborators, Jews underwent Christ's own agony. In other words, persecuted Jews drew unto themselves the world's continued rejection of God Incarnate, who in turn suffered with them. Maritain did not imply that the victims were both conscious and willing agents in a transcendent self-sacrifice as understood by most Catholics.[40] But he did view Jewish suffering as part of the work of atonement.

This "at-one-ment," as one recent theologian puts it, is not just "achieved through the once for all self-offering of the Christ on the cross," but also "continually reenacted and re-experienced as its significance is recognized and accepted for every contingency of human living."[41] Eight hundred years earlier, Saint Anselm had written of the atonement as a painful but necessary completion of the work of creation, for "God should finish what he has begun," rather than leaving a broken world in disorder.[42] Not only had Christ come into the world to effect such an "at-one-ment," to ransom an otherwise unredeemable human race, but the God-man had come from the Jews. Recognizing the Jewish people as Christ-bearers in a world that had not yet experienced the fullness of redemption, Maritain diagnosed "Christophobia" as the motive force behind modern racist antisemitism, the Nazi war against the Jews, and the "passion of Israel."

In putting forth this Christological premise for Jewish victimization, he cited the work not of a Catholic or Protestant theologian, but of Maurice Samuel, a Romanian-born American Jewish writer, who had written that antisemites "must spit on the Jews as 'Christ-killers' because they long to spit on the Jews as 'Christ-givers.'" Maritain welcomed the opportunity to "point out that the most impressive Christian formulas concerning the spiritual essence of anti-Semitism may be found in a book recently published by a Jewish writer, who seems himself strangely unaware of their profoundly Christian meaning."[43]

Maritain saw it as immaterial whether Samuel was himself an observant Jew, as "prophetic intuitions are all the more striking when they pass through slumbering or stubborn prophets, who perceive only in an obscure way what they convey to us."[44] Echoing Maritain's personalism of the 1930s, Samuel argued that Jewish and Christian humanism was under attack in the present war: "Nazism-Fascism says that man exists in and by virtue of *the* machine [*sic*]; Judaeo-Christianity says that a machine must exist for man, or must not exist at all. And everyone who takes this point of view allies himself ultimately with Judaeo-Christianity."[45] With help from Samuel, Maritain came to see antisemitism as essentially a hatred of Christ. How did this realization affect his response to the chaos and carnage of his time and his understanding of Jewish-Christian relations?

Reflecting upon this insight of Christophobic antisemitism, which Maritain claimed his own theological analysis had groped for but not achieved, Maritain saw evidence of a larger phenomenon; a number of Jewish thinkers beginning to draw closer to the Gospel by hearkening back to their own prophetic tradition. His September 1942 *Commonweal* article, "Anti-Semitism as Problem for the Jew" analyzed this aspect of Jewish soul-searching amidst the terrors of Nazi antisemitism. Shortly before *Kristallnacht*, Maritain had criticized secularized German Jews for not returning to their Abrahamic and Mosaic traditions. Now he mourned the modernized Jew, lamenting "that split attitude and that peculiar self-consciousness which sometimes lead the Jew to self-negation."[46]

What once had been Maritain's indictment of Jewish carnality still appears as such but in a more sympathetic vein. His chiding of Jews for forsaking their covenant and failing to live as Jews appears pointed enough to come from a Jewish rather than a Christian critic: "The hated, humiliated, and hunted man cannot help but wonder what are the reasons for the iniquitous wound which is inflicted upon human nature within him. The answer was quite simple for the pious Jew of old, convinced as he was of the divine election of his people. Not so for the rationalistic-minded Jew of today."[47] Maritain saw a degree of Jewish apostasy as, if not instrumental in the coming of the catastrophe, at least as a paralyzing factor behind Jewish responses to it.

Maritain drew two conclusions from the premise that only religious Jews could understand and withstand the apocalyptic fury of antisemitic hatred then underway, one relating to their enduring Jewishness, another to incipient conversion to Christianity. On the one hand, and in reference to the temporal question of the survival of civilization, he argued that only Jews spiritually conscious of their commonality with Christians, but proud of their role in forging western civilization, could weather the assault of Nazi totalitarianism. More importantly, the faithful Jew-as-Jew had an indispensable role to play in saving humanity: "As he has understood that the God of Israel is also the God of mankind, he has likewise understood that in the tidal wave of pagan blood surging up today, our civilization is revealed as a Judaeo-Christian civilization, and that this civilization will perish unless both Christian and Jew come better to perceive the vital part each one plays in its total pattern."[48] Furthermore, the "Jewish" portrayal of antisemitism as Christophobia might save Christians from an antisemitism "more disastrous to the Christian world than to Jewry."[49]

It is difficult to imagine anyone facing a greater peril than the European Jews during 1942 and subsequent years. However, Maritain saw spiritual disaster for Christians in passive complicity in places such as France, "where Christian conscience arises indignant yet powerless against the utter betrayal of human rights which a so-called French government assumes as an added shame."[50] Even with the "purpose of extermination" patently obvious, French policemen had rounded up on behalf of the Germans approximately 13,000 Jews in Paris on 16–17 July. Of those arrested, 8,160 found themselves confined for anywhere from three to six days in an indoor bicycle arena (the *Vélodrome d'Hiver*) without water, food, or toilets.[51] Others caught in the *Aktion* had been sent directly to the transit camp at Drancy, outside of Paris, the final stop before Auschwitz itself.[52]

Faced with horror and helplessness, Christians who otherwise could do little or nothing to stop the atrocities at least could begin to atone by emulating Jews. Maritain urged his coreligionists to see the upcoming Yom Kippur fast as an opportunity to:

> Display before God our brotherly compassion for Israel and make heard our cry on its behalf by praying especially for the Jews and sharing in their penance on this Jewish Day of Atonement. For our relation to the Jewish people is not only a human one, as it is with other suffering national minorities and persecuted peoples, it is also a divine one, a relation of spiritual consanguinity within God's redeeming scheme; a relation that, together with that mysterious drama and rivalry which Saint Paul has depicted, involves and must involve cognate love and charity.[53]

He sought to set something of an example for this showing of Christian respect and compassion for the "'elder race,' for which Christ wept and which is ever dear to His heart."[54]

In September 1942, the "indignant yet powerless" exiled French philosopher confronted his own shame regarding the "*Vel d'Hiv*" roundups in a radio broadcast in which he addressed the Jews of France:

> My Jewish friends, my brothers, allow a Christian to speak to you not only with compassion but with the sacred respect that your sorrows inspire in him. In the depths of suffering into which you have been plunged, you give testimony, in your inexpressible agony, to the grandeur of Israel, of the people to whom promises were made without repentance, of the olive tree onto which all the Christian nations have been grafted. And it is also

for the nations as well that you suffer mysteriously, including France, who finds herself tortured by the same executioners, delivered and betrayed by the same men who are your own persecutors.[55]

Maritain spoke of an essential equality between Jews and Christians, borne out in the same drama of unmerited suffering, and within this drama the mystery of Jews suffering on behalf of the Gentiles. How and why the Jewish victims of Nazi terror and French collaboration had been drawn into this obviously unwanted role of vicarious sufferers remained unclear in this radio address on the "racist persecution in France."

Elsewhere, Maritain offers a clearer explanation, stressing the spiritual, even salvific, import of the Jewish catastrophe, with salvation coming both to and from the Jews. Without discounting the vital need for a temporal Christian-Jewish rapprochement, this earthly reconciliation has only secondary significance compared with the eschatological promise of Jewish integration into the Church. Jewish destiny involved the fullness of being chosen by God and accepting that chosenness in Christ. In his 1941 essay "On Anti-Semitism," Maritain had addressed a growing Jewish comprehension of *their* Jesus, who had lived, preached, and died among them: "The growing solicitude in Israel's heart for the Just Man crucified through the error of the high priests, is a symptom of unquestionable importance. Today in America, representative writers like Sholem Asch and Waldo Frank are trying to reintegrate the Gospel into the brotherhood of Israel. While not yet recognizing Jesus as the Messiah, they do recognize him as the most pure figure in human history."[56] Maritain argues that Jews like Asch[57] hardly realize the extent to which, as they welcome back Jesus (Yeshua), they draw closer to accepting Christ.

One can read this passage simply as a statement of triumphalist expectation that Jews soon would abandon Judaism, but the rest of the paragraph reveals a more complicated picture. Maritain also posits that as they ascend toward Christ, Jews will inevitably bypass, or hopefully meet, Christians falling away from the Truth, for "Israel is beginning to open its eyes, whereas the eyes of many self-styled Christians are blinded, darkened by the exhalations of the old pagan blood suddenly ferociously welling up once more among the Gentiles."[58] Again citing Pascal's pronouncement, dear to Bloy as well, that "Jesus Christ is in agony until the end of the world," Maritain saw apostate Christians as contributing to, if not increasing, that agony with a relapse to barbaric paganism and a murderous assault on Christ through His people. If the conversion of the Jews were truly at hand, it might also, indeed would have to, amount to the *reconversion* of countless Gentiles. While Maritain insisted that the "passion of Israel" not be considered a "co-redemptive passion" for the salvation of humanity, he nonetheless saw it as crucial to "the goading on of the world's temporal life" that would itself eventually find its redemption in its Savior.[59]

As mentioned above, Maritain explained salvation history as something not strictly linear in the way that limited human capacities envision it, but rather as an eternal moment in the mind of God. Many of his statements pointing to the ultimate salvation of the Jews through conversion might today be identified as supersessionist, but he would doubtless recoil from the designation, particularly in its assessment of Judaism as a "spent" or "dead" religion. On the contrary, he insisted on a necessary Jewish role in the reconversion of countless Christians.

While one cannot deny that this view of Jewish identity renders it an instrument of Christian history, it nonetheless avoids a denigration of Jewishness. In sincere admiration and respect for a people still loved by God, Maritain affirmed with Saint Paul that "the gracious gifts of God and his calling are irrevocable."[60] Maritain also acknowledged a profound debt to Jewish artists such as the Russian-born painter Marc Chagall, who in turn considered Maritain anything but disrespectful of Jews and Judaism. Maritain's Jewish friends and acquaintances did not have to agree with his Christian theological instrumentalism to appreciate and extol his political-historical stance on antisemitism and his outspoken solidarity with their plight.

Speaking on the occasion of the philosopher's sixtieth birthday celebration (held several weeks after the fact) in January 1943, Chagall, who had been spirited from France in 1941 with his wife Bella, paid tribute to his Christian friend:

> Though I have followed a different religious path, I nevertheless felt a kind of union with Maritain, and I asked myself: Could not what is possible in the spiritual realm be realized between men in the political field, in the social field, in the world where one war succeeds another, where among all the misunderstanding there is the gravest misunderstanding of all—the two-thousand-year-old misunderstanding which lies behind anti-Semitism, and has led to persecution, and finally the extermination of a people. . . . Since that time he has never ceased to act. He was one of the first men in France who broke the troublesome embarrassed silence which surrounded the "Jewish Ques-

tion." It seemed then, and — alas! — it still seems today, as if good breeding compels silence on this point, always and every-where. Why? . . . A long time ago you, my dear Jacques, and a few other courageous men stood up for the defense of these truths and of these oppressed people, giving to this defense all their minds and all their heart.[61]

Like Chagall, Maritain did not exorcise himself during this time with considerations of competing religious dogmas. What horrified him was the culminating rejection of God-in-man, seen both among the murderers and in the indifference of others. Moreover, he placed the mystery of the salvation of the Jews squarely within the problem of saving a broken world. Maritain saw brokenness not only in the dictatorial realms, but also in the democratic world. His concerns for the future of western civilization demanded the application of spiritual insights to temporal problems. The willful lack of awareness of Jewish suffering among the inhabitants of the supposedly free world could not exist in healthy democracies.

Maritain scornfully rejected the bystander mentality that he some-times saw in the democracies, particularly in areas safely removed from the fighting, and identified it squarely with Christophobia. His January 1943 address in New York on "Racist Law and the True Significance of Racism" discusses Nazi atrocities in detail, offers theological exegesis, and also concentrates on the guilt of bystanders:

What is as appalling as the murders by the assassins and the hor-rors of racist extermination is the inaction of those who could act and the indifference of many honest people. Each morning they read in their newspaper of new atrocities, as regularly as they take in their breakfast. They let out a sigh of indignation, then pass on to other news. They are caught in their routine. This routine of hell is one of the invisible crimes perpetrated on souls throughout the world by Nazi racism. And there is something worse still, and by that I mean the moral complicity that grows little by little, like an insidious leprosy among certain of those who, while condemning the abominations of Hitler, allow them to succeed imperceptibly through antisemitic sentiments. Be-cause it is a fact, and there is no sense in hiding it, that a kind of antisemitism more or less dormant grows in certain social mi-lieus in the democratic countries even as the Nazis pursue their work of extermination.[62]

Maritain wanted this lecture to instill "an inexpressible horror of intellect and of the heart in the face of the human degradation of which racist crimes are the expression, and a resolution to fight to the death against this degradation."[63]

Drawing on such sources as the reports of the American Jewish Congress, and recent articles in the *Jewish Frontier*, Maritain estimated that by the end of 1942, one to two million Jews had already perished, with five or six million still menaced with death in German-occupied Europe.[64] He further itemized these "monstrous fruits of Racist Law," or more to the point "described but a part . . . for one would have to hear all the cries of agony spread over Europe" to truly comprehend a "destruction going beyond the nightmares of the most infernal imagination."[65] His examples included details of large-scale massacres from Riga in the north to Jassy in the south, the "horror and shame" of the roundups and deportations in France, the suicide of Warsaw ghetto leader Adam Czerniakow, and the deportation of the Lodz ghetto inhabitants to their death in poison gas vans at Chelmno.[66]

But even as he described both the nature and extent of Nazi atrocities in horrifically graphic detail, he returned to moral philosophy to emphasize the spiritual destruction waged upon all mankind by the perpetrators: "The evil that covers the heart of the racist and antisemitic executioners in filth inflicts upon our nature a destruction even more dreadful still than the evil suffered by the tortured innocents. The conclusion to be drawn is that today we are seeing hell unleashed on earth. It is the devil, gentlemen, who is leading this dance."[67] The very irrationality of Nazism fed the diabolical nature of racist law, for Maritain a "homicidal idea par excellence." This perverted excellence came from Hitler and leading Nazis such as racial theorist Alfred Rosenberg realizing the power of rejecting even Machiavelli's cynical manipulation of law as a reflection of ethical norms. What remained was a complete contempt for law as an expression of reason and morality, and its final fashioning into nothing less than an instrument of State power and a means of murder.[68]

For Maritain, the problem amounted not only to one of racist antisemitism — itself a species of collective psychosis — but of German national psychology, with Nazism developing "within the rotten parts of the German people." Feeding an "ignoble pride" that could never truly satisfy itself, Nazi racism "needs an enemy to hate and destroy."[69] But Maritain further argued that this distinctly German neo-paganism only directed its hate against all Jews to strike at one Jew in particular:

There is only one thing firmly and unshakably at the heart of German racism and it is Nazi antisemitism: an extreme and paroxytic form of the old German antisemitism. And Nazi antisemitism is in its essence a furious aversion to the Revelation of Sinai and the Law of the Decalogue; above all, it is, as the American Jewish writer Maurice Samuel has well demonstrated, a supernatural fear and hatred that dare not speak their names, of Christianity and the Evangelical Law, and of this King of the Jews, Who is the Word Incarnate, the Word Who was in the beginning — the Word and not the Action! — and Who took bodily form in a virgin of Israel, and Who came to give witness to the truth, and Who proclaimed the Beatitudes to the poor and the merciful, and Who will topple the mighty from their thrones, and Whose kingdom is not of this world and Who will judge us all on love and on charity. Behold the things that make Nazi antisemitism grit its teeth and which excite its rage for destruction. It wants to exterminate the race of Christ from the face of the earth because it wishes to exterminate Christ from human history, it avenges itself on the Jews for the Messiah Who has come from them, and it humiliates and tortures the Jews in searching to humiliate and torture their Messiah in the flesh — it is essentially a Christophobia.[70]

The hatred of Christ present in antisemitism attained a deicidal rage in the Nazi attack on the Jews. But how did Nazi persecution implicate Christians? Should it rouse them to resistance?

Christians needed to defend threatened Jews for a variety of reasons. Beyond "simple human conscience," antisemitism challenged the followers of Christ to reflect on their origins and defend the people of "Christ, the Evangelists, the Apostles, and the first martyrs, and of this Israel of which the sap is holy, said Saint Paul, and onto whose branches we are grafted." Maritain recalled that Pius XI had reaffirmed the historical roots of the Church in the lasting spiritual brotherhood of Jews and Christians. Shortly before the pontiff's death, he pronounced to his flock that "Antisemitism is unacceptable; spiritually we are Semites." Likewise, he had rebuked Nazi racism in his 1937 encyclical *Mit brennender Sorge*. But another imperative for defending the Jews located itself in Christian self-defense. The "antisemitic rage," in seeking to "exterminate the Jews, wishes to impose upon Christ a new passion, in His people, while waiting, or perhaps simultaneously undertaking, to impose the same thing upon His Church. Woe to those who do not grasp these things, they who do not see that the knife is already raised against them."[71] Maritain concluded with both eleventh-hour desperation and faithful confidence that "the Jewish faith in the Messiah to come, the Christian faith in the Messiah already come, crucified, and resurrected, these are the supreme weapons against which racism and antisemitism will break."[72]

During the years in which the Final Solution "unleashed a hell on earth" for Jews and other various victims of Nazi hatred, Maritain devoted his efforts more than ever before to eradicating from his language the residual anti-Jewish stereotypes that had infused even his most impassioned prewar defenses of beleaguered Jews with a certain ambivalence. He maintained a consistently Pauline (and to an extent, Johannine) theological reference point in his exploration of the mystery of Israel. In the light of the extermination of the Jews, however, he began to dignify Judaism as a religion in its own right. He increasingly saw Jewish people as partners in both the rescue of civilization and the work of salvation.

By contrast, even the best intentioned Catholics, writing in defense of persecuted Jews in occupied Europe, could still unreflectively describe Jews as a people more or less opposed to God. For example, Jesuit Joseph Bonsirven's 1942 essay, "The Mystery of Israel," written in France and published in Switzerland, reinforced in the very midst of the genocide this sense of Jewish obliviousness to their divine destiny:

> See therefore how Judaism, closing itself up in a narrow understanding of the Law and withdrawing unto itself, consequently renounces its first calling as God's missionary. Moreover, this concentration, the primacy accorded to the letter of Scripture and the sovereignty of the Law, will have the effect of conceiving the Israelite religion as a kind of completed natural religion and, for all that, attenuating its supernatural character, and closing souls to the intimate interventions of divine grace.[73]

In their theological presuppositions, particularly as expressed before the war, Maritain and Bonsirven certainly would have agreed upon Israel's renounced vocation, be it a "missionary" (Bonsirven) or a "messianic" (Maritain) one.

But Maritain became increasingly uneasy because such formulations contributed to antisemitic hatred and violence. In 1943 he wrote the forward to Father John (Johannes) Oesterreicher's *Racisme-Antisémitisme-Antichristianisme.*[74] Oesterreicher was an Austrian-born convert from Judaism and a refugee from Nazism living at the time in the United States.

As he explained to Oesterreicher, who would later help draft the Second Vatican Council document *Nostra Aetate*,[75] Christians no longer could use the same language in referring to Jews:

> I think that in these days of the passion of Israel, we need to speak of the mystery of its faux-pas in a language sufficiently renewed for not running the risk of causing any injury and in order to keep divine things from getting mixed up in the human melange. This is precisely what you propose to do in insisting as you have on the drama of love between Israel and God. Nevertheless, it seems to me that perhaps the vocabulary could still be amended along this point of view (in the first pages notably). The Acts, Saint John, and Saint Paul all speak of "the Jews" (the Jews persecuted the Church in its infancy, the Jews wanted to kill Paul, etc...etc...) because they were thinking primarily of the rejection of Christ by Israel *as mystical body*, and subsequently characterized Jews in opposition to Christians (who were themselves largely Jews in the beginning). For those of us who do not speak in an inspired language, but that of human and historical narration, I think that we must take care not to speak of "the Jews" in such a case, but of such and such Jews.[76]

And while Maritain went on to cite his 1941 book *The Living Thoughts of Saint Paul* as crucial in forcing him to reconsider the replication of anti-Judaic tropes, the challenge of how to speak of Jews — and *to* Jews — in a new way became particularly acute as he confronted the singular and irrevocable horror of the "passion of Israel."

THIS MASS CRUCIFIXION

On the third of April 1943, Maritain stood before a predominantly Jewish audience and explained why he described the agony of European Jewry as the "passion of Israel." The overall purpose of his address, at the Hotel New Yorker to the 38th Council of the Union of American Hebrew Congregations, involved the "healing of humanity," a topic also addressed by a Protestant and a Jewish speaker. Maritain began with a statement of his "full awareness of and resignation to my own inadequacy," but trusting "that in freely expressing my own views I do not run the risk of hurting the conscience of anyone in the audience." He then proceeded to discuss "the Catholic conception of nature and the temporal order." Most of this discussion would be excised in the published version in the August 1943 *Con-*

temporary Jewish Record, which specified that "a section dealing with some points of Professor Maritain's address dealing with some aspects of Catholic theology has been omitted with his consent."[77]

But a reading of Maritain's original manuscript reveals this section as something other than an exposition of theological points of only academic interest or a lengthy excursus taken out due to limitations of space. Instead, one encounters the most provocative reason why the philosopher saw in the Final Solution the "passion of Israel," as well as the probable reasons the editors of the *Contemporary Jewish Record* chose not to include this section in the published article:

> I believe that the particular vocation of the Jewish people, dispersed among nations, has been to activate and prod earthly history through that passion for justice, that thirst to have God here below, which is deep-rooted in the heart of Israel. Thus the Jewish people, who remain always the chosen people and are always loved "because of their fathers," as St. Paul puts it, despite the misstep through which the Gentile world "entered" into their very privileges, the fact that they have not recognized the One Whom we believe to be their Messiah — the Jewish people are in the depths of this world, both the goad and the scapegoat of the world, which revenges itself on them for the stimulus it receives from them.[78]

One can assume that many Jewish readers, in the very middle of what we today call the Holocaust, would have been disturbed to see Jews described as "both the goad and scapegoat of the world," their slaughter at the hands of the Nazis amounting to an understandable — even if utterly unjust — "revenge."

Maritain's discussion of the world crisis in the published article encapsulated virtually all his wartime writings and offered a carefully worded message of conciliation to Jews on behalf of the Christian world. First he reviewed the history of anthropocentric humanism, reproaching it "not for having been a humanism but for being anthropocentric" and for having left reason "divorced from the supra-rational." This divorce accounted for the modern *"irrationalist* tidal wave: the awakening of a tragic opposition between life and reason" and a contemporary *"counter-humanism . . .* the basest form of which is the cult of race and blood, spreading all over the world the gospel of the hatred of reason, justice, and freedom, and walling the creature up in the abyss of animal vitality."[79] He also interpreted what he called "the data of Judeo-Christian eschatological literature" as indicating in the present crisis not the end, but hopefully "the splendid renewal of the world."[80] But in the interim, Nazism's "diabolical blazing hate" targeted Jews through a "psychopathically disguised Christophobia," leading to an undisguised "passion of Israel . . . taking on more and more distinctly the form of the Cross."[81]

As in other lectures and articles, Maritain hoped that from this new Passion a new understanding of the Crucifixion would arise and that "henceforth Christ should not separate but unite Jews and Christians." But on this occasion, he took more than typical care to avoid offending Jewish sensibilities, taking pains to stress at least the survival of Judaism as a religion rather than its eclipse by Christianity:

> Let us understand clearly what I mean. I am not speaking of any leaning of Judaism toward the Christian creed. I am speaking of a rapprochement in practical attitudes with regard to the world and world history. But from the perspective of a Christian this rapprochement would appear as a first step toward that final state of reconciliation which, as Cornelius a Lapide, the great commentator of St. Paul, put it, should not be called the *conversion* of Israel but rather its *fullness*, *"non conversio, sed plenitudo"* — both the fullness of Israel and of the Church — and which is described by St. Paul as the inutterable riches and vitalization of the world, a universal rekindling of faith and resurrection.[82]

A Jewish interlocutor might be excused for thinking that Maritain's conciliatory conclusion had merely squared the circle. What would be the ultimate future of Judaism after its adherents had supernaturally goaded the world into unleashing an all too natural wave of near total annihilation?

Despite Maritain's desire to avoid conveying anything punitive, using the Passion to encapsulate Jewish suffering is fraught with ambiguities. By reiterating the theme of Jewish crucifixion during the time of the killings, even if from a self-declared philosemitic standpoint, Maritain's representation of the tragedy could not avoid raising difficulties. The idea of a Chosen People punished by the rest of mankind under the permissive eyes of God for its role in sacred history is either incoherent or a mystery. Given his faith, he could hardly relinquish Paul's teaching about Israel's "misstep" and its enduring consequences. His indebtedness to Paul increased after researching and writing his book about the Apostle from whom he had taken the term, *the mystery of Israel*.[83] Maritain's use of this

Pauline teaching always risked raising the question of the responsibility of Jews in their own historical travails. To his credit, Maritain did not obscure the uncomfortable image of Jews "caught in God's trap."

The "passion of Israel" had transformed itself from a dire prophecy in the late 1930s, to a real possibility at the beginning of the 1940s, to a horrendously climactic reality in 1941–1945. Even if most of the rest of the Christian world seemed to ignore it, Maritain's prophetic term now resonated with the sounds of millions of victims' voices. Speaking to France in an early 1944 radio broadcast, he made this explicit, reiterating his earlier image of Jesus Christ abused by the antisemites: "Christ suffers in every innocent person who is persecuted, it is His agony that is exhaled in the cries of the countless human beings who are being humiliated and tortured. All that He has also taken upon Himself, there is not one wound that He has not felt, where He has not dropped a little of His blood, a trace of His pity at each step of the abominable route."[84]

At the conclusion of his address, he read a poem by Raïssa. Here is an excerpt:

> *If we cry abba! Pater!*
> *You do not welcome our cry*
> *It turns back upon us like an arrow*
> *Which has hit an impenetrable target*
> *You plunge us back into the night*[85]

That the Jews of Hitler's Europe should feel as forsaken as the crucified Jesus is understandable. Jacques relied on Raïssa to confront the evil of the mass slaughter of European Jewry by, in a sense, confronting God. To put it plainly, he talked about God, while his wife spoke to God, adding an interrogative counterpoint to what might otherwise remain a speculative, even if impassioned, discourse on what he called the passion of Israel. In his recent commentary on the book of Job, David Burrell writes about how the biblical account of Job's "ranting and raving" can best be read "as an adroit deconstruction of the very enterprise of theodicy itself, precisely by operating in a performative rather than propositional key."[86] With the help of his wife, Maritain managed to strike both keys, the performative and the propositional, in struggling with the "passion of Israel."

The Passion had been invoked periodically for various purposes in French national discourse during Maritain's lifetime.[87] In the present crisis, he hardly stood alone in using the Crucifixion as a metaphor for Jewish suffering and persecution. Might it not also stand as a sign of Jewish-Christian reconciliation? Not only did some Jewish writers and artists on both sides of the Atlantic employ the image of the crucified Jew Jesus during this period, but they did so far more frequently than did their Gentile counterparts.[88] Maritain cited his friend Chagall's 1938 painting known as the *White Crucifixion*: "Despite itself, Israel is climbing the route to Calvary side by side with Christians, and these strange companions are sometimes surprised to find themselves together. As in Chagall's admirable painting, the unhappy Jews are uncomprehendingly carried away in the great whirlwind of the Crucifixion, 'all around the Christ spread out across a lost world.'"[89] But another Jewish artist might use such a motif as a pointed indictment of Christians. Rather than depicting common ground, one might depict the enduring gulf between the elder Abrahamic faith and the younger one. Witness American Joseph Foshko's painting *Forgive Them NOT, Father, For They KNOW What They Do.*[90]

At the time of the commencement of the Shoah, Maritain had entertained the idea of Jews being caught in "God's trap." He categorically rejected the idea, however, that mass murder at the hand of the Nazis was the just punishment of a supposed "deicide race." In his letter to Hayim Greenberg, editor of the *Jewish Frontier* (a letter published in that periodical in August 1944), he offered a view of the Crucifixion both broad and personal. Maritain assumed his own guilt and explicated deicide in the contexts of both the Passion narrative and the outburst of contemporary antisemitic violence. Maritain would not reject the word *deicide*; rather, the term needed to be contextualized, qualified, and deinstrumentalized as a means of hatred against Jews.

For believing Christians, "Christ's crucifixion by God's people" necessarily constituted deicide. As God Incarnate, Jesus had been put to death despite His innocence of any crime. But Maritain insisted that "Christ's condemnation and death are a divine mystery, the most awesome irruption of God's secret purposes in human history, a mystery which can be looked at only in the light of supernatural faith."[91] Therefore, the reader of the Gospels needed to dispense with the idea of a Jewish conspiracy to kill God, on the one hand, and a tragic unfolding of Jewish fate on the other. Maritain argued instead for a more complex, and in his judgment, faithful reading of the four Gospels, the Acts of the Apostles, and Paul's Letters, emphasizing human freedom, divine mercy, and the transformative significance of the Resurrection.[92]

As he delicately put it, one could indeed attribute guilt to "a few persons, the princes of the priests, and to a certain extent, the mob of those days." Christian believers had "good reason to call this guilt a crime of deicide." He then offered a crucial, even if casuistic, distinction: "It was so in fact. But it was not so with regard to the conscience of the judges." Christian scriptural accounts affirmed that no one knowingly killed God Incarnate.[93] Then how could one still speak of Jews as chastised ever since the Crucifixion, as Maritain himself seemed to do? He responded with a historical and scriptural argument. Divine reprobation as such stemmed from a Jewish failure to recognize the risen Christ, a now-culpable ignorance, rather than guilt for having murdered the Messiah. Maritain also saw the reproaches leveled by the earliest (Jewish) Christian writers[94] as "no more anti-Semitic — and no less vehement — than those of Moses." In other words, these words fit into a tradition of Jewish prophetic discourse, and originated before the lasting separation of the Church and the Synagogue made such reproaches increasingly anti-Judaic. The problem of what he termed the "temporary dispossession of Israel" should be seen in the continuity of the relationship between God and His Chosen People. Here Maritain returned to his natural law diagnosis of evil as the corrupted or perverted good, identifying in Jewish unwillingness to believe in Jesus' divinity "the mystery of the solidarity of Israel as a people with its spiritual leaders, for whose fault the people were to pay for centuries."[95]

This perspective on the Crucifixion involves the covenantal relationship between the Jews and God; it thus comprises more of a supernatural mystery than anything else. Hence, Maritain admonished Christians to refrain from intervening in what might best be described as none of their business. His viewpoint was arguably more medieval than modern in this respect. He viewed Jews as in some measure rightfully — even if mysteriously — chastised, yet forbade the Christian mob to touch them: "But over and above all it must be stated that those who want to 'punish' the Jews — who are in the hands of *their* and *our* God—for the murder of Golgotha, make themselves guilty of blasphemy and sacrilege; they stupidly encroach for the sake of their own human wickedness upon the hidden purposes of God, they flaunt the love with which He waits for His people, they offend with their bloody hands eternal Wisdom itself."[96]

In Maritain's view, the term "deicide race" was "pregnant with anti-Semitic potentialities," and should be expunged. The term was a brutal oversimplification of the Passion narrative, and Maritain wanted the Church to assume the leading role in eliminating such dangerous language: "Christian teachers have a duty to rule out such expressions which are definitely

nonsense, as well as to purify carefully their language of similar impropri-
eties due to human thoughtlessness and to the indifference of Gentiles heed-
less of what did not directly concern themselves."[97]

Having not yet mentioned anyone save Jews in his exposition of
the Crucifixion, Maritain then asked the question of who had killed Christ.
He answered that all humanity had killed Jesus, particularly if one viewed
salvation history, as he did, from the perspective of eternity: "Who killed
Christ? The Jews? The Romans? I have killed Him; I am killing Him every
day through my sins. There is no other Christian answer, since He died vol-
untarily for my sins, and to exhaust the justice of God upon Himself. Jews,
Romans, executioners, all were but instruments, free and pitiable instruments of His will to redemption and sacrifice. That is what Christian teachers ought to inculcate in their pupils."[98]

In fact, the only people in the contemporary world who might merit
the designation of "Christ-killers" would be the antisemites themselves. In
reiterating a theological interpretation of racist antisemitism as a Christophobic assault against Jesus' fellow Jews, Maritain in effect reversed the
traditional accusation against the Jews, by accusing antisemites of nailing
Jesus to the Cross: "They are seeking an alibi for their innermost sense of
guilt, for the death of Christ of which they want to clear themselves. . . . In
reality they do not want to be redeemed. Here is the most secret and vicious
root by virtue of which anti-Semitism dechristianizes Christians, and leads
them to paganism." Only by reading and reflecting upon the inspired insight
of Saint Paul, through which Maritain realized "so acutely the essentially
anti-Christian madness of anti-Semitism," could Christians avoid a misunderstanding of the Crucifixion. "The mystery of God's rejection of the chosen people"[99] thus remained a mystery.

Maritain's letter to Greenberg constituted a heartfelt condemnation
of antisemitism, but it also retained a number of traditional Christian conceptions about Jews and the Crucifixion, including an almost complete absence of the Romans in his account of the Passion. His newfound devotion
to expunging potentially antisemitic language from Christian discourse
stopped short of challenging fundamental theological presuppositions. An
ambiguous stance even on the very term *deicide*, albeit while decrying its
often hateful employment, shows that Maritain's confrontation with his
own prejudices had not reached its term. That this process remained unfin-
ished had much to do with the fact of the ongoing war, and within it the
murder of millions of Jews, some of them close friends of the Maritains.
This made working on behalf of the Allied war effort, not quiet reflection,

the overwhelming priority for a devout Catholic philosopher caught up in what he saw as ultimately a religious war: "It is a religious war, not in the sense of the religious wars of the XVIth century, in which men killed each other for the sake of their faith in the God of Heaven and in eternal salvation — today it is for the sake of the temporal salvation of the world, for the sake of man's mission here below that peoples are obliged to suffer death and torture in struggling against the bestiality and hate of the Pagan Empire."[100]

What world would appear after the Pagan Empire's "sovereignty of hate" broke itself upon the power of redemptive Providence? This question had special relevance for the Jews left in the world, and in supramundane terms, for the mystery of Israel. Maritain's reiteration of the "passion of Israel," shrouded in mystery but asserting the close and painful involvement of God, raised the unavoidable question about what many people now called the *genocide*: to what end? Though he did not continue to probe this perhaps unanswerable theological question, Maritain's immediate temporal preoccupations did not exclude an emphasis on theological virtues. As the defeat of the Axis loomed, Maritain asserted that "hope is required of us as a historical duty since hope itself is a dynamic and transforming agent."[101]

To reinvigorate the hope of humanity, he argued that religion and politics would now have to be reconfigured in an organic, rather than antagonistic relationship. Such an organic relationship could only thrive in a polity embracing "Christians and non-Christians — from the moment that they recognize, each in his own way, the human values of which the Gospel has made us aware, the dignity and the rights of the person, the character of moral obligation inherent in authority, the law of brotherly love and the sanctity of natural law."[102] Maritain saw in a democratic framework the pluralistic and personalist prerequisites to a true respect for human dignity.

To this end, and because "what is now at stake is the very spirit of our Judeo-Christian civilization," he hoped that "a rapprochement of all those who believe in God, be they Catholic, Protestant, or Jew, a rapprochement of all those who know that the human person is the image of God, and that this fact is the very basis of human dignity and equality, is to be expected in the temporal field and for the sake of the common good of the earthly city."[103] But this gathering of faiths remained to be seen. Aside from the political uncertainties attendant on the end of a global war, a conflict which would have among its victors both the democracies and the Soviet colossus, there remained the question of the moral integrity of the western world.

Maritain knew that the agony of the Jews would continue until the very end of the war in Europe. He decried the "blind indifference of too many people, Christian at least in name, toward the most appalling mystery of contemporary history — the mass crucifixion of the Jewish people, and that new passion which Christ is now undergoing in His people and race."[104] He spoke these words at a March 1944 Boston University Institute on Post-war Problems. One year later, he found himself neither returning home to France from exile (except for a brief visit in late 1944), nor devoting himself to scholarly reflection in the United States. Both of these possibilities would have to wait. Instead, he would cross the Atlantic to assume the post of French ambassador to the Vatican, from which he would confront anti-semitism once again and try once more to fathom the fullness of the mystery of Israel.

CONCLUSION

By 1942, Maritain's fears of a war of extermination against European Jewry received the worst possible confirmation as news of the Third Reich's systematic Final Solution reached the Allied nations. While Maritain's efforts on behalf of refugees and toward raising public awareness of German atrocities occupied much of his time, he also devoted himself to questioning some of his own assumptions about Jews, Judaism, and Jewish-Christian relations. His opposition to antisemitism deepened into whatever reflective self-criticism he could manage in his overflowing schedule of activist, professor, university president, writer, and broadcaster. He sought to reconcile a curbing of anti-Jewish Christian rhetoric with a preservation of orthodox Christian teachings. More and more, he elevated Judaism to the status of a living religion, demonstrated a heightened respect for an enduring Jewish vocation, and made increasing references to a Judeo-Christian role in salvation history.

Since the beginning of the war, Maritain had taken upon himself the task of fostering hope in others, particularly his compatriots in occupied France, and in particular the increasingly beleaguered Jewish citizens and refugees trapped in his native land. Arguing for the inseparability of democratic freedoms and human dignity, he saw in the eventual victory of the democracies a new beginning of interreligious understanding after a traumatic winnowing of true humanism from anthropocentric errors. Yet even a positive future for Jewish-Christian relations could not mitigate in the immediate sense the cataclysmic evil evident in the "mass crucifixion" of

Europe's Jews. Could antisemitism possibly survive the unveiling of its wholly antihuman and anti-Christian essence? Maritain felt compelled to delve deeper into the mystery of evil, and in particular the divine permission thereof. This philosophical and theological exploration of evil formed an integral part of Maritain's confrontation with what we today call the Holocaust. Intellectually, he avoided explanations that anthropomorphized the subject. Spiritually, though, he sometimes let vent his competing feelings of frustration, powerlessness, and faith.

The resulting theodicy consigned evil to a theological mystery, in which the redemptive promise of incarnate love overcomes otherwise senseless tragedy. Some of Maritain's Jewish contemporaries (and no doubt many more observers today) found his Christological account of the Final Solution — Jesus suffering with the Jewish victims and the Jews in turn suffering for mankind — troublesome. But Maritain's vision of the "passion of Israel" should not be deemed blatantly supersessionist or triumphalist in intent. Nor did Maritain claim that Jewish victimhood in the Shoah constituted a kind of vicarious suffering, making Catholic saints of persecuted Jews. He posited only an unknowing imitation of Christ's atoning sacrifice by these helpless and forsaken victims.

Regarding the role of the Catholic Church faced with the mass murder of Europe's Jews, he often invoked Pius XI during the war but rarely referred to Pius XII.[105] Still, while Maritain lavished little public praise on Pius XII, scholars (including myself) have yet to uncover any pointed criticism of the wartime pontiff's sometimes circumspect stance. Neither reticence nor reverence seems to account for this tendency, for Maritain could question the pope's judgment in other respects, at least privately. For example, he saw the former Cardinal Pacelli as obsessed with communism before, during, and after the war.[106] After 1945, he would add the critique of overindulgence toward an unrepentant Germany to the balance sheet in his estimation of the Holy Father. But he would also insist that Pius XII had been above reproach in his attitudes toward Jews during the war, even as friends such as François Mauriac[107] and particularly Paul Claudel[108] sharply criticized what they saw as a papal silence regarding the murder of the six million. Maritain also specifically took exception to the claim, based on the September 1941 report of Pétain's ambassador to the Vatican, Léon Bérard, that the Pope or any of his immediate subordinates had bestowed a *nihil obstat* upon Vichy's anti-Jewish statutes.[109] That said, Maritain's faith in the Pope's goodwill toward the Jews endured but would be tested in the course of an unanticipated and unwanted sojourn in Rome, as this disciple of Saint Thomas Aquinas reluctantly accepted an appointment as France's first postwar ambassador to the Holy See.

CHAPTER FOUR

SPIRITUALLY, THE EXILE IS NOT OVER:
REFLECTING ON THE HOLOCAUST, 1945–1970

If there is something that I literally cannot bear, that kills me, it is this antisemitism that still brews and doubtless will continue to grow. They [fellow Christians] have not comprehended the divine tragedy, the sacred horror of this Golgotha of a people, even when they have helped them to the point of risking their lives for them. For them the question still poses itself in ignobly human terms. As for me, I feel I have become wedded to the destiny of Israel, and it seems that I will henceforth be a wandering Jew, without a rock on which to rest my head. Spiritually, the exile is not over.

Jacques Maritain, December 1944

As the Second World War came to an end, Maritain agonized both over the mass murder of millions of Jews and the likelihood that his fellow Christians would fail to draw the appropriate spiritual lessons from the carnage. As he wrote the words above — toward the end of 1944 to his friend, the Abbé Charles Journet — he felt this latter issue would never let him rest. Far from rejoicing that the Nazi genocide had neared its end, Maritain already mourned what he saw as continued Christian indifference to both Jewish suffering and the full import of the mystery of Israel as first enunciated by Saint Paul. His anguished concerns had not simply followed the genocide but had anticipated it. Maritain's self-description as a spiritual exile raises the question of whether he considered this incomprehension among his fellow Christians as extending to the Catholic Church, including Pope Pius XII himself.

Some recent historians have portrayed Maritain, who served as France's ambassador to the Vatican between 1945 and 1948, as an oppositional figure within mid-century Catholicism. He sometimes appears as a virtual mirror image of a reigning pontiff indifferent to the fate of Jews during and after the Holocaust.[1] Such interpretations of Maritain's continuing combat against antisemitism might make a potent contribution to historical debates about Pius XII, but they have little to do with the actual facts of Maritain's life and work, and they devote little or no attention to some important questions raised by his continued fight against anti-semitism.

John Conway has commented perceptively about recent scholar-ship on the Christian churches and the Holocaust, identifying a number of studies as "motivated by the eirenic desire to improve Christian-Jewish re-lations . . . written with a 'presentist' agenda, with all the benefits of en-lightened hindsight, an approach that runs the danger of distorting the historical balance of past events."[2] Assuming that Conway's critique has merit, it is worth examining to what extent our understanding of Maritain's historic role in furthering a post-Holocaust Christian-Jewish understanding has been affected by larger historiographical currents.

Making a more accurate and nuanced historical assessment allows us to focus our attention on some crucial questions about Maritain's philosemitism that touch on but ultimately transcend the Pius polemic noted above.[3] First, what lessons did Maritain believe Christians needed to learn from the Holocaust, and how could these lessons best be taught, committed to memory, and acted upon? Second, did Maritain see Pius as contributing to or hindering a necessary rethinking of Christian attitudes toward Jews after the Shoah, and if he disagreed with the Pope in this regard, can we better clarify the nature and extent of that disagreement? Finally, how had Maritain's own views on the Jewish Question changed by the end of his life, and how do they compare with those contained in official Catholic re-statements of Christian-Jewish relations issued before and after his 1973 death (*Nostra Aetate*, 1965; *We Remember*, 1998)?

AMBASSADOR TO THE VATICAN

Maritain's self-understanding as a spiritual exile corresponded with his practical situation at the end of the Second World War. Along with his wife Raïssa and her sister Véra, he had spent the war years in exile in the United States. At the end of the war, he knew he would soon decamp to Rome to assume the post of French ambassador to the Holy See. All that taken into account, the pain of this continued temporal exile paled beside the spiritual one described above. Maritain's conviction that most Christians misunder-stood the spiritual destiny of the Jewish people drew on his own journey in grappling with the Jewish Question from a theological and metahistorical perspective. What did Maritain perceive as the essential meaning of the recent genocidal horrors? What new imperatives presented themselves to Christians?

As we have seen, Maritain's views underwent important changes from the publication of his first essay on the Jewish Question in 1921, in which he decried the negative influence of "Jewish intrigues" in the modern world, to his second one in 1937, in which he pronounced the very impossibility of antisemitic prejudice for faithful Christians. Maritain never succumbed to outright antisemitism himself, but during the 1920s, particularly during the time when he still associated with the reactionary Action Française, he repeatedly venerated "true Israelites" and castigated "carnal Jews." During this relatively brief period he showed a willingness to associate with all but the most vicious antisemites. After the December 1926 papal condemnation of Charles Maurras' movement and writings, however, Maritain increasingly rejected the political precepts of the extreme right, including its often virulent antisemitism. His growing enthusiasm for pluralistic democracy — influenced in a positive sense by his Christian personalism and prompted in a negative sense by the rising fascist threat — helped him articulate a more coherent position of uncompromising opposition to racist antisemitism by the late 1930s.[4]

The "primacy of the spiritual" that guided his break with Maurras also guided his framing of the Jewish Question. Maritain's view, that Jews were a people obstinately and fatally bound to the world "until they change of their own accord," might strike today's readers as somewhat anti-Jewish. For example, one recent study of Holocaust memory in postwar France faintly praises Maritain as "one of the several Catholic intellectuals renovating their faith in direction of friendly condescension rather than hateful contempt for the Jewish people."[5] One cannot help but identify a certain ambivalence in Maritain's philosemitism even during the war. The question here is not whether Maritain subsumed Jewish suffering in a Christian metanarrative (of course he did), but whether his vision of a "forgetful people" finally being made aware of their true Messiah through genocide did indeed constitute something more than "friendly condescension."

Maritain's wartime assertion that "in our time, the passion of Israel is taking on more and more distinctly the form of the cross," points beyond death to resurrection and life everlasting, for Jews and Gentiles alike.[6] As much of Europe lay in ruins, Maritain had high hopes for the western world to engage in a recovery as much spiritual as physical. In early 1946, he finished writing *The Person and the Common Good*, which expanded on some of his wartime lectures. For Maritain, Nazism's ascendancy had demonstrated above all that a "purely biological conception of society" leads inevitably to the cheapening of human life, in which the termination of the undesirables becomes not only tolerated but desired. Indeed, he thought that all principal forms of materialist philosophy of society, whether bourgeois individualism, anti-individualistic communism, or racialist dictatorship, could be said to rest on the same root tendency to "disregard the human person in one way or another and in its place, consider willingly or not, the material individual alone."[7] All three materialist variants were for Maritain disastrous substitutes for the Christian vision.

A new or restored vision of the human person made in the image of God required that Christians in particular draw the appropriate lessons from the Jewish catastrophe. The consequences of a "purely biological conception of society" needed to be confronted. Maritain does so with an astute analysis of persecutor, victim, and Christian observer:

> In our own day we have seen monstrous persecutions: persecutions in which hangmen beyond number scientifically organized cruelty and assassination, bending themselves to the task of debasing man in his body and in his soul, not striking down persons condemned by reason of a faith to which at least they gave witness, but masses of men and women guilty only of the fact of their existence and wiped out like rats. And we have been able to verify the truth of the saying that next to the hangman what men detest most is his victim. Confronted by these great herds of victims left to their fate, the Christian questions his heart, his faith.[8]

During the war, Maritain had argued for religious faith itself as a necessary, if not sufficient, requirement for postwar recovery, since the conflict comprised "the final crisis of a century-old process of secularization." He therefore concluded that "a rapprochement of all those who believe in God, be they Catholic, Protestant, or Jew, a rapprochement of all those who know that the human person is the image of God, and that this fact is the very basis of human dignity and equality, is to be expected in the temporal field and for the sake of the common good of the earthly city."[9] But such a gathering of faiths remained to be seen.

After the recent release of his native France from Nazi captivity, and given his overwhelming desire to see a Christian renewal of western civilization in the wake of war and genocide, one might expect the eminent philosopher to have accepted enthusiastically Charles de Gaulle's July 1944 offer of an appointment to the Vatican embassy. But Maritain, who had kept at arm's length from the Free French leader during the war, suspected him of authoritarian pretensions.[10] With reluctance and misgivings, Maritain accepted the assignment, only after deciding that with France still at war it was "impossible still to shirk one's responsibility in such times."[11] To Yves Simon he confided something less than enthusiasm as he started making his preparations to leave New York in January 1945: "Yves, say many prayers for me, for us, ask of God and the Blessed Virgin their special protection, I am menaced by this service to France and a change in my life that could be for me a terrible sacrifice and which I dread horribly."[12]

Strong apprehensions about the assumption of this diplomatic post persisted, as evidenced by another letter to Simon three weeks later: "You cannot imagine the anguish that I have gone through, I who dreamed of finally returning to pure philosophy and writing my book on ethics, and who knows also that Providence sent me to the New Continent." He consoled himself that this was a "temporary mission,"[13] and he was not alone in this reassurance. Some of the more conservative members of the Curia, including Undersecretary of State Monsignor Domenico Tardini, also cherished this consolation, given his unease about Maritain's political reputation. The new nuncio in Paris, Monsignor Angelo Roncalli (the future Pope John XXIII), had to relay to Tardini Premier de Gaulle's "confidential" assurance that Maritain would not remain in Rome for very long, and that in due time a figure more representative of "the best French diplomatic tradition" — that is to say, a less "political" personage — would replace him.[14]

The transitional nature of the appointment thus well understood by all parties, the new ambassador presented his credentials on the tenth of May 1945, two days after the Second World War in Europe came to an end.[15] Contemplating his appointment as a penitential interlude, Maritain's tone brightened slightly, and he wrote to Mortimer Adler at the end of August: "You know that for my penance and for the sake of the common good I am now involved in the practico-practical realm of Prudence — horribly deprived of intellectual leave and philosophical meditation."[16] And perhaps he refrained from employing another metaphor for his stay, as he had also become acquainted with the Eternal City's summer climate, which he later described to Georges Bernanos as "the worst I have ever known . . . depressing and suffocating. It demands a physical effort which consumes the nerves."[17]

Maritain understood his charge as consisting of facilitating by his presence a rapprochement between the French Fourth Republic and a Holy

See that had maintained cordial relations with Marshal Philippe Pétain's collaborationist Vichy regime.[18] De Gaulle apparently intended his envoy to play a more or less symbolic function. Maritain himself considered the aim of his appointment as less "the achieving of such and such diplomatic negotiation than the gesture itself that he made in selecting me to represent France at the Vatican, and which he regards as significant in and of itself."[19] Maritain's reputation as an illustrious Catholic intellectual and inveterate wartime foe of Vichy made him an ideal figure to represent the French Republic at the Holy See. Likewise, the Holocaust-rescuer Roncalli presented the Vatican's best face in Paris at a time when a sweeping purge of the French episcopate seemed quite possible. But the new ambassador soon embraced more than a symbolic role in French-Vatican relations. He had his own concerns about what he considered an enduring German problem, as well as the resurgence of anti-Jewish violence in East-Central Europe.

In December 1945, Maritain drafted a report to the French Foreign Ministry on the question of the German people's collective responsibility for the crimes of the Nazi regime. According to Maritain, there was no *question* as such: "Let us not speak of Nazi fanatics; suffice to say that the German population as a whole accepted Hitler and the demonic principle that he represented as a convenient tool to be made use of for the grandeur of Germany, and that it hoped for the victory over the world of a regime that accumulated crimes against the natural law." Those who resisted Nazism should not be wishfully described as representing the true Germany in a time of grave emergency; quite the contrary: "Those who fought against Hitler . . . risking captivity or death, were the exceptions and never had with them the heart of the German people." How could one not conclude that, irrespective of Hitler's suicide and the fall of the Third Reich, a German problem remained to menace the peace of Europe, if not the world? Maritain did nothing to assuage this fear, but he rejected a vengeful "solution to the European problem." He opposed "the extermination or the mass resettlement of the German population," even if the German people failed to effect a "spiritual recovery" after their collective abasement.

The ambassador restrained himself from giving full vent to his deep-seated anti-German inclinations, which had become solidified after the rise of Nazism, the unleashing of the war, and the perpetration of the genocide. Even as Maritain pointed to something existentially wrong with the German soul, the possible failure of German national salvation and the dire consequences that might follow still made no sense to him at all: "If this spiritual renewal were not possible, it is because the anti-Christian theory of a racial curse would also hold true for the Germans."[20] Irony if not sarcasm here imbues Maritain's stunning inversion of German racial prejudice being turned upon its practitioners. In the aftermath of Germany's failed bid to dominate the world and annihilate the Jews, Maritain was raising the "German Question."

Could the Catholic Church, in a country with more Lutherans than Catholics, aid Germany in surmounting its present spiritual crisis? Maritain placed less than total faith in the German Catholic bishops, who at Fulda in August 1945 had "recognized that wrongs had been committed by some Germans, but they have evaded the question of their collective responsibility; and silence on such an important point cannot suffice to purify the moral atmosphere, as the Pope himself wishes."[21]

However, Pius's wishes remained less than clear. Almost two years later, in October 1947 Maritain would find himself involved in a behind-the-scenes controversy surrounding Bishop Aloisius Muench's pro-German and anti-French interventions in his dual capacity as both papal representative in occupied Germany and President Truman's liaison with the German Catholic Church. Michael Phayer has good reason to conclude that Pius's indulgence toward Muench reflected a reticence about any need for collective soul-searching as a prerequisite for German spiritual renewal, while Muench's own "philo-Teutonic attitude sickened Maritain," whose misgivings about Muench the Vatican hierarchy consistently ignored.[22] The religious politics of the Occupation and the burgeoning Cold War reinforced Maritain's apprehensions about German collective amnesia. Equally disconcerting, the public spectacle of murderous antisemitic hatred in Poland presented a tangible resurgence of the horror of the Holocaust, and raised the question of a Christian response.

Beyond the issue of German collective guilt and future redemption, the outbreak of antisemitic violence in the heart of Europe, even after the end of the war, gave Maritain's reluctant mission at the Vatican a poignant purpose. The 4 July 1946 Kielce pogrom in Poland, which took the lives of approximately forty Jews, prompted Maritain's action.[23] His astonishment and dismay at the endurance of violent antisemitism led him to approach Vatican Undersecretary of State Monsignor Giovanni Battista Montini, a friend and admirer who had translated *Three Reformers* two decades earlier and who would don the papal tiara almost two decades later as Paul VI. In his 12 July note to Montini, Maritain recalled the:

> Unprecedented fury of humiliation and cruelty that descended
> upon the people of Israel, as it was unwillingly thrown onto the

road of Calvary and formed into the sufferings of its Messiah
. . . not only a crime against justice and natural law . . . but also
a mysterious tragedy which touches upon the divine intentions
before which Saint Paul bended his knee, and in which the hatred against Christ, enveloping at the same time both Christians
and the olive tree among whose branches they have been grafted,
levels itself primarily against the people who gave the world
Moses and the prophets, and from whom Christ came in the
flesh.

Amidst these horrors, he lamented, "the antisemitic psychosis has not van-
ished," adding that "I cannot stop myself for thinking that a proclamation
of the true thought of the Church would be, at the same time as it would be
a work of enlightenment striking down a cruel and harmful error, also a
work of justice and reparation."[24]

Maritain's suggestion that the Catholic Church needed to take some
measure of responsibility for ending antisemitism, and offering a sort of
"reparation," might strike today's ears as delicately put, but in a papal audience four days later, the ambassador found his request rebuffed. He could
expect no further statement, let alone an encyclical. After all, the previous
November, the Pope had granted an audience to a group of seventy Jewish
camp survivors. On that occasion, he expressed his sadness regarding the
human toll of the late conflict: "The abyss of discord, the hatred and folly
of persecution which, under the influence of erroneous and intolerant doc-
trines, in opposition to the noble human and authentic Christian spirit, have
engulfed incomparable numbers of innocent victims, even among those
who took no active part in the war." Pius's judgment that his private remarks from late 1945 sufficed to clarify the Vatican's position on antisemitism remained unshaken even by the Kielce massacre — with its sordid
background of ritual murder accusations and sad aftermath of Polish clerical indifference — which had occurred but a few months later.[25]

Maritain went away from this audience disheartened, though
shortly afterward, on 19 July, he offered a response strikingly similar to
that of Pius. When he received an emergency telegram concerning Kielce
and requesting his intervention at the Vatican from the Jewish Labor Committee in New York, he replied:

Deeply touched by your cable. It is my conviction that any revival of antisemitism would be a shame for humanity. Going to
France for summer vacation. I shall inform my friends about

your request. The Catholic Church has repeatedly condemned racist persecutions and atrocities. I hope you have known the Pope's address to Jewish refugees, November 30, 1945, in which he declared that racist conceptions "cannot be admitted" and "will be numbered in the history of civilization amongst the most deplorable and dishonorable aberrations of human thought and feeling" — see *Osservatore Romano* same date.[26]

So while he clearly emerged from his 16 July papal audience frustrated and disappointed, Maritain also showed himself a supporter of the Pope's response to antisemitism, at least publicly. One must see Kielce therefore not simply as a turning point in Maritain's relations with the Pope, but also as a painful self-exposure of divided loyalties to the Catholic Church and the Jewish people, as he remonstrated in vain with the Pope to better acknowledge and ameliorate the Jews' continued suffering, while insisting to the latter group that the Pontiff and the Church had always cared about them. As his post demanded, Maritain was diplomatic.

A PROBLEM OF LIFE AND DEATH FOR CHRISTIANS

Maritain's private discouragement and personal conflict would not prevent him from further efforts toward changing Catholic teachings and practices, such as a request to amend the prayer *Pro perfidis Judaeis* in the Good Friday liturgy.[27] But as Michael Marrus makes clear, quoting Maritain's correspondence with Journet, by the time the Ambassador left the Vatican almost two years later, in May 1948, he was burdened with a "heart-rending ambivalence" as he felt increasingly disillusioned with a pope for whom he nonetheless retained a "growing affection."[28] One might argue further that Maritain also sought to act in the stead of a pope too preoccupied with political and diplomatic considerations to finally, belatedly offer a categorical rejection of Christian antisemitism on behalf of the Church.

But feeling such private misgivings and assuming such a self-imposed burden should not be equated with ecclesial dissidence, even as Maritain proffered an almost officially Catholic rejection of antisemitic prejudice. Given the recent spate of scholarly allegations that Maritain resigned from the Vatican embassy in "protest" with feelings of "disgust," one can question how far his differences with Pius XII actually extended and how instrumental such divergences actually proved in making up Maritain's mind to leave Rome. This question will be taken up below, along with that of how, during his subsequent years at Princeton, Maritain assimilated this Vatican experience as he continued to confront antisemitism. But first, we should examine how Maritain, in his Seelisberg letter, articulated a definitive rejection of antisemitism on behalf of the Church.

Although he found himself unable to attend the 30 July–5 August 1947 Seelisberg Special International Conference to Combat Antisemitism, an ecumenical meeting in Switzerland, Maritain agreed to provide some opening remarks for the conference. In his letter to the conference participants, Maritain admonished his fellow Christians: "Before being a problem of blood, of physical life or death for Jews, antisemitism is a problem of the spirit, of spiritual life or death for Christians."[29] Charles Molette rightly deems this message "the fruit of a long maturation, of reflections pursued without respite."[30] Maritain's views clearly had matured over the decades. They now contained a far more prescriptive substance than had his prewar interventions on the Jewish Question, which have been criticized by one recent historian on the grounds of "practical opacity."[31] For Maritain in 1947, antisemitism had to be acknowledged as a Christian problem, not necessarily in its origins, but in its hopeful solution, for only "practical measures," not simply a celebration of those few Christians who had "saved honor" by helping Jews, would suffice.[32]

Maritain began his Seelisberg appeal by invoking common self-interest, arguing for the impossibility of postwar recovery without confronting and healing the antisemitic sin persisting from the late conflict. The mention of sin indicates that such "bestial hatred had supernatural eyes." Jews had found themselves victimized, in the final analysis, not as Christ-killers but as Christ-bearers in a world still intent on crucifying him. The ensuing Calvary of the Jews should bond together Christians and Jews in a new, more truly empathetic, and undoubtedly mysterious, way. Therefore, what did Christians need to understand and do about the problem of antisemitism, and more pointedly "how long will they remain asleep?"

First, they needed to see that the self-debasement of the perpetrators constituted a greater spiritual tragedy even than the murder of the innocents. Second, they would have to confront the fact that antisemitism had not necessarily reached a climax in the 1939–45 period, or managed truly to "awaken the conscience of peoples," but continued to spread. Third, the modern project of full assimilation having failed and given way to a more extreme final solution, Christians needed to see the inevitable project of a Jewish state in Palestine as a potential locus for further antisemitism, and needed to accept the fact that Jews everywhere, regardless of their particular national citizenship, would understandably carry a certain loyalty to that new polity whether or not they chose to emigrate to it.[33]

Maritain concluded the Seelisberg letter by demanding that Christians shift the focus of scrutiny from the Jewish Other to the Christian Self. He called for purifying their hearts of residual contempt, changing the very language they had unreflectively used to describe Jews throughout history, and finally making an effort to empathize with Jewish suffering in the Diaspora, including the intermittent pogroms that had prefigured some of the anti-Jewish assaults of the twentieth century. A mutual understanding between Christians and Jews would become possible "thanks to a connaturality" entailed within Christian love. Speaking eschatologically, Christians needed to make the kind of changes that would "prepare for their part the future reintegration which Paul proclaimed."[34] According to historian and Holocaust survivor Jules Isaac, present at Seelisberg, Maritain "said, from a Catholic viewpoint of course, everything I am putting forth in a book on which I am working."[35]

Maritain could see the looming end of a third year in his commitment to represent France at the Holy See[36] when he presided — in the place of an ailing Léon Blum — over the United Nations Economic, Social, and Cultural Organization conference in Mexico City in November 1947. Maritain gave the opening address at this UNESCO conference that gave rise to the Universal Declaration of Human Rights. His speech drew on the experience of World War Two and the Holocaust, while negotiating the new international realities of Cold War antagonism between the democratic west and the communist east and the inclusion of non-western nations in modern international political discourse. Acknowledging the futility of finding common ideological and philosophical ground in the postwar world, a task complicated by the "Babelism of modern thought,"[37] he nonetheless insisted on the urgency of finding common practical ground in a time when the healing of humanity might be preempted by another, nuclear war. Essentially, Maritain argued that only some degree of world governance based on a common appreciation of the nonnegotiable dignity of the human person could forestall future disaster in this time of "international tension and growing antagonisms."[38]

The recent horrific lessons of total war and final genocide demonstrated that the absolute sovereignty of the State must end. This failure of absolute sovereignty made itself clear in three respects. First, Machiavellianism, or *Realpolitik*, had eclipsed morality and ethics, showing once and for all that "the maxim according to which politics must be indifferent to good or evil is a homicidal error." Second, the end of the world conflict necessitated soul-searching and atonement among both persons and nations, and in this regard he devoted particular attention to defeated Germany and this question of atonement: "Given the crimes against humanity committed by Nazi Germany, it grabs us by the throat: it is not good that people leave themselves in perplexity on this subject."[39]

One can hardly suppose that Maritain exempted the Holy Father from this characterization. But Maritain primarily aims this criticism at a German people — and no other specific people — in danger of losing its soul: "More than ever it is necessary to insist here upon the primacy of the spiritual. If in its depths the German conscience does not awaken as one to repentance and to hope, a virile repentance and an upright hope, the German problem will remain charged with misfortune, for the German people itself and for the world."[40] Third, and with less specifics, but with a great deal of resonance at the beginning of the nuclear age, he warned against scientific inquiry and technological achievement divorced from wisdom and "the virtues of the human soul."[41]

Maritain's sorrow and frustration at the beginning of the postwar era make it clear that his ideas about how to achieve human recovery in the wake of global war and genocide were more hopeful than optimistic. But today much of Maritain's reputation is tied to the temporal remedy for spiritual ills advanced in the Universal Declaration of Human Rights, and finds itself tied to the success or failure of that document's assertion of a minimal international consensus on the human basis of the common good. In a world that still experiences endemic oppression and atrocity, should Maritain be branded an inveterate optimist for advancing such ideas?

Strongly critical, Jude Dougherty asserts, "If Maritain has a fault, it lies in his idealism, in his optimism that goodwill and common sense will prevail and that public assessments of the value of religion will result in the same conclusions reached by reflective men in every period of the history of the west." James V. Schall, however, challenges the image of Maritain as "naïve utopian" who dreamed of a world united at "any cost." As for the ideas embodied in the Declaration itself, Bradley Munro wonders specifically how such a conception of a global understanding of human rights has fared in forestalling or responding to events such as the Tienanmen Square Massacre or the Rwandan Genocide.[42] But this line of debate ignores the salient point that Maritain never expected the world to be redeemed by politics or within the limits of historical time. For Maritain, all human striving mattered only insofar as it kept faith with the will of God.

By the time of UNESCO, Maritain had tired of striving at the Vatican in what he had always understood to be a temporary mission. Without forgetting his failure to convince Pius XII to issue a forthright condemnation of antisemitism, his attention returned to the professorial life he had lost in 1940. As he wrote to Yves Simon in February 1948: "It is high time for me to return to my vocation of philosopher."[43] Maritain's final ambassadorial report did not mention the Holocaust or antisemitism, but still criticized the Pontiff, pointing out for example Pius's overwhelming tendency toward political and diplomatic prudence, save in the fight against communism. The French ambassador made little effort to conceal his irritation at "the sympathy and indulgence of Pius XII in regard to the German people, his incessant refusal to envisage the notion of collective responsibility, and finally the role of German influences that exert themselves in the Vatican, and the 'imponderables' coming from the immediate milieu in which the Holy Father lives (his private secretariat and domestic personnel are largely Germanic)."[44]

The recent assertions that Maritain resigned in protest from the Vatican post draw on his unquestionable frustration and disillusionment with papal reticence to push the idea of German collective guilt or make a definitive statement condemning antisemitism. But they find themselves weakened by the facts that his resignation coincided with the expiration of what he had understood as a three-year term,[45] that he had been offered a desirable professorship at Princeton, and perhaps most significantly, that apparently *no one knew he had resigned in protest.* Maritain's close friend Stanislas Fumet, writing in the Catholic periodical *Temps Présent* on 28 May 1948, stated the following: "If Jacques Maritain has asked to be relieved of his functions, the cause thereof is simple: he has given three years of his time to the government and he considers his diplomatic task completed. He has his work as a philosopher to pursue and all his friends have been asking him to get back to it."[46] At a more intimate level, to his confidant Journet, Maritain affirmed his desire to return to academe. He added only secondarily that an otherwise painful severing of ties at the Vatican had been made easier by his discomfort with the Pope's politics. He also related his very warm and memorable last audience with Pius and a constructive final meeting with Montini.[47]

Nor did any inkling of protest apparently reach Jewish circles. Leon Kubowitzki, a leading figure in the World Jewish Congress, who had known Maritain during the war, recalled the philosopher comparing Pius XII unfavorably with Pius XI. Then in 1947 he shared with Maritain a draft memorandum proposing an encyclical on antisemitism. Kubowitzki eventually moved to Israel and adopted the name Aryeh Kubovy, under which he wrote the following reminiscences many years later about his own 1947 mission: "Two years later [in 1949] I heard that Maritain had been conducting a courageous fight on behalf of the encyclical, but that the conservative elements in the Curia had won the upper hand. In spite of many attempts on my part, I have not yet succeeded in obtaining any details about the course of this internal political struggle."[48] This was written in the mid-1960s and published after its author's death. Nonetheless, Randolph Braham cites this source, and only this source, to support the following statement about Maritain as a forthright critic of Pius beginning during the war years: "It would seem that only one Catholic of world stature had the courage to condemn the Pope's silence, the noted French philosopher-the-ologian Jacques Maritain, then living in the United States."[49] Even accepting Kubovy's retrospective account, one cannot claim that Maritain ever offered a courageous condemnation, whatever that might entail, of "the Pope's silence."[50]

But such fragmentary and questionable evidence — questionable both in its hearsay provenance and in its polemical employment — typifies the recent use to which Maritain's Vatican stint has been employed by some scholars. To be sure, this imagining of a protest resignation does not presuppose any intentional distortion of the historical record. But it does amount to a misinterpretation, or more precisely, an irenic over-interpretation of primary and secondary sources amounting to a cumulative misunderstanding among scholars. The historiographical progression can be followed easily: Michael Phayer writes in 2000 the following, which the reader may or may not take as a statement of historical causation: "Realizing that his arguments for a papal-led spiritual reawakening in Europe would come to naught, Jacques Maritain resigned his ambassadorship in 1948."[51] Then, also in 2000, John Pawlikowski cites Phayer and makes an explicit causal point: "Catholic historian Michael Phayer has criticized Pius XII's posture during this period, basing his criticisms in part on the archives of Jacques Maritain, the eminent French Catholic philosopher, who resigned his post as French Ambassador to the Vatican in protest over Pius' immediate post-war stance on German Catholic guilt."[52] Finally, in 2006, Frank Coppa in turn cites Pawlikowski in asserting that "Maritain resigned his post as French ambassador to the Holy See in disgust."[53] By now we find ourselves far removed from Phayer's original and far less dramatic — even if ambiguous — statement, and the only one referencing primary documents.

Tellingly, the invitation to teach at Princeton does not figure into any of the above-mentioned analyses of Ambassador Maritain's resignation, but it certainly should.[54] None of these scholars mentions the philosopher's extreme reluctance to accept the Vatican post in the first place, an acceptance with "*mauvaise grâce*" as Philippe Chenaux aptly puts it, or his insistence that he had only agreed to a temporary mission. Neither do they acknowledge the fact that Maritain eagerly looked forward to resuming his academic life, and that he saw the offer of a Princeton professorship as something he needed to accept lest a similar opportunity not present itself again in either America or his native France. He wrote to Journet that he had no options in France at the time, and needed to seize this opportunity to go to America, a step he considered a providential development. Princeton University President Harold Dodds had asked Maritain for a meeting during a New York stopover on his way back from the UNESCO conference in Mexico City in November 1947. Having by that time given up hope of receiving a chair at the *Collège de France* (the administration of the Collège would reconsider in his favor in 1951, but he declined their offer), Maritain accepted Dodds's invitation to teach moral philosophy in the tradition of Saint Thomas Aquinas.[55] Having also been rejected for a position at the University of Chicago in the late 1930s, due to the objections of positivist and pragmatist philosophy faculty members, and having received a lukewarm welcome as a critic of Franco while visiting the University of Notre Dame during the same period,[56] the Catholic philosopher perhaps savored the fact that his endowed chair at Princeton had been funded by Jewish admirers.[57]

The Maritains returned to the United States in June 1948. That fall, Jacques assumed the post at Princeton, where a professorship with minimal teaching duties allowed him ample time to write further works. One of these, *Man and the State*, expounded on the international ramifications of a politics of the human person based on a common global understanding of human rights.[58] Even during this successful period, Maritain continued to see life as a constant struggle, as he wrote to his friend the Trappist Thomas Merton: "My godfather Léon Bloy was crushed by poverty, I by constant illness around me. For each of my books I could mention a particular illness and anguish against the background of which it was written, that's perhaps why these books are so full of defects, so far off from what they could have been."[59] He himself had a major heart attack in 1954, and at the end of the decade would experience the loss of his household, beginning with his sister-in-law Véra, who succumbed to cancer on the last day of 1959, then on 4 November 1960 losing Raïssa herself, who had always been in precarious health and finally succumbed to a stroke during a visit to Paris.[60]

During these years of reflection and suffering, Maritain pondered the Holocaust, as well as his experience at the Vatican in the late 1940s, and continued to struggle with the meanings of antisemitism from a Catholic perspective. As we have seen, although his relationship with Pius XII had sometimes been an uneasy one, he refused to acknowledge any kind of "papal silence" during the Holocaust. During his Vatican years, he had confined himself to circumspect, private criticisms of Pius's postwar deportment on the German Question and Polish pogroms. Later, as questions about Pius and the Holocaust persisted, he came to the Pontiff's defense — this, less than three years after leaving the Vatican embassy.

In February 1951, he declined a request to write the preface to Léon Poliakov's *Bréviare de la Haine (Breviary of Hate*, English title *Harvest of Hate)*, informing the author that "there is not a shadow of antisemitism in the thought of the Pope." Maritain went further regarding the Vatican's wartime record, admonishing the author: "Let me tell you that a book such as yours, in touching upon the question of the Holy See, calls for you to demonstrate more objectivity and historical exactitude, and to avoid injuring, in speaking of them in too superficial a manner [*en en parlant avec trop de légèreté*], those Christians who took the side of those who were persecuted." François Mauriac in turn accepted the invitation to write the preface of a book that must have undergone substantial revisions, to judge by Maritain's laudatory review of the finished product.[61]

Poliakov's published book managed to strike Maritain in the heart even as its pages presented to his mind a reasoned scholarly explanation for how the Holocaust took shape:

> M. Poliakov's book retraces with an implacable and sure objectivity the stages of the enterprise of extermination. Before such a horror, there is no need for one to raise one's voice; it suffices to *speak*. One can hardly sense, here and there, a restrained shudder, and sometimes, in regard to the executioner, a terrible humor, which grips the heart; Jewish humor, to be precise, but at its most extreme point of tension, and which draws forth tears of blood.[62]

As Maritain read the accounts of how Jews met their deaths, he mourned those he loved who had perished: "I think of those who were so dear to me, of the Jacob family — Manu, my godson, Babet, heroically courageous, and their mother the elderly Madame Jacob — of whom the inner strength, nourished by divine charity, show forth in pure splendor in this supreme test; and to Benjamin Fondane, who comforted his companions until the end with his generous and sparkling thought, and who knew long before what bloody destiny awaited them."[63]

This review of *Bréviare* exposes the continuing ambivalence of Maritain's philosemitism, simultaneously sending different messages to Jewish and Gentile readers. As Maritain embraced and cherished Poliakov's narrative of the dignity of Jewish suffering in the Holocaust, he continued to question the author's characterization of Christianity as a causal factor behind the genocide. Yet rather than challenging the author's argument on its own terms, he held his fellow Christians responsible for any such misunderstanding on the part of Poliakov, or for that matter, other Jews:

> If M. Poliakov, here and there, seems to confound too easily the Church and such and such aspect of the temporal Christian world, we should consider ourselves to be in no position to be scandalized. It is us, Christians, who represent, for sincere spirits on the outside, the exterior appearance based on which they judge the Church; and we mislead them insofar as our comportment is not "without a spot or a wrinkle" [Ephesians 5: 27] but our own sin makes itself visible. Based on the sole fact that there had been, and that there still is, despite everything, a Christian world, the atrocious implementation of the "final solution" should not even have been possible.[64]

Maritain here shows his respect for the Jewish dead, and the living, in turning a scholarly criticism of Poliakov into a moral condemnation of his fellow Christians. As will be seen below, he would not show the same indulgence, or feel conflicted in issuing a straightforward rebuttal, when another Christian made similar claims about the Church's responsibility for antisemitism.

After reading Maritain's schoolmasterly private rebuke of Poliakov, followed by heartfelt but slightly qualified public praise of *Bréviaire de la Haine*, one certainly runs the risk of oversimplification in either recasting the philosopher as a staunch defender of Pius XII and the Catholic Church or continuing to cast him as a "courageous" critic. His strenuous disagreement with English historian and theologian James Parkes over the latter's insistence on the inherently Christian roots of antisemitism further complicates the picture and illustrates Maritain's more than simply reflexive defense of the Catholic tradition and the Church's historical record vis-à-vis the Jews.

The 1954 Maritain-Parkes exchange apparently limited itself to a debate through a third party, Sir Robert Mayer. Reverend Parkes, an Anglican priest, widely published author,[65] and tireless advocate for Jewish-Christian understanding, insisted on the direct, necessary linkage between ancient and medieval Christian prejudice against Jews and modern racist antisemitism. He identified in both forms of anti-Jewish prejudice the irrational antagonism associated with what we might call a working definition of antisemitism, and insisted that "there is no break in the genealogical tree between these nonreligious beliefs of modern man and the religious beliefs of their ancestors. The religious root has still to be uprooted even if (to be magnificently obvious) it is not the most visible part of the tree."[66]

Maritain found none of this argument "magnificently obvious." He might in other circumstances have taken up Parkes's question of "why should we ask the Jew now, when the accepted solution of the Gentiles has proved utterly defective, that he should adopt it?" Did not his Seelisberg letter contain that very question in admonishing Christians to change their own hearts before expecting anything of their Jewish brethren? But the interpretation of Church history offered by Parkes could not be accepted in any form:

> Now medieval antisemitism, nefarious as it may have been, (especially when allied with the greed of princes for money) was essentially impatience against those who prevented by their spiritual obstinacy the advent of Christ's Kingdom on earth. It was *totally different* from racist antisemitism. The latter, nevertheless, may be regarded as an aggravated metamorphosis and secularization of the former. This does not, in my opinion, authorize Rev. Parkes to regard antisemitism as "a creation of the Christian Church."[67]

For Maritain, the issue at stake went beyond a historical disagreement among scholars, for the Church's essential blamelessness for modern antisemitism had not only a historical past significance but also a future eschatological promise.

The Church as the Mystical Body of Christ held itself in readiness for the prospect of Israel's ultimate "reintegration" as proclaimed by Paul. For Maritain, this reintegration entailed a spiritual reawakening, leading to the fulfillment of Jewish vocation:

As concerns the Jews as a whole, I do not see how they will be able to maintain their *spiritual* identity if not by the fire of their religious faith, and at the same time by making this faith of the Old Testament more and more universal or supra-historical, which would mean, despite any intrinsic differences, a kind of rapprochement with Christianity as to practical attitudes. And this very fact would, I think, involuntarily pave the way for that final reintegration of Israel which will be the plenitude both of Israel and the Church, and is the abiding hope of Christianity, and which St. Paul viewed as a miraculous splendor of the world.[68]

Parkes in turn dismissed Maritain's vision of Jewish *telos*, effectively stating that he could pursue no further a dialogue — even through an intermediary — with someone he considered a narrow-minded Catholic: "Maritain speaks as though Jews must make up their minds in accordance with *our* presuppositions. They must make up their minds. But it is *their* presuppositions that matter. So likewise he says that Israel, following the line he thinks right, will draw nearer to the Church. But half the distance between them has to be covered by the Church, not by Israel, and this fact his Roman Catholicism prevents him from admitting."[69]

Is Parkes being fair to Maritain's position? At first glance, one can argue that he is not, because Maritain had in other contexts offered ringing affirmations of the need for Christians to undertake a wholesale reevaluation and revision of their attitudes toward Jews and Judaism. But then again, in the context of this debate, Parkes's shortchanging of such affirmations on Maritain's part is beside the point, for the letters exchanged through Sir Robert disclose more than adequately the real reason for Parkes's dismissal of Maritain's apparently inadequate philosemitism, and this lay in the contested definition of "Church" itself.

The disagreement between Parkes and Maritain really had less to do with Jews and Judaism than the intramural Christian question of theological modernism. These two Christian opponents of antisemitism, each of whom had at the beginning of the century embraced their faith in the midst of the overheated modernist controversy,[70] framed their philosemitic arguments from opposite sides of a presuppositional barricade. Parkes viewed a fallible, culpable Church as implicated in the origins of antisemitism, not only because of his reading of biblical scripture and the historical record, but because he saw the Church as an essentially human institution: "The history of the Church carries no such proof of inerrancy,

and the use of such phrases as the Bride of Christ or Body of Christ to convey the idea of the possession of absolute truth and superhuman authority
by any existing ecclesial organisation is the language not of mysticism but
of emotional sentimentalism. It is unlikely that the world will ever be impressed by such phrases again."[71]

Certainly his more (theologically at least) conservative French
Catholic counterpart[72] could only disagree, not just because he cared less
about which phrases impressed the world, but also because he saw in the
Church-as-Body-of-Christ the only hope for the eradication of antisemitism. Maritain not only saw antisemitism as extrinsic to the Church,
but also antagonistic to it. He therefore had to see in Parkes's avowed lack
of "emotional sentimentalism" nothing more than self-limiting naturalism,
or to borrow from his own words quoted at the beginning of this chapter,
a tendency to see both antisemitism and the Church in "ignobly human
terms."

But despite the sharp differences that flowed from their almost in-
commensurable ecclesiologies, including predictably divergent appraisals
of hierarchical authority, Maritain and Parkes each held himself and his
fellow Christians to a high standard of respect for the Jewish people and
religion, above all. Each affirmed an unabrogated covenant between God
and the Jews. Each frowned (in Maritain's case, at least eventually) on
Christian proselytization of Jews. Maritain could not agree with those aspects of Parkes's writings that anticipated more radical revisionist assertions, including his insistence that the Bible no longer be read liturgically
as "the word of God,"[73] for Maritain's ecclesiology and theology precluded
a strongly critical approach to the canonical texts, not to mention the authority of the Church that had canonized them.

Maritain's Pauline theology and natural law reasoning pointed him
to the conclusion that the key to Israel's destiny lay within the Jewish tradition itself. This did not necessitate on his part a preliminary indictment
of the Gospels, the Church Fathers, and the Church down through the ages.
Did Maritain believe, as Parkes charged, that Jewish presuppositions did
not matter? No, on the contrary: after many years of intellectual and spiritual struggle, Maritain had decided that Jews lacked for nothing in their ultimate ability to recognize in Jesus their messiah. Parkes might have
criticized that perspective in its own right, but instead his animus toward
Maritain's Catholicism prevented him from even trying to make sense of
it. And Parkes likely understood all too well that Maritain's reading of Saint

Paul's theology of Israel relegated antisemitism to the status of a permanent problem, at least within the remaining span of human history.

THE MOST TROUBLING ENIGMA OF HISTORY

Maritain's 1952 retirement from the Princeton faculty allowed him more than ample time for continued research and writing in what he termed the "Elysian" circumstances of an emeritus faculty life finally fully open to contemplation. But only an illness-and-death-ridden-decade in the United States remained before Maritain would return alone to his native land. His final years, after the 1960 death of Raïssa following a massive stroke, would be spent in a hermitage on the grounds of a monastery near Toulouse. There he enjoyed solitude, prayer, and reflection, interrupted only by rare public events such as the ceremony closing the Second Vatican Council, the reforms and documents of which he had done so much to inspire. On that important occasion, as will be seen, he privately regretted that the 1965 final draft of the *Declaration on the Relation of the Church to Non-Christian Religions* (popularly known as *Nostra Aetate*) had been shorn of earlier statements proscribing the use of the word *deicide* and forbidding the teaching of "hatred or contempt for the Jews."[74] A further attempt at confronting the legacy of Christians fostering antisemitism would have to wait until another pontificate that began five years after Maritain's death in 1973.

Maritain's philosophical preoccupations — indeed his "center of gravity" as one writer puts it — became increasingly theological after the Second World War and the Holocaust. The place of evil in and beyond history constituted a significant part of his work after 1945. He had dealt with evil before, including during his 1942 Aquinas Lecture. Here he explained that God permitted — but did not will — evil as a natural corollary of the gift of human freedom. This permission allowed, through grace, the mysterious "consummation of a work of love" connected to the essential destiny of the human person. In *On the Philosophy of History* (1957), he reflected on the horrors of the past, offering the following picturesque and chilling image of Satan's ironic role in the unfolding of redemption:

> The devil hangs like a vampire on the side of history. History goes on, nonetheless, and it goes on with the vampire. It is only in the kingdom of grace, in the divinely assisted life of the Church, that the devil has no place. He plays his own part in the march of the world, and in a sense spurs it. Is he not eager for the better insofar as in his view the better, as a French saying

puts it, "is the enemy of the good"? He does not scruple, on occasion, to court the better in order to destroy some good, not to improve it. And thus he happens to do in his particular way, which is a wrong way, and with perverse intention, what good people omit to do because they are asleep. That which is done is done badly, but it is done.[75]

Lingering over this picture of Maritain's, and looking back upon the Holocaust, might one not ask whether or not that outpouring of evil had done more to discredit antisemitism than had all the good intentions in the world up to that point?

Maritain probably would respond that this kind of question still approached the tragedy in too limited a sense. Rather, he likely would reframe the question metahistorically, concluding as he did in *On the Philosophy of History* that "God turns to a better purpose Evil which He permits but in no way wills or causes. . . . This is the very triumph of God's wisdom and love, and the supreme meaning of human history, to have grace and mercy superabound there where, through the free *nihilation* of the human will, frustrating God's antecedent will, the offense abounded."[76]

As for his long-held belief that the Jewish vocation to stimulate the human conscience drew unto Israel the antagonism of the world, sometimes including an unleashing of violent evil, he clearly felt that Christians could do a better job of emulating their elder brothers: "If we [Christians] really were what we are, and if the world knew us as we are, how pleased it would be to recognize it as its sacred obligation to mow us down, in self-defense."[77] So, for Christians, following Jesus Christ's loving act of sacrificial atonement also means emulating Jesus' fellow Jews, even unto death, making one's unquenchable thirst for the kingdom of God known to an inevitably hostile world. Maritain would continue to expand upon the meanings of evil in his 1962 lectures to the Little Brothers of Jesus, to whom he emphasized that "because of the presence of evil on earth, everything, from the beginning to the end of time, is in perpetual recasting."[78] His own life had been shattered by the death of his beloved Raïssa, and would only be partially recast thereafter.

Jacques not only loved but venerated Raïssa as a true daughter of Israel — their *mariage blanc* (a marriage lived in chastity) had been characterized by a shared household life in which "their" sister Véra played Martha to Raïssa's Mary. The death of the latter left the aged philosopher finally alone, and brought an end to his second American period. He spent the remainder of his days among the Little Brothers, save for occasional and increasingly infrequent visits to the outside world during the 1960s. But first he needed to return to the United States and conclude his affairs there.

The trip gave him the opportunity to offer a remembrance of his closest and dearest collaborator. On 14 October 1961, the Edith Stein Guild honored the Maritains with the Edith Stein Prize. To an audience of almost three hundred at New York's Hotel Commodore, the living honoree paid homage to Stein, the promising philosopher, Catholic convert, and Holocaust victim, whom he and Raïssa once counted as a friend, and he also described his debt to his fellow honoree, his late wife: "I owe her everything good in my life and in my work; moreover she was both a daughter of Israel and a Christian: a double privilege whose significance was rightly (though perhaps with a little bit of exaggeration) emphasized by Leon Bloy when he said: 'It is for us (Gentiles) a matter of difficult effort to be good Christians. But a Jew has only to bend his head to be a saint.'"[79] This last insistence upon a Jewish proximity to sainthood shows how seriously Maritain took the spiritual idea of participation in the divine, and how he applied this not only to his Christian identity, but to his connection with the Jewish people through Raïssa.

In the original 1954 preface to his published *Notebooks*, he had situated the beginning of his intellectual and spiritual journey in his childhood. He then reflected on how his wife, along with Véra, would one day bring him into the consecrated tribe of Israel. Perhaps the two sisters had saved him in a sense analogous to his salvation through Jesus Christ:

> As a child I detested the idea of resembling, as friends of the family used to delight in kindly pointing out, the bust of my grandfather which adorned the mantelpiece of my mother's drawing-room. It was not solely pride, nor revolt at not being "only myself." I had the presentiment of a kind of fatal element, and of what there was of violence and of bitterness, mingled with much grandeur and much generosity, in my hereditary line. If all of this was able to find itself pacified and softened in me, and did not disturb too much the progress of the so marvelously united little flock of our three souls, I think, without speaking of Christian grace, which is clearly the essential, that it was due to the meeting of the traditions of spiritual refinement, of innocence and of nostalgia for the absolute, present in the ancestral line of Raïssa and of Véra. I feel myself thus a debtor to Israel. I do not like, moreover, the grossness of the Gentiles, I would like to be as little as possible a *goïsche kop*; I would like to be a

> Jew by adoption, since I have been introduced by baptism into
> the dignity of the children of Israel.[80]

Referring explicitly to his grandfather Jules Favre, a founder of the laic Third Republic, and implicitly to his father Paul Maritain, a wastrel and a suicide, Maritain saw something deformed if not destructive in his hereditary make-up. He thus saw in his conversion, alongside Raïssa and Véra, a passage into new life, not only becoming a Christian, but also aspiring somehow to be a Jew. Maritain had internalized many of Bloy's dictums, but perhaps none more so than that there was but one real tragedy in life, and that was not to be a saint. By this point in his life, Maritain clearly thought it tragic for a Christian not to embrace in some sense a Jewish identity, given the closeness of "Jewishness" to sainthood, the children of Israel only needing to bow their heads to achieve a privileged closeness to the divine.

This deep identification with Israel, expressed in a spiritual pining, helps explain Maritain's unambiguous support for the fledgling Jewish democracy in the Middle East, for he saw the destiny of the state of Israel as necessarily tied to God's unbroken promises. Writing in 1964, in a postscriptum to *Le Mystère d'Israël*, he regretted that his failing health precluded either writing a substantial chapter on the state of Israel or journeying to that land to conduct the necessary research. Nonetheless, he wanted to make some essential points about this new nation-state. Perhaps most importantly, he saw this as "the sole country to which, taking into account the whole spectacle of human history, it is absolutely, *divinely* certain that a people incontestably has a right: because the people of Israel is the single people in the world to which a land, the Land of Canaan, was given by the true God, the one and transcendent God, creator of the universe and of humanity. And what God gives once is given for all time."[81]

Maritain saw no ambiguity in asserting that this scriptural truth should be taken as an article of faith for Christians and Jews alike. As for the predominantly Muslim Arab world, Maritain saw its hostility to Israel as an uncharacteristic failure to exhibit "this resignation to an event testifying to the will of Allah that is such a profoundly characteristic trait of Islam." It would be better for all concerned if the group of surrounding Arab states could "decide one day without too much trouble to 'give' to the Jews that which, from its point of view, it regards as its own, but which God, by an event that has undoubtedly come to pass, and for the good and peace of the world, asks it to give up."[82] Maritain did not clarify where in either Arab history or the Qur'an itself he found this axiomatic character-istic of Muslim Arab quietude.

While Maritain showed, for all his personalist and pluralist con-victions, as little sympathy for the displaced Palestinian Arabs of his day as the slaughtered Canaanites of yore, he justified total support of Israel on two bases: the destiny and mission of the Jewish people, and the terrible sufferings they too long had endured. As he put it, for Jews, "the temporal destiny of the State of Israel, while not perhaps being identical with their own, essentially involves their heart and their soul; and in and of itself moreover, while being temporal and 'secular,' inevitably has a spiritual function and a spiritual mission."[83] He also contemplated the meaning of Jewish survival throughout history, asking,

> Are we not permitted to think that well before any problem ex-plicitly posed in regard to the Gospel one day stirs the con-science of Israel, well before one day it is a question for her of an *agonizing reappraisal* of her attitude toward Jesus, it is in her *physical comportment*, in her manner of reacting, through the implacable dialectic over which she prevails, to the difficulties and to the enigmas of history, that in fact Israel, even without yet knowing it, is getting closer to the great day which according to Saint Paul will be for the world as a resurrection among the dead, and which the Spirit of God makes us await with such a grand desire?[84]

Maritain again equated the immediate or anticipated danger of Jew-ish annihilation and promise of ultimate survival with the apocalyptic prospect of the day of resurrection and reintegration forecast by Paul. How else could one explain the otherwise unlikely survival for almost two thou-sand years of a people who both refused to recognize deliverance in the arms of their messiah or acknowledge defeat at the hands of their enemies? The Shoah had marked the climax of this mysterious dialectic:

> And I think also of this Holocaust of six million Jews annihilated by Hitler and the Nazi racism that has marked our epoch with a gaping wound, and which has revealed a sort of enigmatic and terrifying similarity between the passion of the people of God on the march, in the night of the world, toward its final destiny, and the Passion of the Son of God accomplishing, in the great sacred night of eternal designs, the work of redemption of hu-mankind.[85]

If Maritain therefore saw the Holocaust as the "passion of Israel," he saw the coalescence of an Israeli state as the commencement of Israel's resurrection.

But Maritain's confidant, Charles (now Cardinal) Journet privately questioned what he read as an espousal of Israel's supposed right of conquest by divine sanction: "The achievement of the state of Israel — due not to the methods of Gandhi but to violence — is that what God wanted or permitted?" He further asked whether one should equally validate the conquests made by Muslims and Christians "in the name of holy war?"[86] But Maritain disagreed with his friend's critical premises, denying that he thought the Israeli state itself had a divine sanction, or that military conquest really described what had happened in 1948. It simply amounted to a group of survivors of near extermination seeking to survive on their ancestral land, and in so doing, serving to foreshadow if not stimulate the *parousia*: "What the surrounding peoples are being asked to recognize, is not at all a conquest in the name of holy war or in the name of a messianic mission, it is establishing something in order *to be able to exist*, as I just said. . . . Should not a Christian see in the return of the Jews to the Promised Land a *preamble*, as far off as it might be, to the final reintegration?"[87] Both the movement of Jews in history and the changing attitudes of Christians would play a part in reaching the *eschaton*.

For Maritain, history would move toward its conclusion based on events not only in Jerusalem but in other places, including Rome. Perhaps the most public triumph in his long life came to him as an octogenarian, when at the close of the Second Vatican Council in 1965 Pope Paul VI lauded him as the doyen of Catholic intellectuals, presenting him with a special letter to the world's writers and scientists. But Maritain continued to feel misgivings about the inadequacy of his Church's response to antisemitism, particularly as the response found itself mired in politics. Indeed, he had already felt disappointed when during a historic 1964 visit to the Holy Land, Paul VI relegated to the Dean of the College of Cardinals, Eugène Cardinal Tisserant, the task of lighting six candles — one for each of the six millions — at the Yad Vashem Holocaust memorial in Jerusalem.[88]

Bernard Doering accurately recaptures Maritain's mood when he refers to the "watered down" declarations of *Nostra Aetate* that finally condemned Christian antisemitism, but left crucial words and phrases from the 1964 draft on the cutting-room floor.[89] Indeed, the former ambassador to the Vatican wrote to Journet on 7 October 1965 that "I have suffered a real wound in seeing that the words 'and condemn' after the word 'deplore' (hatred, persecution, manifestations of antisemitism) have been suppressed."[90] Maritain saw a bowing to political considerations — not only the resistance of certain conservative members of the curia but also the fear of offending Arab opinion (including Christian Arab opinion) in the Middle East — as continuing to play a negative role in the Catholic Church's ability to formulate a complete and final denunciation of antisemitism; perhaps the new pope's approach to this issue even compared unfavorably with the anti-antisemitic stance of Pope Pius XI almost thirty years earlier.

Maritain had an apocalyptic vision of Jewish-Christian relations. He saw Jewish-Christian reconciliation as a prelude to the Second Coming, and his expressed hopes in this regard made him impatient at half-measures of achieving a better understanding between Christians and Jews. Maritain looked upon the Second Vatican Council not only with frustration at its incomplete rejection of anti-Jewish prejudice, but also with an overall mixed view of what it had achieved in its intention to bring the light of the Gospel to bear on the problems of the modern world.

His assessment of the wider impact of the Council's reforms took form in his 1966 book *The Peasant of the Garonne*, which further emphasized his consternation at what he saw as a widespread temporalization of eschatological hopes, a "frenzied modernism" among laity and clergy alike that threatened the spiritual integrity of Catholicism. Before the publication of the book, Thomas Merton heartily praised his friend's arguments, sadly agreed with his conclusions, and connected this denial of the transcendent to a failure to learn from the Holocaust:

> We are so foolish and we think this earth is our home (well, it will be that after the resurrection) but there is now all the incredible nonsense that is being preached about a religionless religion, about total commitment to the modern secular world, etc. etc. it would make you sick if you saw it. One would think there had never been a Calvary, an Auschwitz, a Dachau . . . These poor idiots have simply determined that it is now time to be very optimistic, and the gamble succeeded, everybody likes it (Christians I mean). It is the thing. Léon Bloy would be able to say a thing or two about this rage.[91]

Despite Merton's support, as well as that of other friends, this book earned Maritain the lasting enmity of many liberal Catholics, who saw in this work evidence of either senility or a return to right-wing hostility against modernity. Unfortunately, Maritain's complex, impassioned, and irritated response to his changing times contradicted the ineffable myth of a consistently liberal Maritain who had advocated progressive change for its own sake.

FINAL REFLECTIONS ON THE MYSTERY OF ISRAEL

Toward the end of his life, Maritain offered some final reflections on the mystery of Israel. At this point, it is worth asking what Maritain, based on his own mature understanding of Christian-Jewish relations, might have made of subsequent Vatican statements and initiatives, such as the 1998 document, *We Remember*, given the fact that some of the same scholars who have lionized Maritain have taken the Catholic Church to task for what they see as the inadequacies of this document.

In *On the Church of Christ*, Maritain reasserted the essential and necessary purity of the Church, and presented his metahistorical interpretation of the relationship of both Christians and Jews to the Body of Christ. He continued to assert the innocence of the Church in the historic hatreds against Jews, as opposed to the misdeeds of its members and even some of the Church Fathers such as John Chrysostom. Generally speaking, however, he distinguished between the religious leadership and the general populace in this regard: "The hatred of the Jews in the Middle Ages was the deed of the populace and of many in the [emerging] bourgeoisie and in the nobility, and of many in the lower clergy. The high personnel of the Church, the Papacy above all, remained free from it."[92] Some of the intemperate outbursts of Chrysostom and other early Christians bore bitter fruit by this period, with a half-educated lower clergy and the ignorant masses cherishing a smoldering hostility toward a people charged with the murder of God Incarnate: "The idea of the 'deicide-people' and the religious hatred of the Jewish people are linked like flesh and bones."[93]

What had once been the marginalization of Jews as members of a bad religion eventually became the dehumanization of Jews as members of a bad race. It seems difficult to narrate the subsequent history of anti-semitism — that is, its appearance as a racist prejudice seeing the Jew as an essentially implacable enemy of humankind — without acknowledging the institutional Church's responsibility for teaching contempt of Jews and Judaism. But the question of responsibility really hinges on the degree of continuity between medieval and modern variants of the prejudice. Indeed, scholars such as Parkes and, later on, Rosemary Radford Ruether[94] do not even speak of anti-Judaic/antisemitic variants.

Maritain drew a distinction, however, and saw the early modern period as historically crucial in making a case for discontinuity. A transition took place from an official discriminatory policy among the popes, which held that "legal constraint must be employed to protect the faith," to an increasingly unmitigated hatred in an increasingly post-Catholic and incipiently secular society. Thus Yosef Hayim Yerushalmi observes that "while the Christian tradition of 'reprobation' continued into the modern era, the Christian tradition of 'preservation' fell by the wayside and was no longer operative."[95] Maritain adopted a similar position. Although he deemphasized the "tradition of reprobation," he argued in effect that modern antisemitism should be seen as symptomatic of the Church's loss of influence and control in modern society and culture. The Church had lost its control over Jews and Christians alike:

> If others had without doubt the same sentiments as [Louis XIV's court preacher Bishop] Bossuet the episcopal body as a whole kept itself free from the religious hatred of the Jewish people. The hatred was intense in Luther. The Renaissance marked the beginnings of its disappearance. But Voltaire showed that anti-Judaic rage can very well not be of a religious order and that it is easy to secularize hate. On the side of the Church, it was toward the recognition by Christians of the dignity of Israel and of the bonds of friendship that must be established between them and it that the wind began to blow. Before the interruption of the first Council of the Vatican almost all the Fathers of the Church had signed the *Postulatum pro Hebraeis* presented by the two Lémann brothers, and one knows the remark of Pius IX to these latter: *Vos estis filii.*[96]

In Maritain's historical analysis, Protestantism and the Enlightenment play crucial roles in undermining a bedrock Christian respect and love for Jews. Indeed, forces of modernity work to curtail what he sees as the Church's movement toward a new understanding between Catholics and Jews, undertaken even under the pontificate of Pius IX.[97]

Maritain's diagnosis of modern antisemitism as crucially linked to the breakdown of what had once been called Christendom not only hearkens back to the substance of early works such as *Three Reformers* but fully anticipates the position in *We Remember*, the Vatican statement acknowledging the long roots of antisemitism but distancing the Church itself from the "neo-pagan" assault on the Jews. He maintains that God's disavowal of antisemitism is based on an enduring, unbreakable, and long-suffering love for His chosen people:

> God is patient. He does not charge the Jewish people with what the Christians call its obstinacy, and which the Jews call their fidelity — it is not their fault that the bandage was formerly put over their eyes by their high priests, and reinforced again by all the persecutions which they have suffered from Christians. But God has ever before His eyes that which is at the origin of their obstinate waiting for the Messiah already come: His love betrayed and insulted by the house of Israel, when He sent His Son and when Jerusalem did not know the time of her visitation. Who would venture to say that in Him love gave way to the thirst for vengeance and reprobation? This would be blasphemy.[98]

One encounters so often in Maritain's theological-historical explanation of antisemitism a logically compelling yet precariously balanced combination of factors: God's perfect and unchanging love, the Jews' imperfect vision of the risen Christ, and the hatred of Christians cursing yet reinforcing Jewish "obstinacy" through the ages.

A long historical standoff between faiths ensues. One resists God's call; the other at once reiterates and obscures that call. This impasse persists for centuries, only to be broken by the challenge of modernity to both faiths. Modernity presents the strange combination of doubt, self-edification, and horror. In the wreckage of this modern world, a broken world in which humanity carries open wounds that long predate the modern age, God's love is inseparable from the Cross, even and especially for the Jewish people: "To be loved by God can mean to have to sweat blood. *It is the love of God* which abandoned it during centuries to the abominable treatment of the Gentiles; we are the blindest of the blind if we do not understand this. And this love is always there, the Jews can count upon it."[99]

Maritain does not consider the special love of God toward the Jews in any way inferior to that shown toward Gentiles who believe in Christ. How could God's perfect love have gradations? One thus beholds different aspects of one and the same supreme *caritas*:

> And in spite of the different forms under which it manifests itself, the love of God for His new people and for the ancient one in its descendants of today is, as I have said, a single and unique love because in the eternal divine vision the two constitute but

a single and same people of God, the fact remains that fallen in
to human history the things which constitute but one in the divine vision and in the divine love are delivered over to the dialectic from below, with the bloody oppositions which are
proper to it and its miserable limping progress.[100]

Maritain's philosophy of history, with its insistence on both the divine permission of evil and human moral growth through suffering and atonement,
depends on a fulfilling moment in which Jews and Christians come together
before God. The Holocaust had pushed the dialectic of modern Jewish history toward a terrible conclusion. In "a civilization formerly Christian," a
new radical and profane opposition between Jewish emancipation and
racial antisemitism ended in the fires of "the Nazi extermination camps."[101]
What afterward but hope?

In his final years, his body weakened and his spirit battered, the
eldest of the Little Brothers of Jesus (he pronounced his vows in 1970)
dared to hope that the Jewish and Christian travels through history had just
taken their last separate steps: "And then the hour arrived when the blind
dialectical opposition finally relaxed a little, in order to let pass a ray of
light. It seems to me very significant that these two events of such great
bearing — on the Jewish side the return of a portion of the Jewish people
to the Promised Land, on the Christian side the second Council of the Vatican — took place at almost the same time. . . . They mark, each in its own
manner, a reorientation of history."[102]

But Maritain knew painfully that the human person does not live
on historical hope alone. The old student of Saint Thomas still *distinguished
in order to unite*. The convert emulator of Saint Paul humbled himself before the sacred mystery that had already shown so terribly much, yet somehow still too little, apocalyptic fulfillment:

The *cross of survival* carried by the Jewish people and the *cross
of redemption* carried by the Church are very far still from being
ready to join each other. But later, much later without doubt,
when there will come the historical catastrophe from which will
arise for a time a renewed human universe, that day, which will
be as a prelude to the resurrection of the dead, the cross of survival (for it will be the old olive tree of Israel which will flower
again in its entirety, ["all Israel shall be saved," Romans 11:26]
and the cross of redemption (for it is the new people of God
which will assume everything in the light of Christ) will recognize themselves finally and will constitute but a single cross, in

order to offer salvation to the men of all the earth, and perhaps in order that, before the end of time, the earth itself may pass through a moment in which it will be given to it to know the peace which the Lamb of God gives.[103]

Shifting his focus from his reader to his God, Maritain asked to discern the "unity which the Father Who is in Heaven had in view from all eternity." He dedicated himself to sharing this vision, or whatever part of it he could yet grasp, with others in need of understanding.

Sharing this vision had a practical import. In a letter written in 1967, he had replied to a young woman, a convert to Catholicism who had written him as he was leaving for his summer vacation in the Alsatian village of Kolbsheim. There he and his wife had spent happier times as the guests at the chateau of Alexander and Antoinette Grunelius, and there Raïssa's body now rested in the small cemetery. Having rested on a mattress during the long automobile drive from Toulouse, he disobeyed his physician's standing orders and immediately put to paper his reply to the young "Jewish Christian's" feelings of both joy and painful dislocation:

> "Maladjusted," you say, of course! A true Christian is never "adjusted." — "Uprooted" from your people according to the flesh? Yes, undoubtedly, and that is the price of the marvelous privilege ["to be at the same time of the race of Jesus and of His Spirit"] of which I just spoke. One must bless this condition, not bemoan it, it *obligates* you thus to march toward sanctity, in the footsteps of Saint Paul, and toward the love of this Cross by which man became co-redemptor with Jesus: for the salvation of the world and the accomplishment of Israel. Until the reintegration of Israel, you form the humble suite of servitors of these prophets (no one is a prophet in his country). And you can only "uproot" yourself in this little flock of souls (there is one just the same, and more than people realize) absolutely given in themselves to Jesus and uprooted for the world.[104]

Maritain looked upon this girl with sincere love and sanctified envy. He saw in her anxieties about trying to renegotiate her identity both the promise and the pain known by Raïssa and her sister, his two companions in that little flock that comprised a part of a larger more mysterious one. As he sought a glimpse of the eternal Kingdom, he saw himself struggling through faith and reason toward a more perfect love, hoping to learn

how to live as both a Christian by conversion and a Jew by participation
— until such a time as the distinction would have lost all meaning.

CONCLUSION

Given his earnest hope that something positive would arise from the Shoah,
Maritain's postwar activities arguably assumed an evangelical dimension
regarding the lessons of the Holocaust. Not only Jewish people, but the
Church itself needed to change before a new age, before a true reintegration, could show itself. This Catholic philosopher, haunted by the legacy
of the Holocaust, has become an iconic figure in the history of Catholic-
Jewish relations, and has been cited as epitomizing Catholic progressivism
and philosemitism in the face of papal silence and/or intransigence. Some
of the scholars who praise Maritain in this regard lament the shortcomings
not only in Pius XII's policies, but also the inadequacies of contemporary
Church documents such as *We Remember*. Because the 1998 document denies a causal connection between Christian anti-Judaism and Nazi antisemitism, these writers claim that little has changed within the Catholic
Church. Pawlikowski, for example, regrets that *We Remember* leaves the
strong impression that there was *no* inherent connection between Nazi ideology and classical Christian anti-Judaism and anti-Semitism,"[105] and Braham describes *We Remember* as erring "by failing to emphatically admit
the institutional guilt of the Church and by staunchly defending the wartime
position of Pope Pius XII."[106] But might they not be criticizing Maritain as
well?

Indeed, Maritain also denied a close historical connection between
traditional anti-Judaism and Nazi antisemitism, and he publicly defended
Pius XII as often as he privately criticized him. As I have taken pains to
show, Maritain's engagement of the Jewish Question in the wake of the
Holocaust should be less easily categorized and instrumentalized. My attempt has been to provide something other than a simplistic snapshot of
one Catholic's encounter with the Jewish Other, therefore critiquing and
where necessary refuting the misuse of Maritain in the "Pius Wars." For
example, while Braham's identification of Maritain as the only courageous
Catholic opponent of Pius XII is based on only one source, and a posthumously published account of decades old hearsay at that, some crucial con-
tentions do not rely on evidence at all. Phayer asserts about Maritain's
assumption of the Vatican post: "Whatever motivated De Gaulle, it is certain that Maritain's views on the danger of antisemitism motivated him to

accept the position."[107] But he neglects to support this contention — which contradicts all the available documentary evidence cited above — with any citation of sources whatsoever.

Maritain's historical and theological challenge to his fellow Catholics was to enter into a crucial dialogue with Jews without compromising the key elements of the faith tradition of either group. It took him decades to arrive at this point, and he never achieved an entirely unproblematic position. Even so, a truer appreciation of the problems within his ambivalent philosemitism promises to reveal more than all the polarized polemics of the so-called Pius Wars ever will. The *real* Maritain, the devout Catholic driven by love and assailed by hate, the philosopher searching for truth on a pathway beset with contradictions, still has much to teach us. Perhaps, spiritually, Maritain's exile is not yet over.

CONCLUSION

What has this study revealed about Maritain's fight against antisemitism and his response to the Holocaust? First, his public opposition to anti-semitism materialized gradually during the antifascist struggle of the 1930s, drew on Catholic arguments against racism, increased in urgency during the Nazi genocide, and after 1945 focused on the need for Christians and others to draw appropriate lessons from the Holocaust. But Maritain's desire to confront the legacy of Christian anti-Judaism (or Christian anti-semitism as some scholars have put it) should not be overstated, as does the apocryphal story of his protest resignation from the Vatican embassy in 1948. While he privately criticized some of the reigning pontiff's decisions in the wake of the Holocaust, by and large, he defended Pius XII's attitude toward Jews and considered the Pope free of any taint of anti-semitism.

Second, Maritain's own changing attitude toward Jews in the modern world did not involve a dramatic transformation from an antisemite to a philosemite, because he had never, even during his early association with the extreme rightist Action Française, embraced the antisemitism rampant in his day. By the 1930s, his politics changed to embrace democratic pluralism, and he decisively rejected the emerging racist — if not eliminationist — antisemitism favored by the extreme right. Nonetheless, his primarily theological framing of the Jewish Question as the mystery of Israel led him to retain a number of anti-Judaic stereotypes, including a yet unresolved ambivalence about their responsibility for their own travails. Examining the "passion of Israel" through Maritain's eyes only highlights the problematic nature of his evolving philosemitism.

Third, the case of Maritain points to the inherent instability of the concept of philosemitism, a term loaded with meanings potentially at war with one another: overt sympathy for a traditional Jewish identity, but muted disapproval of at least some aspects of Jewish distinctiveness; generosity of sentiment toward the "people of Israel," but expectations of conversion to Christianity; denunciation of criminal violence against the "race of Moses and Jesus," but a belief in the salvific value of the victims' suffering. Instead of celebrating an unrealistically progressive Maritain, we can learn more from his insistence on struggling with the tensions within his philosemitism, for that struggle, not simply his good intentions toward

Jews, makes him almost unique for his time and rightfully influential there-after. Not all Jews have appreciated Maritain's philosemitic impulse. Jewish theologian Arthur Cohen went so far as to brand Maritain's expression "a murderous love."[1] In spite of lofty motivations, we cannot but acknowledge an uncomfortable aspect to the Christian-Jewish encounter that continues to the present day.

Believing themselves to be chosen in Christ, many Christians have long felt discomfort with, and anxiety about, a non-Christian Chosen People. Can we entirely separate Maritain from this characterization? Maritain's translation of the Jewish Question into the mystery of Israel, which characterized his attitude toward Jews for most of his life, points to a strug-gle for meaning, truth, and grace in the face of a seemingly insoluble mys-tery that can touch the very center of Christian faith and history. His labors to love more fully his Jewish neighbors, and to understand and alleviate their suffering, always comprised more striving than attainment. Notwith-standing the ambiguities of Maritain's philosemitism that I have pointed out, given the raging antisemitism of his time, his strong public rejection of anti-Jewish hatred must be commended. Maritain anticipated and helped direct some significant strides that have been taken by Catholics and other Christians since the Shoah: the mitigation of a "teaching of contempt,"[2] as well as the rejection by most Christians of a crude supersessionism or "re-placement theology."

Even as he worked tirelessly in the world against antisemitism and for Jewish-Christian reconciliation, for Maritain, the mystery of Israel was essentially eschatological. He wrestled with a theological mystery that can-not be avoided when examining the long story of Jewish-Christian rela-tions. His Catholic understanding of this problem, while it may seem triumphalist in today's postmodern, secular western world, never embodied arrogance or complacency, but rather testifies to a Christian conscience dis-turbed by a difficult, painful issue. At the beginning of this book, I empha-sized the central importance of conversion for Maritain, his own and that of others. The very pluralism he came to advocate, an ever more prevalent fact of life in our present western (or northern?) world, casts conversionist overtures by Christians in a questionable light, especially as concerns Christian "missions" to Jews.

Maritain's own journey of self-understanding demonstrates how he reconciled soteriological hope with deepening respect for Jews and Ju-daism. As the decades passed, he became increasingly hesitant to prosely-tize them. Today, historians can write of Maritain's early years as a

converter of Jews in either condescending ("the Meudon conversion machine")[3] or outright unfair ("Maritain saw the good Jew… as the convert")[4]
terms. But by the time of the Shoah, his views on true conversion had
changed so much that he could see faithful Jews playing a role in redeeming
apostate Christians.

Notwithstanding his transformed views of Jews and Judaism, Maritain never repudiated his orthodox Christian belief that Jesus is the savior
of all humanity and that faith in Christ is normative for salvation. His recognition of an enduring Jewish vocation did not acknowledge coequal Jewish
and Christian covenants — or for that matter a "double covenant"[5] — that
would unavoidably undercut the universalistic claims of Christianity. He
never equated the Synagogue with the Church, even if he analogized them.
He saw Jews as incipient Christians, not necessarily in a worldly sense, but
in a proleptic sense — eschatologically deferred. Maritain does not quite
"fit" the irenic historiography of Jewish-Christian relations or the predominantly liberal theology that underpins it.

While a Christian respect for Jewish disbelief in Jesus as the Messiah seems a reasonable enough prerequisite for discussion and reconciliation at this point in history,[6] can Christian faith in Jesus Christ be seen as
anything other than supersessionism or triumphalism? A prominent historian of antisemitism once asked me if I thought Maritain was a supersessionist; I replied that he worked hard not to be one. My interlocutor did not
press the issue, but I suspect that the inevitable rebuttal from some scholars
would run as follows: Maritain did not work hard *enough*.

As we have seen, James Parkes's insistence on separating what he
saw as true Christian faith from the oppressive weight of historic Christianity put him at odds with Maritain on the question of the Christian roots
of antisemitism. Parkes saw antisemitism embedded in the very origins of
the Church, while Maritain offered what Gavin Langmuir calls "a discul-
pation of Christian faith by insisting on the contrast between anti-Judaism
and antisemitism."[7] But as we also found, the debate over historical continuity can overshadow another deeper point of contention, which is theological. The heart of the argument between Parkes and Maritain really
involved the designation of the Church as the "mystical body of Christ,"
something the former rejected and the latter upheld.

Some recent scholars, such as Rosemary Radford Ruether, have
called for a radical revision of Christology as a prerequisite for improving
relations between Christians and Jews in the wake of the Holocaust.
Ruether argues that Christians need to understand Jesus as but "another

story," or more pointedly, as "the paradigm of salvation for Christians," in order for Christian belief to "cease to be an assault on the right of Jews to exist." Some parts of the Gospels "may simply be unusable and will have to be put aside or relativized historically."[8] While this relativizing of Christian scriptures may be well-intentioned, what distinctively Christian beliefs would remain? Maritain can be criticized on a number of fronts, and from a number of perspectives, but he never confused Christian doctrine with ameliorative praxis. Dismantling Christian belief is likely to lead to secularism, not reconciliation.

The delicacy of upholding Christian faith claims in a post-Holocaust world makes itself apparent in an ongoing controversy regarding the treatment of the Jewish covenant in the United States Catholic Catechism for Adults. In August 2008, the United States Conference of Catholic Bishops voted to recommend to the Vatican the removal of the following statement from the Catechism: "Thus the covenant that God made with the Jewish people through Moses remains eternally valid for them." Fearing that this statement "might be understood to imply that one of the former covenants imparts salvation without the mediation of Christ," the bishops opted to replace it with this citation of Romans 9:4–5: "To the Jewish people, whom God first chose to hear his word, 'belong the sonship, the glory, the covenants, the giving of the law, the worship and the promises; to them belong the patriarchs, and of their race, according to the flesh, is the Christ.'"[9] Abraham Foxman doubtless spoke for many Jewish readers when he voiced his resentment at this change, asking, "When did the Catholic Church decide that our covenant was finished?"[10]

But how can Christian self-understanding avoid any contradiction whatsoever of Jewish self-understanding? Witness one recent attempt by three Catholic theologians to reconcile fully the imperative of making continued progress in Christian-Jewish dialogue with an assertion of "the universal saving significance of Jesus Christ":

> The Catholic Church does not teach that explicit personal confession of faith in Jesus is necessary for salvation. It teaches that Christ saves everyone. If Jews are in covenant with the God whom Christians understand to be triune, then they are in relationship with the Father, Son and Spirit and are related to the saving power of Jesus Christ, even if that is not how Jews experience that relationship. Can any relationship as intimate as a covenant with the triune God not be salvific?[11]

This statement, while trying to offend no party, may offend all. Do Jews *really* want to be told they are in a "covenant with the triune God"?

Maritain held to his assertion that an orthodox Catholic Christian faith need not contradict a love for one's Jewish brothers and sisters. His unwillingness to exchange what he saw as truth for praxis[12] perhaps will be misconstrued by many in a pluralistic culture, but even when Maritain spoke in front of Jewish audiences in the 1940s, he showed an awareness of this risk, and proceeded to share his convictions anyway. In a time of unprecedented horror, when Jews rightfully felt forsaken, he wanted to demonstrate that a Catholic conscience could utterly reject antisemitism and uphold the covenantal kinship between Christians and Jews. This is not to argue that this kinship, particularly as outlined by Saint Paul, can ever be rendered unproblematic. Andrew Das, in his recent book, *Paul and the Jews*, stresses the interfaith impasse:

> If a modern Christian . . . maintains Paul's perspective as normative for his or her own personal worldview, then disagreement will be inevitable. If the Christian claims Paul's emphasis on faith in Christ as the sole means of salvation in the world to come, then such a Christian is as much at odds with a Jew who rejects Jesus as the Jewish Messiah as the Jewish Paul was at odds with his own brothers and sisters in the first century. May such disagreements be expressed with the mutual respect and humility that is required in this post-Shoah generation.[13]

Maritain accepted this disagreement and emphasized the eschatological promise, as he hoped and believed that at the end of time Jews and Christians alike would recognize Jesus as the Jewish Messiah and the savior of the world. The reader can choose to remain indifferent to, or to take offense at, the expression of this belief. Or the reader can choose to find comfort in the light of this hope.

NOTES

INTRODUCTION

[1] Gutman, *The Jews of Warsaw*, 307.

[2] Chagall, "In Honor of Jacques Maritain."

[3] Ibid.

[4] Maritain did not use the word *Holocaust* to describe the Nazi mass murder of Europe's Jews (nor did almost anyone else until the 1960s), except in the post-script to his 1965 collection of essays on the mystery of Israel, when he evoked "cet holocauste de six millions de Juifs anéantis par Hitler et le racisme nazi qui a marqué notre époque d'une plaie béante, et qui a révélé une sorte d'énigmatique et terrifiante similarité entre la passion du peuple de Dieu en marche, dans la nuit du monde, vers sa destinée finale, et la Passion du Fils de Dieu accomplissant, dans la grande nuit sacrée des desseins éternels, l'œuvre de la rédemption du genre humain." See J. Maritain, *Le Mystère d'Israël et autres essais*, 252. We can see here that even in employing the word *Holocaust*, Maritain implicitly retains his designation of that event as the "passion of Israel." As most readers will already know, the word *holocaust* has its roots in the Greek term for "burnt offering," and hence something pleasing to God (or a deity). But while we can acknowledge the potential offensiveness of the term, particularly for Jews, I agree with Dominick LaCapra that "here one is in an area where no easy, uninvolved, or purely objective choices are available." LaCapra further points to the danger of alternative word choices such as *annihilation* (whence comes the Hebrew *Shoah*) or *final solution*, either of which might "inadvertently repeat Nazi terminology." LaCapra, *Representing the Holocaust*, 45. So, understanding the risks implicit in using *Holocaust*, *Shoah*, *Final Solution*, and *Passion of Israel*, I will employ all of these terms in this book, but will devote my interpretive efforts to the last of these designators, the one used by Maritain.

[5] See note 7 below.

[6] Catholic Bishops of France, "Declaration of Repentance."

[7] "Catholic historian Michael Phayer has criticized Pius XII's posture during this period, basing his criticisms in part on the archives of Jacques Maritain, the eminent French Catholic philosopher, who resigned his post as French Ambassador to the Vatican in protest over Pius' immediate post-war stance on German Catholic guilt." Pawlikowski, "The Canonization of Pope Pius XII," 222. Phayer himself puts it somewhat less dramatically: "Realizing that his arguments for a papal-led spiritual reawakening in Europe would come to naught, Jacques Maritain resigned his ambassadorship in 1948." Phayer, *The Catholic Church and the Holocaust*, 182. See also Coppa, *The Papacy, the Jews, and the Holocaust*, 213.

[8] Maritain contributed an essay — which joined pieces by Paul Claudel, Joseph Bonsirven, and others — titled "L'impossible antisémitisme" to Daniel-Rops, ed., *Les Juifs*.

[9] Cf. Maritain's 1944 radio address "The Passion of Israel," reprinted in J. Maritain, *Messages (1941–1944)*, 119–22.

[10] An otherwise excellent collection of essays on Maritain and the Jews devotes only seven of its almost three hundred pages directly to the Holocaust, with another seven mentioning Adolf Hitler. I refer here to Royal, ed., *Jacques Maritain and the Jews*.

[11] According to sociologist Alan Edelstein, *philosemitism* can be defined as a "belief system that 1. sees Jews in a positive light . . . 2. may take a multitude of forms, depending on the time, place, and situation . . . 3. has attitudinal and behavioral components . . . 4. in its weakest sense, entails anti-anti-Semitism . . . 5. may or may not lead to overt actions . . . 6. may or may not be consistent . . . [and] 7. may exist for numerous reasons — self-interested, religious, political, economic, or humanistic motives." Edelstein, *An Unacknowledged Harmony*, 19. While Edelstein's definition of *philosemitism* establishes rather broad parameters, he rightly avoids defining philosemitism as the opposite of antisemitism. He might have gone further, however, by pointing out how philosemites and antisemites both essentialize Jews based on "otherness." Zygmunt Bauman reflects on a traditional essentializing about Jews, or "allosemitism," in contact with modernity: "The Jews, already inherited by modernity in their capacity of ambivalence incarnate, were predestined for their role of the eponymical weed. . . . Modern practice stands out from all other practices for its obsessive preoccupation with ordering, and all ordering is about neat divisions and clear-cut categories, casting all ambivalence, automatically, as the prime and most awesome of weeds. Making order is a synonym for the fight against ambiguity. Making modern Europe was synonymical with allosemitism veering toward its antisemitic pole." Bauman, *Life in Fragments*, 219. As will be seen, the case of Maritain shows that allosemitism can veer toward another pole, and this has much to do with an individual's engagement with or interrogation of modernity.

[12] Quoted in Doering, *Jacques Maritain and the French Catholic Intellectuals*, 10.

[13] Barré, *Jacques et Raïssa Maritain*, 13–33; McInerny, *The Very Rich Hours*, 7–11.

[14] J. Maritain, *Notebooks*, 60.

[15] R. Maritain, *The Memoirs of Raïssa Maritain*, 15. The reference is to the first of the two memoirs, originally published in 1942.

[16] J. Maritain, *Integral Humanism*, 244.

CHAPTER ONE

Epigraph: J. Maritain, "*À propos de la question juive*," 62.
[1] Poliakov, *The History of Anti-Semitism, Volume Four*, 278–79.
[2] Cf. Kruger, *The Spectral Jew*.
[3] Hyman, *The Jews of Modern France*, 173–74.

⁴ Cf. Weber, *France: Fin de siècle*, 9–26.

⁵ Michel Winock writes that "les milieux les plus traditionnellement enclins au rejet du judaïsme — les catholiques — connaissent au long des années trente une évolution dans le sens de l'esprit démocratique et de la tolérance. S'il ne fallait retenir qu'un nom, Jacques Maritain est exemplaire, puisque ce philosophe est passé de l'Action Française à un humanisme militant qui exclut toutes les formes du totalitarisme et réfute toutes les justifications de l'antisémitisme." Winock, *La France et les Juifs*, 214.

⁶ "M. Jacques Maritain est marié à une Juive. Il a enjuivé sa vie et sa doctrine. Sa théologie, sa dialectique sont falsifiées comme le passeport d'un espion juif. M. Maritain, corps et âme, représente ce que les Allemands appellent avec tant de raison un 'Rassenschander,' un souilleur de la Race." Rebatet, "Juifs et Catholiques," *Je suis partout* (n. 384), 1 April 1938, in J. Maritain, *L'impossible antisémitisme*, 169–70.

⁷ Marrus, "A Plea Unanswered," 10.

⁸ "Why is it, in the debates which we know took place, that the Church did not listen to the better claims of its members' voices? Before the war, Jacques Maritain, both in articles and in lectures, tried to open Christians up to different perspectives on the Jewish people. He also warned against the perversity of the anti-Semitism that was developing." Catholic Bishops of France, "Declaration of Repentance."

⁹ I refer here specifically to the 29 December 1926 papal ban on Catholics reading the *Action française* newspaper and several of Maurras' own writings, which for all intents and purposes aimed at banning French Catholics from participation in the Action Française movement. The respective italicization of the newspaper and the non-italicization of the movement are customary among most English-speaking historians.

¹⁰ After tracing the gestation of a "*génération intellectuelle*" born in the 1880s, coming of age during the Church-State conflict of the first decade of the new century, rallying to the *Union Sacrée* during the Great War, and seeing itself as simultaneously Catholic, Thomist, and Maurrasian until the moment of the papal condemnation, Chenaux concludes: "Avec Maritain, l'intellectuel catholique . . . fait son entrée dans la vie publique sous le signe du combat contre le naturalisme maurrassien." Chenaux, *Entre Maurras et Maritain*, 225–28.

¹¹ On the use and abuse of antisemitism and associated terminology, see Judaken, "Between Philosemitism and Antisemitism."

¹² J. Maritain, "*À propos de la question juive*," 61–62.

¹³ Ibid., 62.

¹⁴ Ibid., 62–63.

¹⁵ Ibid., 63–64.

¹⁶ Bernard Lazare's 1894 book *L'Antisémitisme, son histoire et ses causes* is available in English translation, with an informative preface by Robert Wistrich. See Lazare, *Antisemitism: Its History and Causes*, 149, 162, 182.

¹⁷ J. Maritain, "*À propos de la question juive*," 64.

[18] Ibid., 65–66.

[19] A Thomist of a later generation described such virtue ethics as follows: "To define the obligations of man is certainly a legitimate, even estimable, and no doubt necessary undertaking. With a doctrine of commandments or duties, there is always the danger of arbitrarily drawing up a list of requirements and losing sight of the human person who 'ought' to do this or that. The doctrine of virtue, on the other hand, has things to say about this human person; it speaks to both the kind of being which is his when he enters the world, as a consequence of his createdness, and the kind of being he ought to strive toward and attain to — by being prudent, just, brave, and temperate. The doctrine of virtue, that is, is one form of the doctrine of obligation; but one by nature free of regimentation and restriction. On the contrary, its aim is to clear a trail, to open a way." Pieper, *The Four Cardinal Virtues*, xi–xii. Obviously, such a "doctrine of virtue . . . one by nature free of regimentation and restriction" presupposes an objective moral reality upon which to draw — that is, natural law.

[20] J. Maritain, "*À propos de la question juive*," 68.

[21] "There are good reasons to say simply that Jacques Maritain was — at least for the earlier part of his career — an anti-Semite." Hellman, "The Jews in the 'New Middle Ages,'" 89. Michael Phayer also identifies Maritain with anti-semitism, but only goes so far as to portray Maritain as a Catholic convert "washed by the waters of French anti-Semitism." Phayer, *The Catholic Church and the Holocaust*, 178.

[22] Shain, *Antisemitism*, 5.

[23] Jaurès and Clemenceau quoted in Poliakov, *The History of Anti-Semitism, Volume Four*, 54, 64.

[24] Quoted in Goyet, *Charles Maurras*, 264.

[25] See Schloesser, *Jazz Age Catholicism*. Maritain, along with his wife, figures as a prominent case for Schloesser's thesis that various French Catholic artists and intellectuals advanced a "Catholicity" that engaged rather than rejected modernism.

[26] As the philosopher would put it in 1941, "Before being captured by Saint Thomas Aquinas, I underwent some great influences, Charles Péguy, Bergson, and Léon Bloy." J. Maritain, *Social and Political Philosophy*, 331.

[27] "I will be a socialist and live for the revolution." He made this declaration in an 1898 letter to the husband of the family cook, François Baton. J. Maritain, *Notebooks*, 8. On Maritain's earliest years, see McInerny, *The Very Rich Hours*, 7–11; and Barré, *Jacques et Raïssa Maritain*, 13–33.

[28] See Royal, "Péguy, Dreyfus, Maritain." On the later years of the Maritain-Péguy friendship, which soured for a time when Maritain prevailed upon Péguy to pressure his anticlerical wife to normalize their marriage, see the letters in *Péguy au porche de l'Église*.

[29] Doering, "Maritain's Idea of the Chosen People," 19.

[30] Maritain wrote the following in his notebook in early 1906, shortly before his baptism "The great obstacle to Christianity is the Christians. This is the thorn which pierces me. The Christians have abandoned the poor — and the poor among

the nations: the Jews — and Poverty of the soul: authentic Reason. They horrify me." J. Maritain, *Notebooks*, 26. Perhaps it is worth noting that the year 1906, which saw the Maritains convert to Catholicism, also saw both the exoneration of Dreyfus and the implementation of the Combes anti-clerical legislation, no doubt reducing the image, in many people's minds, of the Catholic Church as a monstrous, potent force of reaction.

[31] R. Maritain, *We Have Been Friends Together* (1941), 68. See also Barré, *Jacques et Raïssa Maritain*, 66–74, which among other things details the *Jardin des Plantes* suicide pact between the two students, as well as Suther's biography, *Raïssa Maritain: Pilgrim, Poet, Exile*. See also Stock, "Students versus the University."

[32] Barré, *Jacques et Raïssa Maritain*, 78.

[33] Schloesser, *Jazz Age Catholicism*, 67, 69–70.

[34] Bloy, *Pilgrim of the Absolute*, 263.

[35] Bloy, *Le Salut par les Juifs*, 15–16.

[36] Ibid., 25.

[37] Ibid., 7.

[38] Ibid., 85. No wonder that while one scholar can write that Bloy "venerated the suffering Jew" and offered "an idiosyncratic vision of the Jewish people radically opposed to that propagated in Drumont's *Libre Parole*," another identifies him as "one of the most extreme and vociferous anti-Semites of turn-of-the-century France." See respectively Schloesser, *Jazz Age Catholicism*, 68; and Hellman, "The Jews in the 'New Middle Ages,'" 91. Hellman elaborates in his next sentence on Bloy: "He attacked the high profile of Jews in that loathsome, materialistic, and money-grubbing world in which he passed as a stranger, as an 'ungrateful beggar' living off the donations of friends and acquaintances." Without reconciling these perhaps irreconcilable interpretations, Pierre Vidal-Naquet puts it thus: "Il va sans dire que les Juifs réels, qu'il fussent religieux ou athées, français ou étrangers, ne demeuraient pas indemnes sous les coups de cet instrument de la fureur divine que voulait être Léon Bloy." Vidal-Naquet, "Jacques Maritain et les Juifs," 24.

[39] R. Maritain, *We Have Been Friends Together*, 124. Jacques Maritain writes in his 1927 introduction to Raïssa's Bloy anthology: "I know it is as easy as it would be unjust to sketch of Bloy a heinous caricature, using for documents absurd bits of gossip, or lining up a certain number of texts chosen from a work that includes a great diversity of matter, part of which has vituperation as its main object." Bloy, *Pilgrim of the Absolute*, 8.

[40] Chenaux, "*Léon Bloy et sa postérité*," 48–52.

[41] Péguy quoted in Royal, "Péguy, Dreyfus, Maritain," 211.

[42] I think the term *rapprochement,* used by Vidal-Naquet and Chenaux, best captures the extent of and the intentionality behind Maritain's relationship with the movement. See Vidal-Naquet, "Jacques Maritain et les Juifs," 28; Chenaux, *Entre Maurras et Maritain*, 14, uses the term to describe the relationship between Catholics in general with the Action Française.

[43] Note that Maritain and Maurras did not share entirely an antipathy to the

same "modern world." Both demonstrated a certain political antimodernism —
opposing either tacitly or expressly the liberal democratic regime of the Third Republic, including its secularizing tendencies. But they diverged in that only Maurras lambasted literary and artistic modernism and only Maritain seethed when
encountering the bulk of modern philosophical thought. Thieulloy, *Le Chevalier
de l'Absolu*, 111.

[44] McInerny, *The Very Rich Hours*, 91.

[45] Ibid., 60–65.

[46] Goyet, *Charles Maurras*, 208. On Maurras' literary associations more generally, see pages 147–209.

[47] Jacques Maritain to Yves Simon, 31 August 1941, JM 29/17, Jacques Maritain Center, University of Notre Dame. Among Maritain biographers, McInerny
finds such explanations "unconvincing," while Doering is more sympathetic, emphasizing the improbability of the association in the first place: McInerny, *The
Very Rich Hours*, 65; Doering, *Jacques Maritain and the French Catholic Intellectuals*, 8. See also Barré, *Jacques et Raïssa Maritain*, 130–97.

[48] For Maritain and other Catholics, allying with "royalists" had little to do
with royalism per se, and this alliance in turn meant much more to Maurras and
his colleagues by the 1920s than did the residual link with French royalism, a consideration supported in a recent essay by Brian Jenkins: "La relation que l'Action
française entretenait avec l'Église catholique était politiquement bien plus signi-
ficative que son attachement symbolique à la famille royale de France." Jenkins,
"L'Action française," 130. Nor did this alliance necessarily bespeak a proto-fascist
inclination. In the same volume, Maurras biographer Bruno Goyet points out how
in the 1920s the Action Française, whatever its formative influence on later French
fascism/s, evaluated Mussolini's March on Rome in terms quite congenial to a
French Catholic traditionalist understanding of both French and European politics.
For example, the *Action française* on 28 October 1922 offered the following appraisal of Italian fascism: "Maçonnique, le Fascisme est d'essence anticléricale et
anticatholique." Quoted in "La 'Marche sur Rome': version originale sous-titrée.
La reception du fascisme en France dans les années 20." (85)

[49] Arnal, *Ambivalent Alliance*, 84. See also Prévotat, *Les Catholiques et l'Action Française*. For a poignant example of Maritain's conversionary hopes for
Maurras, see the 11 January 1927 letter from Jacques Maritain to Charles Maurras
reprinted in *Actes du cinquième colloque Maurras*, 650–53.

[50] Hanna, *The Mobilization of the Intellect*, 118. Maritain had also confided
to Maurras that various peace proposals circulating in autumn 1914 were evidently
inspired by freemasonry. Letter, Jacques Maritain to Charles Maurras, 18 October
1914, *Cercle d'Études Jacques et Raïssa Maritain*, Kolbsheim, France. Although
his anti-bourgeois and anti-liberal diatribes would fade with time, a discernable
anti-German bias would remain. This blanket condemnation of the German nation
would only intensify during the Second World War, when Maritain wrote the following: "As long as the unfortunate German people recognizes its temporal sacra-

ment in Thor and Odin, or in Luther and Hitler, it will labor in vain. It can move hell to draw therefrom the most perfect machinery of murder and of death; it will so far remain an ill-starred people." J. Maritain, "Ten Months Later," 33. Indeed, after the Shoah, Maritain insisted on the collective guilt of the German nation, going so far as to argue that "the German population as a whole accepted Hitler and the demonic principle that he represented as a convenient tool to be made use of for the grandeur of Germany." J. Maritain, ambassadorial report, 9 December 1945, Dossier Ambassade I, *Cercle d'Études Jacques et Raïssa Maritain*, Kolbsheim, France.

51 Quoted in Neher-Bernheim, *Éclats d'une Amitié*, 84–85.

52 J. Maritain, *Three Reformers*, 28.

53 On the Villard bequest and the wartime correspondence with Maritain, see J. Maritain, *Notebooks*, 100–132.

54 Ibid., 130.

55 Maritain deserves his reputation as a humble contemplative, as he and Raïssa lived under a mutual vow of chastity and shared a life as Benedictine oblates with her sister Véra into the 1950s. Cf. Mougel, "*A propos du mariage des Maritain.*" His ideal philosophical life, personified in Saint Thomas Aquinas, included humble prayer, assiduous study, and vigorous debate, all animated by a loving disposition, to be sure, but also entailing an uncompromising, sometimes combative, commitment to truth. For example, in the days following Hiroshima and Nagasaki, he could write Mortimer Adler of hurling atomic bombs in the tradition of Saint Thomas: "Did you read the excellent article of Father Eschmann in the Modern Schoolman? Not only is Konick pretty well demolished and you and I have our revenge upon his vicious attacks, but the issue appears in all its importance, Eschmann revives the good old tradition of great scholastic controversies, pulverizing adversaries with atomic bombs; there is matter for one century of struggle and annihilating discussion, I like that." Jacques Maritain to Mortimer Adler, 31 August 1945, *Cercle d'Études Jacques et Raïssa Maritain*, Kolbsheim, France.

56 J. Maritain, *Antimoderne*, 14. Schloesser aptly concludes, "Like coffee table books that lie unexamined beyond their alluring covers, this book's brazen title has been referred to more often than its contents have been actually explored." Schloesser, *Jazz Age Catholicism*, 162. Schloesser's book convincingly illustrates Maritain's eager engagement with some of the avatars of modern culture in the 1920s, notably Jean Cocteau, showing the limits of the antimodernist tag that has been placed upon the "early Maritain." But Charles Blanchet makes an excellent case for seeing Maritain's interrogation of modernity as a lifelong venture: " . . . il y aura chez Maritain, d'un bout à l'autre de sa vie un affrontement avec modernité . . . [mais] . . . ce n'est pas une position figée, statique, établie une fois pour toutes dans un rejet radical." In the 1920s, according to Blanchet, Maritain posed the following questions about modernity:

    1) Does the break with *telos*/finality allow one to see any meaning in human existence?

    2) Does radical autonomy not contradict human nature?

3) Can a total break with the past lead to anything but intellectual barbarism?

4) How can the subjective self know anything once it has broken with being/metaphysics?

Blanchet, *"Maritain face à la modernité,"* 11, 14–15.

[57] J. Maritain, *Three Reformers*, 35.

[58] Ibid., 79.

[59] Ibid., 118–19.

[60] Barré, *Jacques et Raïssa Maritain*, 449–50; Weber, *Action Française*, 160.

[61] J. Maritain, "Abraham, hou, hou," 13–14. An excerpt from Maritain's 1926 *Réponse à Jean Cocteau*, this comprised the first selection in a 1965 anthology he compiled of his writings on the Jews. (The otherwise comprehensive collection did not include his 1921 essay *"À propos de la question juive,"* which incidentally has still not been published in English translation.)

[62] Ibid.

[63] Ibid. On Maritain's testimony for the defense at Maurras' trial, see Barré, *Jacques et Raïssa Maritain*, 449–50.

[64] Neher-Bernheim, *Éclats d'une Amitié*, 116–17.

[65] J. Maritain, "Rapport sur le sionisme."

[66] Ibid., 28.

[67] Hellman, "The Jews in the 'New Middle Ages,'" 98.

[68] Neher-Bernheim, *"Rencontre de deux personnalités,"* 14. Maritain's mention of Feinberg in a 10 June 1909 journal entry gives a sense of this genuine affection and attempt at conversion: "In the evening, departure of Absalom for Darmstadt, then for Palestine. He accepts, before leaving, as a remembrance of me, a medal of Our Lady of Victories, and promises to keep it always." J. Maritain, *Notebooks*, 52. What one would give for a corresponding journal entry from Feinberg.

[69] Barré, *Jacques et Raïssa Maritain*, 450. Nor did Vatican officials, according to Sergio I. Minerbi, even agree with Maritain's premises concerning Zionism. Having "adopted most of the arguments of the Arabs," the Vatican considered Zionism either irreligious or antireligious, a threat to established Christian interests in the region, unacceptable in that it sought to establish a Jewish government, and a movement aiming at "radical changes" and an "accelerated modernization . . . damaging to moral values" among the local population. Minerbi, *The Vatican and Zionism*, 198.

[70] Jacques Maritain to Henri Massis, 1 October 1925, *Cercle d'Études Jacques et Raïssa Maritain*, Kolbsheim, France.

[71] Jacques Maritain to Henri Massis, 4 March 1927, *Cercle d'Études Jacques et Raïssa Maritain*, Kolbsheim, France.

[72] The 29 December 1926 decree promulgated by Pope Pius XI had been formulated as early as 1914 during the pontificate of Pius X, whose hesitancy, along with the coming of war, sufficed to shelve the condemnation. Seven of Maurras'

books, together with his newspaper, were now placed on the Index. Doering, *Jacques Maritain and the French Catholic Intellectuals*, 29. Arnal describes Maritain as a leading intellectual whose defection from the Maurrasian camp had a crucial role in ensuring the success of the condemnation among French Catholics: "Maritain's book was an important turning point in the conflict. . . . The shift of his intellectual skills to the Vatican camp constituted a serious blow to the Action Française and marked his emergence as the leading papal theologian in France." Arnal, *Ambivalent Alliance*, 128. While Arnal makes an important observation about the political episode, another historian analyzes the intellectual process: Maritain had begun to move away from what Schloesser calls the "deep anxieties and the need to divide the world into absolute oppositions" that prompted the use of such terms as *charnelle* in his 1920s writings. Schloesser, *Jazz Age Catholicism*, 79.

[73] J. Maritain, *Une Opinion*, 72. He also remonstrated behind the scenes to convince Maurras to submit to the Pope and sought the help of a leading theologian in this effort. When Maritain convened the fifth annual Thomist retreat at Meudon on 24–28 September 1926, he asked Maurras to visit with the retreat chaplain Father Reginald Garrigou-Lagrange: "Maurras came one morning for an interview with Fr. Garrigou from which I had hoped a great deal, but which produces nothing because of the weakness of Father before the obstinacy of this man." J. Maritain, *Notebooks*, 158.

[74] Thieulloy, *Le Chevalier de l'Absolu*, 124.

[75] Jacques Maritain to Charles Maurras, 11 January 1927, *Cercle d'Études Jacques et Raïssa Maritain*, Kolbsheim, France.

[76] Chenaux, *Entre Maurras et Maritain*, 147–55. On Blondel's long acquaintance with Maurras, rejection of Thomism, alignment with Social Catholicism, and efforts to dampen French Catholic enthusiasm for the Action Française, see Sutton, *Nationalism, Positivism, and Catholicism*, 123–62.

[77] English translation: J. Maritain, *The Things That Are Not Caesar's*. Maritain's profession of the primacy of the expansively spiritual over the merely political did not entail an apolitical stance or a pendulum swing to the extreme left, but as Charles Blanchet describes it, something altogether more ambitious: a metaphysical reawakening and the establishment of a new civilization. See Blanchet, "Maritain face à la modernité," 25.

[78] Chenaux, *Entre Maurras et Maritain*, 154–55.

[79] Thieulloy, *Le Chevalier de l'Absolu*, 132–33.

[80] J. Maritain et al., *Pourquoi Rome a parlé*, 332–33.

[81] Ibid., 358, 361, 378. On Joan of Arc and the Action Française, see Hanna, "Iconology and Ideology."

[82] J. Maritain et al., *Clairvoyance de Rome*.

[83] Doering, *Jacques Maritain and the French Catholic Intellectuals*, 37–39.

[84] Georges Bernanos to Jacques Maritain, 21 April 1928, in *Correspondance de Georges Bernanos*, 321–22.

[85] Doering, *Jacques Maritain and the French Catholic Intellectuals*, 44–59, 144–46.

[86] Ibid., 45–51.

[87] After they met in 1928, Maritain gave crucial initial support to Emmanuel Mounier, the founder of the journal *Esprit* who saw a politics of the human person as *imago Dei* as a spiritually revolutionary answer to what Joseph Amato calls "a soulless world that refused youth's hopes, that denied the poor's needs, and even resisted acknowledging life's mystery." Amato, *Mounier and Maritain*, 129. John Hellman counters Amato's emphasis on the confluence of Maritain's and Mounier's personalist ideas for a Christian renewal of western civilization with a reminder that Maritain's enthusiasm for a journal that began appearing in 1932 had more or less soured by the end of 1933. Maritain objected to Mounier's broad ecumenism, as well as his openness to Third Force and *Ordre Nouveau* political tendencies within the *Esprit* group, or as Maritain put it "perfect 'Kerenskyist' foolishness." Hellman, "Maritain and Mounier," 160. See also Hellman, *Emmanuel Mounier and the New Catholic Left*.

[88] McInerny, for example, calls *Distinguish to Unite, or The Degrees of Knowledge* Maritain's "acknowledged masterpiece." McInerny, *The Very Rich Hours*, 119.

[89] *Pour le bien commun* can be found in English translation, with an introduction by Bernard Doering. See J. Maritain et al., "For the Common Good." The year 1934 also saw the formation in Paris of a Jewish-Christian group dedicated to fighting antisemitism, "L'Union civique des croyants," in which Maritain and some of his coreligionists such as journalist Stanislas Fumet accepted the invitation to join with Jews such as Grand Rabbi Julien Weill. Schor, *L'Antisémitisme en France*, 246.

[90] Maritain et al., "For the Common Good,"13, 18.

[91] These writings included J. Maritain, *À propos de la répression* (April 1934); *Pour la justice* (October 1935, after Mussolini's invasion of Ethiopia); and *Pour l'honneur* (November 1936, after Interior Minister Roger Salengro was driven to suicide by the slanders of the extreme right). Schor, *L'Antisémitisme en France*, 4–8.

[92] Daniel-Rops, ed., *Les Juifs*.

[93] J. Maritain, "Sur l'antisémitisme" [Untitled manuscript], 476–77n.

[94] Doering, *Jacques Maritain and the French Catholic Intellectuals*, 148–51.

[95] *Correspondance Fondane-Maritain*, 39n; René Schwob, "Être Chrétien," 317–26.

[96] J. Maritain, "L'impossible antisémitisme," 72–73

[97] Ibid., 92.

[98] Ibid., 74.

[99] Ibid., 97, emphasis in original.

[100] Ibid., 76–77.

[101] Ibid., 78. Note that when this essay was published in English under the title "The Mystery of Israel" in 1941, Maritain changed the first part of this quoted pas-

sage: "The Jews chose the world" (*Les Juifs ont choisi le monde*) in the 1937 original becomes "The Jews (I do not mean the Jews individually, but the mystical
body of Israel at the moment when it struck against the rock) the Jews at a crucial
moment chose the world." J. Maritain, *Ransoming the Time*, 153. This question of
"choice" also figures prominently in Esther Starobinski-Safran's interpretation of
the same essay. She more favorably evaluates Maritain's ability at this point to
make a clear distinction between a punishment event and a lasting state of punishment. Starobinski-Safran, "Judaïsme, peuple juif, et état d'Isräel," 225. One can
argue on the contrary that he still struggled with this problem during the Shoah itself.

[102] Thieulloy, *Le Chevalier de l'Absolu*, 106.

[103] J. Maritain, "L'impossible antisémitisme," 91.

[104] Ibid., 100–101.

[105] J. Maritain, *Integral Humanism*, 7.

[106] Ibid., 39–40, 51, 145.

[107] Ibid., 32, 34.

[108] Ibid., 190.

[109] J. Maritain, *Notebooks*, 169.

[110] The 19 June 1938 broadcast is quoted in Vidal-Naquet, "Jacques Maritain
et les Juifs," 40.

[111] On this subject, see Rohr, "The Use of Antisemitism."

[112] Doering, "Jacques Maritain and the Spanish Civil War," 506–10.

[113] Quoted ibid., 519–20.

[114] Quoted in J. Maritain and R. Maritain, *Jacques and Raïssa Maritain: Oeuvres Complètes*, 16:1086.

[115] J. Maritain, "L'impossible antisémitisme," 81.

[116] J. Maritain, "The Menace of Racialism," 70; *Casti Connubii*.

[117] John LaFarge to Jacques Maritain, 26 May 1937, John LaFarge, SJ, Papers.
Maritain himself had long stressed the catholicity of Catholicism, writing in 1922,
for example: "Consider how the thinking elite is focused, more markedly than at
any other moment in the past two centuries, on Christianity, and how the Catholic
faith appears more demonstrably than ever, amidst the universal failure of human
systems, as the only stable light, as the only honest intellectual force, always new
and alive in its permanence." J. Maritain, *Antimoderne*, 218. For a longer exposition of this usage, see Schloesser, *Jazz Age Catholicism*, 167–70.

[118] See Passelcq and Suchecky, *The Hidden Encyclical of Pius XI*.

[119] Maritain wrote this letter to Journet on 6 February 1939. *Journet-Maritain
Correspondance*, 2:787.

[120] See Coppa, "The Hidden Encyclical of Pius XI."

[121] *Humani Generis Unitas* quoted in Passelcq and Suchecky, *The Hidden Encyclical of Pius XI*, 249. The book includes the encyclical reprinted in its entirety.

[122] Paul Mazgaj evokes this disenchantment with Maurras as a quintessential
man of inaction, describing how Brasillach "discovered a circle of young Action
Française alumni, indebted to Maurras but increasingly impatient with the back-

ward-looking and geographically inward focus of his movement" when he joined the *équipe* at *Je suis partout* and "found an especially kindred spirit in Lucien Rebatet." Mazgaj, *Imagining Fascism*, 184.

[123] For example, Jesuit Joseph Bonsirven, an influential biblical scholar, and one of the contributors to *Les Juifs,* would write a 1942 essay on "The Mystery of Israel" that reinforced, in the very midst of the genocide, the theme of Jewish obliviousness to their divine calling. For Bonsirven, this amounted to a renounced, but latent, "missionary" vocation, whereas Maritain termed it a "messianic" one. Most importantly, Bonsirven wrote his essay as a contribution to a book intended to counteract antisemitism and persecution in Vichy France, a book prepared clandestinely by Catholic *résistant* clergy also involved in *Témoignage Chrétien,* and smuggled to Switzerland for publication. See Bonsirven, "Le Mystère d'Israël." On the background to this book, see Lubac, *Christian Resistance to Anti-Semitism*, 108–10. Bonsirven's influence on Maritain can be discerned for example in J. Maritain, "L'impossible antisémitisme," in which the latter cites the former's books among other "contributions catholiques à l'étude de la question d'Israël." (95)

[124] Maurras, *Le Bienheureux Pie X*, 217–20. Maritain quoted in Vidal-Naquet, "Jacques Maritain et les Juifs," 54.

[125] Vicki Caron sums up the change in French antisemitism from the turn of the century to the outbreak of the Second World War: "While the animosity aimed at Jews in middle-class professions had begun well before the Dreyfus affair, the tendency to link Jews to the political left, which climaxed in the vitriolic attacks on Blum, together with the theme of Jewish war-mongering, were more specific to the interwar years." Caron, "'The Jewish Question' from Dreyfus to Vichy," 198. Caron's assessment, accurate in situating antisemitism socially, politically, and economically, might be enhanced by mention of the cultural construction of the Jew-as-vermin (or even bacillus) — seen most strikingly in the novels of Céline, for example.

CHAPTER TWO

Epigraph: J. Maritain, "Les Juifs parmi les nations," 103–4.
[1] J. Maritain, *The Twilight of Civilization.*
[2] J. Maritain, *Christianity and Democracy*, 17.
[3] Littell, *The Crucifixion of the Jews*, 4.
[4] Jacques Maritain to Mortimer Adler, 26 June 1940, *Cercle d'Études Jacques et Raïssa Maritain*, Kolbsheim, France.
[5] J. Maritain, "Europe is Already Saved!"
[6] J. Maritain, "Les Juifs parmi les nations," 103–4.
[7] Ibid., 148.
[8] Ibid., 104–5.
[9] Ibid., 106.
[10] Ibid., 107–8.

[11] Ibid., 108.

[12] The December 1937 electoral defeat of Romania's governing National Liberal Party at the hands of the Iron Guard and allied right-wing parties led to "the installation of an expressly anti-Semitic government headed by the notorious A. C. Cuza and the ultra nationalist Transylvanian poet Octavian Goga." Fischer-Galati, "The Legacy of Anti-Semitism," 20.

[13] J. Maritain, "Les Juifs parmi les nations," 109.

[14] Ibid., 107–10.

[15] Ibid., 111.

[16] Ibid., 113–14.

[17] Ibid., 117.

[18] See Chapter One.

[19] J. Maritain, "Les Juifs parmi les nations," 118.

[20] Ibid., 107.

[21] Ibid., 124.

[22] Ibid., 128–32.

[23] Ibid., 133.

[24] Ioanid, *The Holocaust in Romania*, 18.

[25] Dariusz Libionka explains that this complicity often appeared at first glance as a condemnation of antisemitism, but in reality amounted to an encouragement of anti-Jewish sentiments: "The 'Catholic' differed from the 'nationalist' approach to the Jewish problem in its critical appraisal of brute force as a method of political struggle. That the Church and the Catholic press 'condemned' the increasing violence of anti-Jewish attacks was not, however, synonymous with depriving their instigators and participants of the moral right to come out in defense of the Polish national interest. . . . Thus, on the eve of the war, advocates of the 'de-Judaization' of culture and the economy, of the introduction of religious schools and *numerus clausus* at universities, of Aryan sections at public institutions, and finally of the emigration of Jews, whether voluntary or forced, dominated among the Polish clergy. And the Catholic press, even of the more elevated variety, did not offer any guidance for proper Polish-Jewish coexistence but instead anticipated a rapid escalation of the conflict." Libionka, "Antisemitism, Anti-Judaism," 236–37.

[26] Ibid., 134–41.

[27] Ibid., 145.

[28] Ibid., 149.

[29] Ibid., 148.

[30] Barré, *Jacques et Raïssa Maritain*, 453; Iswolsky, *Light before Dusk*, 197–98.

[31] See Doering, *Jacques Maritain and the French Catholic Intellectuals*, 85–125, for a detailed account of Maritain's conflict with Claudel, and what Doering describes as a "campaign of denunciation in Rome."

[32] Rebatet, "Juifs et Catholiques," 169–70. When in 1944 Maritain's close friend the artist Max Jacob, himself a Jewish Catholic convert, died at Drancy —

the French "antechamber to Auschwitz" — *Je Suis Partout* offered the following obituary: "Jew by race, Breton by birth, Roman Catholic by religion, sodomist by habit." Quoted in Lottman, *The Left Bank*, 163.

[33] Letter from Raïssa Maritain to Pierre and Christine Van der Meer de Walcheren, 9 April 1938, in J. Maritain, *L'impossible antisémitisme*, 171–72.

[34] J. Maritain, "Réponse à André Gide sur les Juifs," 168.

[35] Gide, "Les Juifs, Céline, et Maritain," 157–64.

[36] One recent study concurs that "Gide misread Maritain. . . . Despite the Nazis' policies toward Jews in Germany, Gide adhered to his own long held view that the Jews in France were an alien minority which, if not wholly unassimilable, was widely at variance with his own 'identity' as a Frenchman." Cornick, *Intellectuals in Politics*, 173. See also Carroll, "Poetics and the Ideology of Race."

[37] J. Maritain, "Réponse à André Gide," 165–68.

[38] See Chapter One.

[39] McInerny, *The Very Rich Hours*, 133.

[40] Thieulloy, *Le Chevalier de l'Absolu*, 55–56, quoting the title of Floucat, *Pour une restauration du politique*.

[41] Doering, *Jacques Maritain and the French Catholic Intellectuals*, 156.

[42] Ibid., 151.

[43] Maritain had written the preface for Erik Peterson's *Le Mystère des Juifs*.

[44] Corte, "Jacques Maritain et la 'question juive,'" 179–86.

[45] Ibid., 186–94.

[46] J. Maritain, "Le Mystère d'Israël," 195–96.

[47] Ibid., 199.

[48] Ibid., 200–201.

[49] Ibid., 203–11.

[50] Ibid., 214–15.

[51] Levinas, "L'essence spirituelle," 175.

[52] Ibid., 178.

[53] *Correspondance Fondane-Maritain*, 37.

[54] Ibid., 12–13. Fondane was denounced as a Jew and sent to Drancy in March 1944. Although Jean Paulhan and other literary luminaries prevailed upon the French authorities to secure his release, he refused to leave his sister Line alone to her fate. He died in a gas chamber at Auschwitz on 3 October 1944.

[55] John LaFarge to Jacques Maritain, 3 April 1938, *Cercle d'Études Jacques et Raïssa Maritain*, Kolbsheim, France.

[56] J. Maritain, *A Christian Looks at the Jewish Question*; Jacques Maritain to Mortimer Adler, 16 October 1939, *Cercle d'Études Jacques et Raïssa Maritain*, Kolbsheim, France.

[57] "Jews Urged to Honor Pius XI and Mundelein: Rabbi S. S. Wise Lauds Their Fight against Anti-Semitism," *The New York Times*, October 23, 1939.

[58] J. Maritain, *A Christian Looks at the Jewish Question*, 89–90

[59] J. Maritain, *Twilight of Civilization*, 19.

[60] J. Maritain, *Notebooks*, 170–71.

[61] Maritain found himself associated with the late pontiff in a laudatory American review of his book *A Christian Looks at the Jewish Question*: "He reminds all such mistaken souls as are touched with the lunacy of anti-Semitism that, in the words of the late Pope Pius XI, spiritually we are Semites," and that "anti-Semitism is a movement in which we as Christians can have no part whatsoever.'" Cournos, "A Catholic to Jews." Incidentally, this is the review to which Maritain refers in his 16 October 1939 letter to Mortimer Adler, *Cercle d'Études Jacques et Raïssa Maritain*, Kolbsheim, France.

[62] Chenaux, "Maritain, G. B. Montini, et l'ultime Pie XI," 238. According to Garrigou-Lagrange, in a series of admonitory messages relayed through Abbé Journet, the new Pope, Pius XII — who as Cardinal Eugenio Pacelli had served as Pius XI's papal secretary of state — had ongoing misgivings both about Maritain's sympathy for the Spanish Republicans and his misplaced optimism regarding "mass conversion" of the Jews. See Barré, *Jacques et Raïssa Maritain*, 464–65.

[63] J. Maritain, *Twilight of Civilization*, 9.

[64] Ibid., 11.

[65] Ibid., 13.

[66] Ibid., 14.

[67] Maritain would continue to draw attention to the similarities between the two ostensibly opposing ideologies, seeing in the August 1939 Nazi-Soviet Pact a cruel vindication of his viewpoint: "And when we took pains ceaselessly to explain that here was a question of two opposite aspects of the same evil, of two horns of the same devil, only those understood who attached some importance to the philosophy of history. Now the whole world understands, in the shattering clarity of events. One has only to see in one's mind Herr von Ribbentrop, the promoter of the anti-Comintern agreements, decorated with the Order of Lenin; it is sufficient to see Stalin and Ribbentrop shaking hands while they smile at each other the cynical smile of accomplices." J. Maritain, "Europe is Already Saved!"

[68] J. Maritain, *Twilight of Civilization*, 17.

[69] Ibid., 18.

[70] Ibid., 19–20.

[71] Ibid., 21.

[72] Ibid., 24–25.

[73] Ibid., 28.

[74] Ibid., 24–35.

[75] Ibid., 39–44.

[76] On Maritain's wartime years in New York, which he spent teaching philosophy at Columbia and Princeton, serving as president of the university-in-exile *L'École Libre des Hautes Études*, and delivering public lectures and radio broadcasts to occupied France, see Mougel, "Les années de New York," 7–28.

[77] J. Maritain, *Twilight of Civilization*, 28.

[78] J. Maritain, "Ten Months Later," 31.

[79] J. Maritain, *Christianity and Democracy*, 17.

[80] The book was published in English as *France, My Country, Through the Disaster*; Fourcade, "Jacques Maritain, inspirateur de la Résistance," 38–39.

[81] Bloch, *Strange Defeat*.

[82] Ibid., ix.

[83] Jacques Maritain to Mortimer Adler, 26 June 1940, *Cercle d'Études Jacques et Raïssa Maritain*, Kolbsheim, France.

[84] J. Maritain, *France, My Country*, 1–2.

[85] Most recently, Ernest R. May makes this point: "Overall, France and its allies turn out to have been better equipped for war than was Germany, with more trained men, more guns, more and better tanks, more bombers and fighters." May, *Strange Victory*, 5–6.

[86] J. Maritain, *France, My Country*, 3.

[87] Ibid., 4.

[88] Pertinax, *The Gravediggers of France*. Pertinax was the pseudonym of journalist André Géraud.

[89] J. Maritain, *France, My Country*, 5.

[90] Ibid., 7.

[91] Ibid., 8.

[92] Ibid., 24.

[93] Ibid., 36.

[94] Ibid., 38.

[95] Cf. Marrus and Paxton, *Vichy France and the Jews*: "Vichy measures against Jews came from within, as part of the National Revolution. They were autonomous acts taken in pursuit of indigenous goals." (13)

[96] J. Maritain, *France, My Country*, 61.

[97] Ibid., 66.

[98] Ibid., 68. While the bishops of France may not have "chained" the Church to this "state clericalism" and its targeting of Jews, they did not initially contest it either: "The Assembly of Cardinals and Archbishops (A.C.A.), meeting in Lyon on August 31, 1940, had been discreetly informed in advance of the proposed [Jewish] statute and this issue was included on the agenda. No protest was voiced. Apparently as a result of the intervention of Cardinal Gerlier, it was decided not to do anything which might damage the government's ability to rebuild the nation." Laborie, "The Jewish Statutes," 104. On Catholic responses to Vichy antisemitism in the aftermath of the defeat, see also Adler, "The French Churches and the Jewish Question"; and Crane, "*La Croix* and the Swastika."

[99] J. Maritain, *France, My Country*, 97.

[100] Ibid., 92.

[101] Ibid., 108–9.

[102] Ibid., 109.

[103] Lubac, *Christian Resistance to Anti-Semitism*, 49.

[104] *Cahiers du Témoignage Chrétien, I: "France, prends garde de perdre ton âme,"* November 1941.

[105] Jackson, *France: The Dark Years, 1940–1944*, 357–59.

[106] J. Maritain, *France, My Country*, 85.

[107] "Ultra-Modernist," *Time*, 31 May 1948.

[108] Jacques and Raïssa's American friend, editor, and translator Julie Kernan remembers that "Jacques was submerged in work," that "he dedicated much effort to the help of his exiled compatriots," and that he "spoke out and championed the Jews as he had always done." But she also confirms the fare at the salons: "There were always tea and cakes, but Jacques himself leaned to peanuts and ginger ale, which for a Frenchman of his generation were pleasantly exotic." Kernan, *Our Friend, Jacques Maritain*, 120, 125, 128, 132.

[109] Mougel, "Les années de New York," 16–18.

[110] Kernan, *Our Friend, Jacques Maritain*, 125.

[111] On the *École Libre* see Loyer, "La débâcle"; and Zollberg, "The *École Libre* at the New School, 1941–1946."

[112] Fourcade, "Jacques Maritain et l'Europe en exil." Johnson also tried unsuccessfully to bring Marc Bloch to the United States, securing him an exit visa, but failing to do so for his wife and children. See Rutkoff and Scott, "Letters to America."

[113] Marino, *A Quiet American*, 46.

[114] Mougel, "Les années de New York," 27; Lacouture, *De Gaulle: The Rebel*, 374.

[115] J. Maritain, *Christianity and Democracy*, 58.

[116] Jacques Maritain to Mortimer Adler, 24 August 1942, *Cercle d'Études Jacques et Raïssa Maritain*, Kolbsheim, France.

[117] Ousby, *Occupation*, 183.

[118] Lubac, *Christian Resistance to Anti-Semitism*, 105–6. The Maritains mistakenly thought at first that Bergson had died a baptized Catholic; see "Bergson Pupil Says He Died a Catholic," *The New York Times*, 13 January 1941.

[119] Fourcade, "Jacques Maritain, inspirateur de la Résistance," 17.

[120] J. Maritain, *France, My Country*, 113–14.

[121] J. Maritain, "The End of Machiavellianism."

[122] Ibid., 9.

[123] Ibid., 4.

[124] Ibid., 11–12.

[125] Ibid., 12.

[126] Ibid., 13–14.

[127] Ibid., 15.

[128] On the sequence of events between these dates, see Friedländer, *The Years of Extermination*, 263–88.

[129] J. Maritain, "The End of Machiavellianism," 16.

[130] Ibid., 17.

[131] Ibid., 19–21.

[132] Aron, "Jacques Maritain and the Quarrel Over Machiavellianism," 53–64.

[133] Morgenthau, "The Evil of Politics and the Ethics of Evil," 17.

[134] J. Maritain, "The End of Machiavellianism," 22, 25, 31–33.

[135] Fourcade, "Jacques Maritain et l'Europe en exil," 17, 36.

[136] J. Maritain, *The Living Thoughts of Saint Paul*, 1.

[137] Ibid.

[138] Ibid., 3, 7, 18.

[139] Ibid., 44, 54–55.

[140] Ibid., 78.

[141] Ibid., 71.

[142] Ibid., 82–86.

[143] Klenicki, "Jacques Maritain's Vision of Judaism and Anti-Semitism," 73.

[144] Jacques Maritain to John Oesterreicher, 23 July 1943: Monsignor John Oesterreicher Collection.

[145] J. Maritain, *The Living Thoughts of Saint Paul*, 82.

[146] Jacques Maritain to John Oesterreicher, 23 July 1943: Monsignor John Oesterreicher Collection. This sentiment is echoed, many years later, by Swedish theologian Krister Stendahl, one of the scholars responsible for a "new perspective" on Paul and Judaism in the 1970s: "But the glorious secret that was whispered into the ear of Paul the Apostle, the Jewish apostle to the Gentiles, was that God in his grace had changed his plans. Now it was the 'No' of the Jews, their non-acceptance of the Messiah, which opened up the possibility of the '*Yes*' of the Gentiles. . . . The central issue claiming Paul's attention is that of the inclusion both of Gentiles and Jews." Stendahl, *Paul among Jews and Gentiles*, 28. Yet another scholar more recently cautions against reading Paul (or we might add, Maritain) as someone who did not consider faith in Jesus Christ as normative for salvation, which in effect would amount to a "questionable double covenant theory, that God has a special plan for the Jewish people apart from faith in Christ." Das, *Paul and the Jews*, 192.

[147] J. Maritain, *The Living Thoughts of Saint Paul*, 97.

[148] Ibid., 111.

[149] Ibid., 133, 137, 139, 143.

[150] J. Maritain, "World Trial," 343.

CHAPTER THREE

Epigraph: J. Maritain, "World Trial," 345.

[1] In summer 1942, the American public started hearing of a Nazi mass murder program that entailed not only a series of atrocities but had as its goal the systematic destruction of European Jewry. On the 29th of June 1942, CBS radio correspondent Quincy Howe reported the following: "A horrifying reminder of what this war means to certain noncombatants comes from the World Jewish Congress in London today. It is now estimated that the Germans have massacred more than one million Jews since the war began. That's about one sixth [*sic*] of the Jewish

population in the Old World." The following day, the *New York Herald Tribune* carried the following headline: "NAZI SLAUGHTER OF MILLION JEWS SO FAR CHARGED; World Congress Leaders Tell London of Systematic Massacre over Europe." Quoted in Lipstadt, *Beyond Belief*, 166. Yet only in December did the Allied powers issue "their confirmation and condemnation of 'Hitler's bestial policy of cold-blooded extermination,'" in other words "the official imprimatur that had been awaited" by Rabbi Stephen S. Wise and the World Jewish Congress. (186)

[2] Historians such as Philippe Burrin and Christopher Browning assert that Hitler decided on the Final Solution in early October 1941, a time falling incidentally midway between the launch of Barbarossa and the meeting at Wannsee, marking the transformation of a set of anti-Jewish policies including ghettoization, deportation, and localized killings into a systematic policy of *Vernichtigung,* or annihilation. Browning in particular links the Führer's decision to "Nazi victory euphoria" in the racial and ideological war against Soviet Russia. See Browning, *Nazi Policy, Jewish Workers, German Killers*, 26–27. Without contradicting this judgment, Ian Kershaw emphasizes the gradual yet relentless momentum of a cumulative decision process within the same time frame: "Hitler's decision to the deportation of the German Jews [in mid-September 1941] was not tantamount to a decision for the 'Final Solution.' It is doubtful whether a single, comprehensive decision of such a kind was ever made. But Hitler's authorization of the deportations opened the door widely to a whole range of new initiatives from numerous local and regional Nazi leaders who seized on the opportunity now to rid themselves of their own 'Jewish problem,' to start killing Jews in their own areas. There was a perceptible quickening of the genocidal tempo over the next few weeks. The speed and scale of the escalation in killing point to an authorization by Hitler to liquidate the hundreds of thousands of Jews in various parts of the east who were incapable of work. But there was as yet no coordinated, comprehensive programme of total genocide. This would still take some months to emerge." Kershaw, *Hitler, 1936–45*, 481.

[3] Browning, *Ordinary Men*, xv.

[4] J. Maritain, "The Crisis of Civilization," 154.

[5] John 4:22.

[6] J. Maritain, *Saint Thomas and the Problem of Evil*, 18.

[7] Ibid., 1.

[8] Ibid., 8–9.

[9] Ibid., 12.

[10] Ibid., 13.

[11] Ibid., 14.

[12] Ibid., 19.

[13] Ibid., 33.

[14] Ibid., 35.

[15] J. Maritain, "The Conquest of Freedom," 641.

[16] J. Maritain, *Saint Thomas and the Problem of Evil*, 38.

[17] Ibid., 39.

[18] The word *genocide* originated with the Polish Jew Rafael Lemkin, who escaped the Nazis and eventually found refuge in the United States. Lemkin "coined the word . . . from the Greek word *genos* ('people' or 'tribe') and the Latin *cide* ('killing'), in 1942." Dwork and Van Pelt, *Holocaust: A History*, 150.

[19] J. Maritain, "On Anti-Semitism," 572.

[20] Romans 11:8.

[21] J. Maritain, *Saint Thomas and the Problem of Evil*, 4.

[22] J. Maritain, "On Anti-Semitism," 564.

[23] Ibid., 566.

[24] Jacques Maritain to Hannah Arendt, 30 September 1942, *Cercle d'Études Jacques et Raïssa Maritain*, Kolbsheim, France.

[25] The question of antisemitism in wartime France, and among French Catholics in particular, should be studied with an attention not only to the phenomenon of anti-Jewish prejudice during *les années noires* but also the upsurge of *maréchaliste* sentiment in mid 1940 and the ongoing influence of interwar xenophobia: "The Pétainist adulation helps to explain the attitude of Christian France to the promulgation of the *Statut des Juifs* of October 3, 1940—the ordinance which made second-class citizens of the Jews of France. At this early stage of the 'New Order' the clergy was unable to separate the attitude of the Church to the new regime from its relation to the 'Jewish problem.' . . . Since the thirties, a growing element of the population had been advocating an end to Jewish immigration. Now the ordinances of October fortified those xenophobic tendencies." R. Cohen, "Jews and Christians in France," 329. In the same volume, Michael Marrus emphasizes indifference within the Church: "The Jews were easily forgotten in this atmosphere of *reconquista,* what was seen as a re-Christianization of France." Marrus, "French Churches," 310. Pierre Laborie also highlights indifference as a factor in French popular acquiescence during the early stages of Vichy antisemitic policies: "Without denying the existence of a fundamental anti-Semitism at the heart of middle France—an anti-Semitism rekindled by the crisis of national identity in the 1930s — it is equally possible to interpret the indifferent attitude toward the Jews in the France of 1940 and 1941 as a symptom of more complex phenomena." Laborie, "The Jewish Statutes," 110. Laborie, like other scholars, points to the events of 1942 — in particular the 29 May yellow-star order in the Occupied Zone and the July Vel d'Hiv roundup in Paris, along with an ongoing "processus de détachement à l'égard du régime" — as decisive. Laborie, *La France des années troubles*, 147. On the other hand, Vicki Caron dissents from much of the above historical reasoning, convincingly arguing that historians have exaggerated popular indifference to Vichy antisemitism, particularly professional associations already pressing for laws of exclusion, and less convincingly asserting that the events of 1942 provoked public displeasure primarily because they stemmed from "German rather than French dictates." Caron, "French Public Opinion," 379, 485.

²⁶ Jacques Maritain to Yves Simon, 31 August 1941, JM 29/17, Jacques Maritain Center, University of Notre Dame.

²⁷ J. Maritain, *The Rights of Man and Natural Law*, 4, 5, 10, 20.

²⁸ On Maritain's friend Charles Journet's struggle to wage moral combat against the Nazi persecution and extermination of the Jews in the face of the political neutrality of his native Switzerland and in intermittent conflict with a Swiss episcopate that "avait alors plutôt tendance à soutenir le gouvernement dans une politique de neutralité poussée parfois à l'extrême," (14) see Boissard, *Quelle neutralité face à l'horreur*. The founder and editor of the theological journal *Nova et Vetera*, the future cardinal also served as a conduit between French Catholic *résistants* such as the *Témoignage Chrétien* group in Lyon and the Allied nations. To cite one example of his clandestine work, but one particularly relevant to the present study, it was thanks to Journet that Maritain's essay "The End of Machiavellianism" found its way onto the pages of the April–June 1942 issue of *Cahiers du Témoignage Chrétien*. (216)

²⁹ J. Maritain, *The Rights of Man and Natural Law*, 23.

³⁰ Ibid., 30.

³¹ Ibid., 48.

³² Ibid., 53.

³³ Ibid., 67.

³⁴ Guéna, "La Passion d'Israël," 16–17; N. Peterson, ed., *From Hitler's Doorstep*, 7, 579.

³⁵ Jacques Maritain to Yves Simon, 9 December 1942, JM 29/17: Jacques Maritain Center, University of Notre Dame.

³⁶ R. Maritain, *The Memoirs of Raïssa Maritain*. The quotation comes from page 110 of her *We Have Been Friends Together*, originally published in 1942.

³⁷ J. Maritain, *Saint Thomas and the Problem of Evil*, 2–3.

³⁸ J. Maritain, "Ten Months Later," 33.

³⁹ J. Maritain, "On Anti-Semitism," 572.

⁴⁰ For a discussion of "vicarious suffering" as it was understood in Maritain's time, see Burton, *Holy Tears, Holy Blood*. Raïssa Maritain is one of the women studied in the book.

⁴¹ See Dillistone, "Atonement," 50–53.

⁴² Anselm, "Why God Became Man," 317.

⁴³ J. Maritain, "On Anti-Semitism," 568.

⁴⁴ Ibid.

⁴⁵ Samuel, *The Great Hatred*, 109.

⁴⁶ J. Maritain, "Anti-Semitism as Problem for the Jew," 159.

⁴⁷ Ibid.

⁴⁸ Ibid., 163.

⁴⁹ Ibid., 165.

⁵⁰ J. Maritain, "Atonement for All," 155.

⁵¹ Poznanski, *Jews in France during World War II*, 256–62.

[52] According to one historian, none of the approximately four thousand children held at Vel d'Hiv survived the war. At Drancy, they had imagined they would soon be sent to a mysterious place called "'Pitchipoi,' a name derived from East European folklore. Pitchipoi, it turned out, was Auschwitz." Hyman, *The Jews of Modern France*, 173–74.

[53] J. Maritain, "Atonement for All," 155–56.

[54] Ibid., 156.

[55] J. Maritain, "La persécution raciste en France," 45–46. Maritain would be incensed when Vichy racist law continued to be applied in liberated French territory, namely the *départements* of Algeria, which after the Anglo-American invasion of November 1942 fell under the governance of Admiral François Darlan, and after Darlan's assassination, General Henri Giraud until General Charles de Gaulle supplanted Giraud. See Maritain's 25 April 1943 letter to the editor of the *New York Times*, "Cremieux Law Upheld," which insisted that "if an attempt were made to justify the abrogation of the Cremieux decree merely as a measure of appeasing the anti-Semitic feelings developed by German propaganda and by the servility of the Vichy regime toward Nazi Germany, such an argument would deserve only to be branded as unworthy of the cause for which the free peoples are fighting. . . . Anti-Semitism is the vehicle of all Nazi poisons, and in no event must any concession be made to it." Vichy had abrogated the Loi Cremieux on 7 October 1940, four days after the promulgation of the first anti-Jewish statue. Peschanski, "Les statuts des Juifs," 24–25. It took the remainder of 1943 for the Gaullists to secure the restoration of the 1870 law that had granted French citizenship to Algerian Jews, and this occurred over the expressed resistance of President Roosevelt, who almost pathologically distrusted General de Gaulle. See Lacouture, *De Gaulle: The Rebel*, 431; Marrus and Paxton, *Vichy France and the Jews*, 196–97.

[56] J. Maritain, "On Anti-Semitism," 570.

[57] Asch's 1939 novel, *The Nazarene*, draws a parallel between the Nazi persecution of Jews and the crucifixion of Jesus through the character Hermanus, the commander of the German auxiliaries under Roman command in Judea. His men are sadists who eagerly await Pilate's orders to scourge the prisoner: "The commander of the German horsemen was a man with an evil face and cold, murderous eyes. He was the terror of the Jews. His name was Hermanus. It was to Hermanus and his men that the prisoner was delivered. . . . They stood on their tip-toes straining like bloodhounds who expect a bone to be thrown to them. When they heard that the pale, thin man was accused of setting himself up as the Jewish king, they burst into wild howls of laughter." And the German officer himself crucifies Yeshua the Nazarene: "Hermanus, the terror of Israel, lifted a hammer and a nail, and he began to hammer the nail through the Rabbi's flesh, through the palm of his hand, into the cross . . . slowly, steadily, blow by blow, as if he found delight in the swing of his arm, as if he could not bear the thought that his pleasure would end soon." Asch, *The Nazarene*, 656, 680.

[58] J. Maritain, "On Anti-Semitism," 570.

59 Ibid., 570–72.

60 Romans 11:29.

61 Chagall, "In Honor of Jacques Maritain."

62 J. Maritain, "Le Droit raciste," 180–81.

63 Ibid., 165.

64 Ibid., 173–74.

65 Ibid., 173.

66 Ibid., 173–80.

67 Ibid., 166.

68 Ibid., 167, 171.

69 Ibid., 182–84.

70 Ibid., 184–85.

71 Ibid., 188.

72 Ibid., 189–90.

73 Bonsirven, "Le Mystère d'Israël." On the creation of this book, intended to counteract antisemitic propaganda in Vichy France, see Lubac, *Christian Resistance to Anti-Semitism*, 108–10.

74 Oesterreicher, *Racisme-Antisémitisme-Antichristianisme.*

75 See Oesterreicher, "Declaration," 1–136, which offers important context on the drafting of *Nostra Aetate*.

76 Jacques Maritain to John Oesterreicher, 23 July 1943, Monsignor John Oesterreicher Collection.

77 J. Maritain, "World Trial," 339.

78 J. Maritain, "The Healing of Humanity."

79 J. Maritain, "World Trial," 341.

80 Ibid., 343.

81 Ibid., 344–45.

82 Ibid., 347.

83 J. Maritain, *The Living Thoughts of Saint Paul*, 78–88.

84 J. Maritain, "The Passion of Israel," 122.

85 R. Maritain, "Il en est temps," 125.

86 Burrell, *Deconstructing Theodicy*, 19. See also Tilley, *The Evils of Theodicy*.

87 For examples taken from the Dreyfus Affair, the Great War, and the Second World War, respectively, see the following: Griffiths, *The Uses of Abuse*; Becker, *La guerre et la foi*; Crane, "*La Croix* and the Swastika."

88 Amishai-Maisels, "Christological Symbolism of the Holocaust," 461.

89 J. Maritain, *Messages*, 121–22, 161. The last phrase comes from the book later published by Raïssa Maritain, *Chagall ou l'orage enchanté*, 113.

90 Baigell, *Jewish Artists in New York*, 71–72.

91 J. Maritain, "The Christian Teaching."

92 After the war, Maritain explained to Journet in a 15 November 1948 letter his understanding of the redemptive role played by a Jewish rejection of Jesus as

messiah: "Le faux-pas des Juifs n'a pas été *voulu* de Dieu, mais *permis*. Il ne devait pas se produire en vertu d'un scénario fixé d'avance. Il s'est produit en vertu du péché de la Synagogue éternellement vu. . . . *Si* Jésus avait été reconnu par Israël (et c'est bien dans cette intention qu'il lui a été envoyé), si les Juifs avaient reconnu et suivi leur Messie, que serait-il arrivé? Le Peuple aurait-été l'apôtre de l'Évangile? Aurait souffert persécution avec Jésus? Jésus aurait été crucifié par les Gentils [*sic*] (de par un péché dont ils auraient eu la première initiative, et qu'on peut juger bien probable, vu la méchanceté humaine)? Il y avait bien d'autres moyens de rédemption possible que le Calvaire. La première intention de Dieu, en voulant l'Incarnation, c'était que son Fils prît sur lui toutes nos langueurs et tous nos péchés, jusqu'à la mort s'il le fallait, absolument jusqu'à bout. Ce n'était pas qu'il fût mis à mort *par les Romains à l'instigation des Juifs après la trahison de Judas etc. . . . . Dans ce plan divin éternellement fixé nous trouvons l'exemple le plus éminent de la permission divine du mal *pour un bien plus grand*. Le péché de la Synagogue (dû à la première initiative néantante de la créature) a été permis pour un *mode* de rédemption (par le Sang, et parce que la Pierre d'angle a été rejetée par le peuple élu) qui est *meilleur* et plus *beau*, plus riche et plus glorieux en signification infinies, que si les Juifs avaient reconnu leur Dieu et coopéré avec lui au salut du monde." *Journet-Maritain Correspondance*, 3:724–25.

[93] J. Maritain, "The Christian Teaching."

[94] This designation should be applied to the Jewish-Christian writers of the Gospels themselves, as modern scholarship identifies the Gospel of Matthew — like the other synoptic ones, Mark and Luke — as "a late first-century Jewish-Christian document." Even the language used to castigate "the Jews" in the Gospel of John, in which we can perceive the sharpest evidence of a divergence between post-Second-Temple Judaism and an incipient Christian Church, "probably reflects the pain and anger of the Jewish-Christian Johannine community, a tiny group within a small minority community, as it became separated — divorced in a sense — from the larger Jewish community" around the year 100. Geller, "Transitions and Trajectories," 561–62. As will be seen in the next chapter, Maritain resisted a conflation of New Testament scriptural language concerning Jews and Judaism with the patristic, medieval, or modern manifestations of anti-Jewish antagonism yet to come.

[95] J. Maritain, "The Christian Teaching."

[96] Ibid.

[97] Ibid.

[98] Ibid.

[99] Ibid.

[100] J. Maritain, "Religion and Peace," 302.

[101] Ibid., 305.

[102] Ibid., 307.

[103] Ibid., 309.

[104] Ibid., 311.

[105] An example of Maritain's infrequent praise of Pius XII can be found in his September 1942 radio address, "The Racist Persecution in France": "Nous savons que le Pape est intervenu pour demander merci, que les évêques de France ont protesté, et pareillement les chefs des églises réformées." J. Maritain, "La persécution raciste en France," 42. But in terms of an active resistance to Nazi racism, Maritain thought more often of the example of Pius XI. That pope is cited authoritatively four times in the address "Le Droit Raciste et la vraie signification du racisme," beginning with Maritain pointing to the "consolation de penser que cette œuvre de condamnation doctrinale a été accompli avec une souveraine autorité par le pape Pie XI." (168) Maritain approvingly states, "Pie est tenu à affirmer l'inviolabilité du Droit Naturel," (170) and says that "il continue en affirmant la vérité explicitement niée par Hitler et le Droit Raciste . . . ces droits de la personne humaine," (171) concluding that "les chrétiens qui ont entendu la parole de Pie XI . . . ont compris que leur Dieu est soufflété et outragé par la rage antisémite." (188) Indeed, Maritain sees fit to mention the sixteenth-century Pope Paul III's intervention in the controversy surrounding the Spanish treatment of the indigenous inhabitants of the Americas. (182–83) But as for the reigning pontiff, one finds no word at all.

[106] On Maritain, Pius XI, Cardinal Pacelli and the "*mythe de la guerre sainte,*" see Doering, "Jacques Maritain and the Spanish Civil War." Maritain was relieved if not surprised that Pius XII did not endorse the Nazi German war against the Soviet Union, confiding to his notebook on 29 July 1941: "Le Pape dans son discours ne dit pas un mot de Russie. Le mythe de la guerre sainte est ainsi liquidé. *Deo gratias.*" *Journet-Maritain Correspondance*, 3:184. Regarding Pius XII's post-1945 anticommunism, see Kent, *The Lonely Cold War of Pope Pius XII.*

[107] In an article in *Figaro* on 1–2 February 1948 titled "La vérité devenue folle (Truth becomes Mad)," Mauriac contemplated the recent assassination of Gandhi to ask whether Pius XII had during the war exhibited the kind of moral leadership associated with the slain Mahatma: "Cet unique feu qui vient de s'éteindre, dans quel endroit du monde va-t-il se rallumer? Sur quelle colline? . . . Mais si, au cours de cette guerre dont nous feignons d'être sortis, quelqu'un, sur une des collines de la Ville éternelle, avait refusé de manger et de boire. . . . Pourquoi aucune folie de cet ordre n'a-t-elle jamais été tenté sur l'une des collines de la Ville éternelle? Pourquoi . . . jamais ce jeste, cet acte inimaginable qui aurait fait tomber à genoux les frères ennemis?" Quoted in *Journet-Maritain Correspondance*, 3:922.

[108] In a 13 December 1945 letter to Maritain, with whom he had reconstructed a friendly acquaintance after their public sparring in the late 1930s, Claudel complained that instead of a "protestation solennelle du Vicaire de Christ . . .nous n'avons entendu que de faibles et vagues gémissements" in response to the spectacle of "enfants juifs massacrés par les nazis." We have no evidence that Maritain agreed with these condemnations leveled privately by Claudel, but (as will be seen) he did agree with another assertion of Claudel's, that in the postwar era nothing should now impede Pius XII's condemnation of murderous antisemitism. Doubt-

less, Claudel's final admonitory flourish stuck with France's new ambassador to the Vatican, as he connected the deaths of one-third of the world's Jews with the text in the Book of Revelation describing a third of the world covered in blood: "C'est ce sang dans l'affreux silence du Vatican qui étouffée tous les Chrétiens. La voix d'Abel ne finira-t-elle pas par se faire entendre?" Claudel, "Une lettre de Paul Claudel à Jacques Maritain," 1–2.

[109] Maritain expressed his consternation at this report being taken at face value in a 1951 letter to historian Léon Poliakov, cited in Poliakov, *Mémoires*, 287–88. Whereas Maritain offers a blunt rejection of the substance and import of the Bérard report, Henri de Lubac goes into more detail in his wartime memoir, pointing out that the papal nuncio, Bishop Valerio Valeri, publicly contradicted the Marshal in front of other diplomats when the Vichy head claimed that the Holy See had expressed no objection to Vichy's anti-Jewish laws. Lubac further cites an October 1941 confirmation of Valeri's objection by the Vatican secretary of state Cardinal Maglione, concluding that "the opposition between the orientation of the Vichy government and the thought of Pius XII was patent." Lubac, *Christian Resistance to Anti-Semitism*, 82–97. Historians, dealing in this case with a preponderance of hearsay, have diverged in their judgments of Bérard's veracity and hence the usefulness of this document. Michael R. Marrus relies on Bérard's report when he states that a "largely unconcerned" Vatican "effectively gave them [Vichy's leaders] a green light to legislate as they chose against Jews." Marrus, *The Holocaust in History*, 180. W.D. Halls, on the other hand, more pointedly questions the source, stating that "Bérard's own political position was plain," and that as an outspoken advocate of Franco-German collaboration it "was almost certain that at first he personally approved of the [anti-Jewish] laws." Therefore, Halls only sees in the Vichy ambassador's report "the alleged papal reaction to the persecutions in 1941." Halls, *Politics, Society, and Christianity in Vichy France*, 108, 127.

CHAPTER FOUR

Epigraph: *Journet-Maritain Correspondance*, 3:293.

[1] See, most notably, Phayer, *The Catholic Church and the Holocaust*; Pawlikowski, "The Canonization of Pope Pius XII"; and Coppa, *The Papacy, the Jews, and the Holocaust*.

[2] John Conway, review of Spicer, ed., *Anti-Semitism, Christian Ambivalence, and the Holocaust*.

[3] For a critical overview of the "Pius Wars" see Sanchéz, *Pius XII and the Holocaust*. Sanchéz offers a moderate judgment amidst the generally polarized historiography on the wartime pontiff: "He was a prisoner of his equivocation, his scholarly exactness, his inability to become his own person and rise above the tradition-bound concepts of the imperial papacy. And not only was his personality a factor in his reputation, it was also one in his alleged silence." (130)

[4] See the title essay in J. Maritain, *L'impossible antisémitisme*.

[5] Moyn, *A Holocaust Controversy*, 72.

[6] J. Maritain, "La Passion d'Israël," 119–22.

[7] J. Maritain, *The Person and the Common Good*, 48, 64–66.

[8] J. Maritain, "Blessed are the Persecuted."

[9] J. Maritain, "Religion and Peace," 304, 309.

[10] See Blanchet, "Jacques Maritain, 1940–1944."

[11] J. Maritain, notebook entry, 11 July 1944, in *Cahiers Jacques Maritain* 4 *bis* (June 1982): 10.

[12] Jacques Maritain to Yves Simon, 8 January 1945, in *Cahiers Jacques Maritain* 4 *bis* (June 1982): 13.

[13] Jacques Maritain to Yves Simon, 29 January 1945, in *Cahiers Jacques Maritain* 4 *bis* (June 1982): 17–18.

[14] See in particular the 13 January 1945 letter from Angelo Roncalli to Domenico Tardini, the 18 January letter from Tardini to Roncalli, and the 29 January letter from Roncalli to Tardini in Blet, et al., edd. *Actes et Documents*, 676, 679, 686. I am grateful to Joel Blatt for assisting with the translation of these letters from the original Italian.

[15] McInerny, *The Very Rich Hours*, 140.

[16] Jacques Maritain to Mortimer Adler, 31 August 1945, *Cercle d'Études Jacques et Raïssa Maritain*, Kolbsheim, France.

[17] Jacques Maritain to Georges Bernanos, 5 October 1947, quoted in Barré, *Jacques et Raïssa Maritain*, 532.

[18] On the first day of 1945, a new nuncio presented his credentials in Paris: Monsignor Angelo Roncalli, the future Pope John XXIII. *Cahiers Jacques Maritain* 4 *bis* (June 1982): 6.

[19] Jacques Maritain to Yves Simon, 29 January 1945, *Cahiers Jacques Maritain* 4 *bis* (June 1982): 18.

[20] Maritain ambassadorial report, 9 December 1945, *Cercle d'Études Jacques et Raïssa Maritain*, Kolbsheim, France.

[21] Jacques Maritain to [Foreign Minister] Georges Bidault, 10 May 1946, quoted in Molette, "Jacques Maritain et la Conférence de Seelisberg," 214.

[22] Phayer, *The Catholic Church and the Holocaust*, 152–55. On Muench's lack of sympathy for Jews whose bad behavior, as he saw it, continued to provoke German antisemitism, see Brown-Fleming, *The Holocaust and Catholic Conscience*.

[23] Phayer, *The Catholic Church and the Holocaust*, xiv–xv, 180.

[24] Jacques Maritain to Giovanni Battista Montini, 12 July 1946, *Cahiers Jacques Maritain* 23 (October 1991), 31–33.

[25] Coppa, *The Papacy, the Jews, and the Holocaust*, 212; Phayer, *The Catholic Church and the Holocaust*, 180–82. Jan Gross offers an unsparing judgment of the Catholic Church in Poland: "When the people of Kielce lost their way, the hierarchy of Poland's Catholic church [*sic*] abdicated its responsibility to offer spiritual guidance and simply coasted along. . . . Priests could not and would not condone murder, but Catholic hierarchs said that Jews were communists and that they had

brought all their misfortunes upon themselves. The bishops even missed an opportunity simply to keep quiet when one of their own ranks [Teodor Kubina] made an honorable statement." Gross, *Fear*, 152–53.

[26] Telegram, Jacques Maritain to Jewish Labor Committee, 19 July 1947, RG-67.001M Reel 7, Jewish Labor Committee Records, United States Holocaust Memorial Museum Archives. The printed date of 12 July on the original telegram from the JLC has been changed by hand to 16 July, which corresponds with the date listed in the Maritain-Journet correspondence. Accordingly, as the reply on this microfilm is undated, I follow the Maritain-Journet volume's date of 19 July for the reply, as the editors of that collection use Maritain's unpublished notebook entry to verify the date, and to point out that Maritain submitted his reply to Montini for suggestions, which led to the insertion of the mention of the November 1945 papal remarks. *Journet-Maritain Correspondance*, 3:912–14.

[27] See the 12 April 1948 memorandum from Jacques Maritain to Giovanni Battista Montini reprinted in Chenaux, *Paul VI et Maritain*, 104–7. Maritain's request gained a measure of success in 1956 under Pius XII, when the Congregation of Rites restored the long-suppressed practice of genuflecting for the "faithless" Jews (*perfidis* means "faithless" or "unbelieving" rather than "perfidious") during the prayer. Flannery, *The Anguish of the Jews*, 87. In 1960, John XXIII removed the word itself.

[28] Marrus, "The Ambassador and the Pope," 14–18. Regarding Maritain's relationship with Pius XII, Marrus emphasizes the "supersessionist theological context that was, at the time, inescapably associated with any Vatican-level discussion of the Jews," and which required the linkage of "any declaration about the Jews with an assertion of Catholic rectitude and universal spiritual hegemony." Marrus, "A Plea Unanswered," 10.

[29] J. Maritain, "Lettre à la Conférence du Seelisberg," 226. The text of the "Address to the Churches" that emerged from the conference, intended to "prevent any animosity toward the Jews which might arise from false, inadequate or mistaken presentations or conception of the teaching and preaching of the Christian doctrine . . . and . . . to promote brotherly love toward the sorely tried people of the old covenant," can be found in Rittner et al., edd., *The Holocaust and the Christian World*, 245–46. Maritain's words resonated with a French Jewish participant at Seelisberg who had lost his wife and daughter in the Holocaust and who would play a key role in Jewish-Catholic relations before the Second Vatican Council. Abbé Charles Journet wrote to Maritain about his Seelisberg letter: "It made a strong impression. Jules Isaac told me afterward: 'He said, from a Catholic viewpoint of course, everything I am putting forth in a book on which I am working.'" *Journet-Maritain Correspondance*, 3:576.

[30] Molette, "Jacques Maritain et la Conférence de Seelisberg," 222.

[31] Ventresca, "Jacques Maritain and the Jewish Question," 60, 65. Ventresca borrows the phrase "practical opacity" from Ralph McInerny, invoking a line of thought that has long lauded Maritain as a metaphysician while either dismissing

or excoriating his "political" interventions. Later in the article, however, Ventresca examines the Seelisberg address and sees reason to relax the charge of "practical opacity" maintained in other quarters (cf. note 43 in this chapter), offering the following measured assessment: "We must be careful not to exaggerate the problem of practical opacity, nor should we underestimate the potential Maritain's prophetic vision had for realm [sic] of practical, concrete action."(68)

[32] J. Maritain, "Lettre à la Conférence du Seelisberg," 225.

[33] Ibid., 226–29.

[34] Ibid., 230–31.

[35] Charles Journet to Jacques Maritain, 2 August 1947, *Journet-Maritain Correspondance*, 3:576.

[36] Doering, *Jacques Maritain and the French Catholic Intellectuals*, 212. McInerny describes the Vatican stint in words that can be read either wryly or profoundly: "When Maritain accepted appointment as the French ambassador to the Vatican, he agreed to serve for three years. Those years may have been the most heroic expression of his patriotism as a Frenchman." McInerny, *The Very Rich Hours*, 160.

[37] J. Maritain, "La Voix de la Paix," 157.

[38] Ibid., 148.

[39] Ibid., 153.

[40] Ibid., 154.

[41] Ibid., 155–56.

[42] For recent analyses of Maritain's vision of a common global understanding of human rights, see Tester, "A Theory of Indifference"; and Munro, "The Universal Declaration of Human Rights." Scholars have long disagreed on the philosophical basis of what some call Maritain's excessive optimism. See Dougherty, *Jacques Maritain: An Intellectual Portrait*, 24–25, and Schall, *Jacques Maritain: The Philosopher in Society*, 210.

[43] Quoted in Barré, *Jacques et Raïssa Maritain*, 532.

[44] Reprinted in *Cahiers Jacques Maritain 4 bis* (June 1982): 91–96.

[45] Kernan, *Our Friend, Jacques Maritain*, 145–46.

[46] Quoted in *Cahiers Jacques Maritain 4 bis* (June 1982): 28.

[47] Jacques Maritain notebook entry, 3 June 1948, in *Journet-Maritain Correspondance*, 3:628n.

[48] Kubovy, "The Silence of Pope Pius XII," 25.

[49] Braham, "Remembering and Forgetting: The Vatican, the German Catholic Hierarchy, and the Holocaust," 237.

[50] To the extent that Pius XII had remained silent during the Holocaust, Maritain insisted that the Pope's motives were unimpeachable: "Quant à Pie XII, il serait pareillement injuste, et gravement injuste, d'attribuer à de l'indifférence son silence à l'heure de la persécution hitlérienne: non seulement il a contribué par ses efforts à sauver beaucoup de persécutés, mais quand j'étais à Rome je me suis informé en haut lieu sur les raisons de ce silence, et je sais qu'il n'a été dû qu'à la

crainte d'augmenter gravement la persécution s'il élevait la voix. Le Pape avait consulté des communautés juives allemandes, et c'est cela même qu'elles avaient répondu. Qu'il ait eu tort ou raison de suivre cet avis, et d'abstenir d'un grand témoignage qu'il aurait souhaité rendre et qui eut été à sa gloire, mais qui aurait causé des milliers de vies humaines sacrifiées en surcroît, qui de nous peut en juger? Son motif a été ce qu'il a tenu pour une obligation de conscience, et c'était un motif profondément humain." J. Maritain, "Lettre de Jacques Maritain à André Chouraqui (1969)."

[51] Phayer, *The Catholic Church and the Holocaust*, 182.

[52] Pawlikowski, "The Canonization of Pope Pius XII," 222.

[53] Coppa, *The Papacy, the Jews, and the Holocaust*, 213.

[54] Peter Kent offers a more balanced and accurate judgment on Maritain's departure from the Vatican embassy in part by taking into account the offer of a professorship at Princeton: "It was perhaps fitting that Jacques Maritain resigned his ambassadorial post to accept a position at Princeton University; the climate at the Vatican was becoming less sympathetic to his personal outlook and values." Kent, *The Lonely Cold War*, 202.

[55] Barré, *Jacques et Raïssa Maritain*, 532–33.

[56] Ibid., 358–60.

[57] Ibid., 535.

[58] J. Maritain, *Man and the State*.

[59] Jacques Maritain to Thomas Merton, Good Friday 1951, *Cercle d'Études Jacques et Raïssa Maritain*, Kolbsheim, France.

[60] Barré, *Jacques et Raïssa Maritain*, 546–53.

[61] Poliakov, *Mémoires*, 287–88.

[62] J. Maritain and R. Maritain, *Jacques and Raïssa Maritain: Oeuvres Complètes*, 10:1153.

[63] Ibid., 1159.

[64] Ibid., 1160.

[65] Parkes's first major work is still his most influential: *The Conflict of the Church and the Synagogue*. See also Parkes, *Anti-Semitism*. Chertok, *He Also Spoke as a Jew*, offers the most extensive, as well as the most idiosyncratically psycho-historical, biography of Parkes to date.

[66] James Parkes to Robert Mayer, 19 August 1954, Jacques Maritain Center, University of Notre Dame.

[67] Jacques Maritain to Robert Mayer, 9 November 1954, Jacques Maritain Center, University of Notre Dame.

[68] Ibid.

[69] Robert Mayer to Jacques Maritain, 21 December 1954, Maritain Center, University of Notre Dame.

[70] On Maritain and modernism, see chapter one above. On Parkes, see Everett, *Christianity Without Antisemitism*, 57–65, as well as Chertok, *He Also Spoke as a Jew*, 130–32.

[71] Quoted in Everett, *Christianity Without Antisemitism*, 137.

[72] One hesitates to place Maritain lightly in either a conservative or liberal category theologically speaking, but certainly in comparison with Parkes, the conservative label sticks. To be sure, the "conservative" designation can be taken in a more pejorative direction, as is the case with Alan T. Davies, who writes that "Maritain's imagination carries him well beyond the church fathers, who could see in Judaism no worth whatsoever, except as a foil for Christian polemics. But the substance of his doctrine remains one with Augustine, Cyprian, Eusebius, and the other intellectual progenitors of a long tradition of theological anti-Judaism. At heart, Maritain is a conservative, even if his view contains some transitional elements." Davies, *Anti-Semitism and the Christian Mind*, 84. Davies chides Maritain for embodying the limited traditionalist outlook of someone who "approaches the problem essentially as a Catholic dogmatist," (82) echoing Parkes's dismissal. But he also draws cautionary attention to the consequences of Parkes's theological radicalism: "That which Parkes really seems to be celebrating, in his peculiar trinitarianism, is not Jewish or Christian religious faith, but human progress."(141)

[73] Richmond, *Campaigner against Antisemitism*, 263–66.

[74] Doering, *Jacques Maritain and the French Catholic Intellectuals*, 165–67.

[75] J. Maritain, *On the Philosophy of History*, 54.

[76] Ibid., 90. Pages 85–93 comprise the section of this book that concentrates on "The Destiny of the Jewish People."

[77] Ibid., 149.

[78] J. Maritain, *God and the Permission of Evil*, 86.

[79] J. Maritain, "At the Edith Stein Guild," 1212.

[80] J. Maritain, *Notebooks*, 4.

[81] J. Maritain, "Post-scriptum," in *Le Mystère d'Israël*, 243.

[82] Ibid., 244–45.

[83] Ibid., 246–47.

[84] Ibid., 250.

[85] Ibid., 252.

[86] Charles Journet to Jacques Maritain, 22 October 1965, reprinted in *Cahiers Jacques Maritain* 23 (October 1991): 33–35.

[87] Jacques Maritain to Charles Journet, 27 October 1965, reprinted ibid., 36–38.

[88] Barré, *Jacques et Raïssa Maritain*, 571.

[89] Doering, "Maritain's Idea of the Chosen People," 34.

[90] Jacques Maritain to Charles Journet, 7 October 1965, excerpted in *Cahiers Jacques Maritain*, 23 (October 1991): 35n.

[91] Thomas Merton to Jacques Maritain, 6 October 1965, *Cercle d'Études Jacques et Raïssa Maritain*, Kolbsheim, France.

[92] J. Maritain, *On the Church of Christ*, 167.

[93] Ibid.

[94] Ruether, *Faith and Fratricide*.

[95] Yerushalmi, "Response to Rosemary Radford Ruether," 103. On page 104,

Yerushalmi's words can be seen as more or less identical to those Maritain would have chosen had he been asked to radically condense his position on the origins of modern antisemitism in *On the Church of Christ*: "The slaughter of Jews by the state was not part of the medieval Christian world order. It became possible with the breakdown of that order."

[96] J. Maritain, *On the Church of Christ*, 168–69.

[97] But that papal reign also saw the Edgar Mortara affair, an international controversy surrounding the Papal States authorities' kidnapping of a baptized Jewish boy. See Kertzer, *The Kidnapping*. Maritain does not mention the Mortara case at all.

[98] J. Maritain, *On the Church of Christ*, 172.

[99] Ibid., 173.

[100] Ibid.

[101] Ibid., 173–74.

[102] Ibid., 174.

[103] Ibid., 174–75.

[104] J. Maritain, "Lettre à un Juif Chrétien (1967)."

[105] Pawlikowski, "The Vatican and the Holocaust," 15.

[106] Braham, "Remembering and Forgetting: The Catholic Church and the Jews during the Nazi Era," 38.

[107] Phayer, *The Catholic Church and the Holocaust*, 177.

CONCLUSION

[1] For Arthur Cohen, a historic survey of philosemitism shows that "the registry of authentic Christian humanism is quickly exhausted and even such reflected not a comprehension of the Jews and their world in itself, but rather an agonic leap of *caritas*." He goes on to evoke the "murderous love" characteristic of philosemitic Christians, extending this indictment to Maritain and his mentor: "Even Leon Bloy and Jacques Maritain (with whom I several times discussed 'the Jewish question') were clearly philosemites but only up to the possibility of the conversion of the Jews. Both could be contemptibly small-minded in their aspersions upon the materialism they imputed to Jews and Judaism in general." A. Cohen, "The Holocaust and Christian Theology," 479–80.

[2] Isaac, *The Teaching of Contempt*.

[3] Burton, *Holy Tears, Holy Blood*, 93.

[4] Hellman, "The Jews in the 'New Middle Ages,'" 98.

[5] Catholic theologian David Tracy sees in Maritain's and Hans Urs von Balthasar's intimations of successive covenants a well-intentioned but risky theological gambit, as "it does become questionable whether the history of the effects of Christian theological fulfillment language or law-gospel language or even the New Covenant language can really be retrieved without seeming to imply that God's covenant with the chosen people, the Jews, is abrogated and that Judaism

becomes, in the new covenantal Christian perspective, a spent religion." Tracy, "Religious Values after the Holocaust," 95–99. For an endorsement of a "double covenantal perspective" that seeks to avoid such an intimation of successive covenants see Pawlikowski, "Christian Theological Concerns after the Holocaust," 41.

[6] See for example, Meier Soloveichik's essay "No Friend in Jesus," 32: "Does truth as traditionally understood still exist? Traditional Jews, like Catholics, know the answer to the question. In the end, this is what unites Jews and Christians. Because they believe in truth, traditional Jews cannot and will not find a friend in Jesus—but because they do believe in truth, they can find a friend in followers of Jesus such as [Pope] Benedict. A friendship founded on our mutual resistance to relativism is one that can unite us despite our theological differences. That will have to do until our debate over Jesus is resolved by God himself."

[7] Langmuir, *History, Religion, and Antisemitism*, 28. According to Maritain's friend, John Oesterreicher, "We — Jacques Maritain and I — were of one mind in considering Hitler's fury sui generis. It was light-years away from any previous hostility toward the Jewish people, however bitter and brutal." Oesterreicher, "Cher ami et maître," 258.

[8] Ruether, *Faith and Fratricide*, 256.

[9] O'Brien, "Bishops Vote to Revise U.S. Catechism."

[10] Quoted in Burke, "Catechism Edit 'Troubling,' Jewish Leaders Say."

[11] Boys, et al., "Theology's Sacred Obligation."

[12] This is not to claim that Maritain rejected practical human acts in the service of advancing Christian-Jewish relations; on the contrary, Mary C. Boys, a Catholic nun and professor at the liberal Protestant and ecumenical Union Theological Seminary, states that her institution "explicitly organized a service for Yom Kippur" for the first time in October 2003. See Boys, "Learning from Each Other." Maritain took this kind of step sixty-one years earlier: "The suggestion has been made that we Christians might display before God our brotherly compassion for Israel and make heard our cry on its behalf by praying especially for the Jews and sharing in their penance on this Jewish Day of Atonement. For our relation to the Jewish people is not only a human one, as it is with other suffering national minorities and persecuted peoples, it is also a divine one, a relation of spiritual consanguinity within God's redeeming scheme; a relation that, together with that mysterious drama and rivalry which Saint Paul has depicted, involves and must involve cognate love and charity." J. Maritain, "Atonement for All," 155–56.

[13] Das, *Paul and the Jews*, 195.

BIBLIOGRAPHY

The following archives hold manuscripts consulted or referenced for this study:

Cercle d'Études Jacques et Raïssa Maritain, Kolbsheim, France.

Jacques Maritain Center, University of Notre Dame.

John LaFarge, SJ, Papers, Georgetown University Library Special Collections.

Monsignor John Oesterreicher Collection, Monsignor William Noé Field Archives & Special Collections Center, Seton Hall University.

United States Holocaust Memorial Museum Archives.

This bibliography includes books, articles, and published correspondence.

The sources for published correspondence are set in boldface type.

Actes du cinquième colloque Maurras. Non Possumus. La crise religieuse de l'Action Française. Deuxième Partie. Aix-en-Provence: Centre Charles Maurras, 1986.

Actes et Documents du Saint Siège Relatifs à la Seconde Guerre Mondiale, Volume 11, La Saint Siège et la Guerre Mondiale, Janvier 1944–Mai 1945, ed. Pierre Blet, Robert A. Graham, Angelo Martini, and Burkhart Schneider. Vatican City: Libraria Editrice Vaticana, 1981.

Adler, Jacques. "The French Churches and the Jewish Question: July 1940– March 1941," *Australian Journal of Politics and History*, 46 (2000): 357–77.

Alexander, Martin S., ed. *French History Since Napoleon*. London: Arnold, 1995.

Amato, Joseph. *Mounier and Maritain: A French Catholic Understanding of the Modern World*. Ypsilanti, MI: Sapientia, 2002.

Amishai-Maisels, Ziva. "Christological Symbolism of the Holocaust," *Holocaust and Genocide Studies* 3 (1988): 457–81.

Anschen, Ruth Nanda, ed. *Freedom: Its Meaning*. New York: Harcourt, Brace, 1940.

Anslem, Saint. "Why God Became Man" [*Cur Deus Homo*], in Davies and Evans, eds., *Anselm of Canterbury: The Major Works*.

Arnal, Oscar. *Ambivalent Alliance: The Catholic Church and the Action Française, 1899–1939*. Pittsburgh: University of Pittsburgh Press, 1985.

Aron, Raymond. "Jacques Maritain and the Quarrel Over Machiavellianism," in Mahoney, ed., *In Defense of Political Realism*.

Asch, Sholem. *The Nazarene*, trans. Maurice Samuel. New York: Carroll & Graf, 1984.

Baigell, Matthew. *Jewish Artists in New York: The Holocaust Years*. New Brunswick, NJ: Rutgers University Press, 2002.

Bankier, David, and Israel Gutman, eds. *Nazi Europe and the Final Solution*. Jerusalem: Yad Vashem, 2003.

Barré, Jean-Luc. *Jacques et Raïssa Maritain: Les mendiants du Ciel*. Paris: Stock, 1995. (Translated recently into English: *Jacques and Raïssa Maritain: Beggars of Heaven*, trans. Bernard E. Doering. Notre Dame, IN: University of Notre Dame Press, 2005.)

Bauman, Zygmunt. *Life in Fragments: Essays in Postmodern Morality*. Oxford: Blackwell, 1995.

Becker, Annette. *La guerre et la foi: De la mort à la mémoire*. Paris: Armand Colin, 1994.

————, Danielle Delmaire, and Frédéric Gugelot, eds. *Juifs et Chrétiens: entre ignorance, hostilité et rapprochement (1898–1998)*. Annette Lille: Université Charles-de-Gaulle-Lille 3, 2002.

"Bergson Pupil Says He Died a Catholic," *New York Times*, 13 January 1941.

Blanchet, Charles. "Jacques Maritain, 1940–1944: le refus de la défaite et ses relations avec le général de Gaulle," *Cahiers Jacques Maritain* 16–17 (1988): 39–58.

————. "Maritain face à la modernité," in Bresolotte and Mougel, eds., *Jacques Maritain face à la modernité*.

Blobaum, Robert, ed. *Antisemitism and its Opponents in Modern Poland*. Ithaca, NY: Cornell University Press, 2005.

Bloch, Marc. *Strange Defeat: A Statement of Evidence Written in 1940*, trans. Gerard Hopkins. New York: W. W. Norton, 1968.

Bloy, Léon. *Léon Bloy, Pilgrim of the Absolute: Selection by Raïssa Maritain* (Introduction by Jacques Maritain), trans. John Coleman and Harry Lorin Binnse. New York: Pantheon, 1947.

————. *Le Salut par les Juifs*. Paris: Éditions G. Crès, 1906.

Bonsirven, Joseph. "Le Mystère d'Israël," in Lubac et al., *Israël et la foi chrétienne*.

Boissard, Guy. *Quelle neutralité face à l'horreur: Le courage de Charles Journet*. Fribourg: Editions Saint-Augustin, 2000.

Boys, Mary C., "Learning from Each Other—A Christian Perspective," http://www.jcrelations.net/en/?item=2368 (accessed 24 August 2008).

————, Philip A. Cunningham, and John T. Pawlikowski, "Theology's Sacred Obligation," *America* 187, 12 (21 October 2002): 12–16, http://www.umanitoba.ca/stpauls/pub/pdf/1.pdf (accessed 30 August 2008).

Braham, Randolph L. "Remembering and Forgetting: The Catholic Church and the Jews during the Nazi Era," in Braham, ed., *The Vatican and the Holocaust.*

———. "Remembering and Forgetting: The Vatican, the German Catholic Hierarchy, and the Holocaust," *Holocaust and Genocide Studies* 13 (1999): 222–51.

———, ed. *The Tragedy of Romanian Jewry.* Boulder, CO: East European Monographs, 1994.

———, ed. *The Vatican and the Holocaust: The Catholic Church and the Jews during the Nazi Era.* Boulder, CO: East European Monographs, 2000.

Bresolette, Michel, and René Mougel, eds. *Jacques Maritain: face à la modernité.* Toulouse, Presses Universitaires du Mirail, 1995.

Brown-Fleming, Suzanne. *The Holocaust and Catholic Conscience: Cardinal Aloisius Muench and the Guilt Question in Germany.* Notre Dame, IN: University of Notre Dame Press, 2005.

Browning, Christopher R. *Nazi Policy, Jewish Workers, German Killers.* Cambridge: Cambridge University Press, 2000.

———. *Ordinary Men: Reserve Battalion 101 and the Final Solution in Poland.* New York: HarperCollins, 1992.

Burke, Daniel, "Catechism Edit 'Troubling,' Jewish Leaders Say: Deletion of Passage on Moses in Catholic Handbook Questioned," *The Washington Post*, 13 September 2008, http://washingtonpost.com/wp-dyn/content/article/2008/09/12/AR2008091203077pf.html (accessed 16 September 2008).

Burrell, David B. *Deconstructing Theodicy: Why Job Has Nothing to Say to the Puzzle of Suffering.* Grand Rapids, MI: Brazos, 2008.

Burton, Richard D. E. *Holy Tears, Holy Blood: Women, Catholicism, and the Culture of Suffering in France, 1840–1970*. Ithaca, NY: Cornell University Press, 2004.

Cahiers du Témoignage Chrétien, I: "France, prends garde de perdre ton âme," November 1941.

Caron, Vicki. "French Public Opinion and the 'Jewish Question,'" in Bankier and Gutman, eds., *Nazi Europe and the Final Solution*.

———. "'The Jewish Question' from Dreyfus to Vichy," in Alexander, ed., *French History Since Napoleon*.

Carroll, David. "Poetics and the Ideology of Race: Style and Anti-Semitic Representations in Céline's Pamphlets," *Poetics Today* 16 (1995): 253–81.

Casti Connubii, Encyclical of Pope Pius XI on Christian Marriage, 31 December 1930, http://www.vatican.va/holy_father/piusxi/encyclicals/documents/hfp-xienc31121930casti-connubiien.html (accessed 17 August 2006).

Catholic Bishops of France, "Declaration of Repentance," 30 September 1997, www.bc.edu/research/cjl/meta-elements/texts/documents/catholic/french_repentance.htm (accessed 10 February 2005).

Chagall, Marc. "In Honor of Jacques Maritain," *Jewish Frontier*, February 1943.

Chenaux, Philippe. *Entre Maurras et Maritain. Une génération intellectuelle catholique (1920–1930)*. Paris: Les Éditions du Cerf, 1999.

———. "*Léon Bloy et sa postérité*," in Becker et al., eds., *Juifs et Chrétiens: entre ignorance, hostilité et rapprochement (1898–1998)*.

———. "Maritain, G. B. Montini, et l'ultime Pie XI," in *Montini, Journet, Maritain: Une Famille d'Esprit*. Brescia, Italy: Istituto Paolo VI, 2000.

———. *Paul VI et Maritain: Les rapports du "Montinianisme" et du "Maritanism."* Rome: Édizioni Studium, 1994.

Chertok, Haim. *He Also Spoke as a Jew: The Life of the Reverend James Parkes*. London: Vallentine Mitchell, 2006.

Claudel, Paul. "Une lettre de Paul Claudel à Jacques Maritain," in *Bulletin de la Société Paul Claudel* 143 (1996).

Cohen, Arthur A. "The Holocaust and Christian Theology: An Interpretation of the Problem," in Kulka and Mendes-Flohr., *Judaism and Christianity*.

Cohen, Richard I. "Jews and Christians in France during World War II: A Methodological Essay," in Kulka and Mendes-Flohr., *Judaism and Christianity*.

Conway, John. Review of Spicer, ed., *Anti-Semitism, Christian Ambivalence, and the Holocaust*, in *Association of Church Historians Newsletter*, 14:1 (January 2008): 1.

Coogan, Michael D., ed. *The Oxford History of the Biblical World*. Oxford: Oxford University Press, 1998.

Coppa, Frank J. *The Papacy, the Jews, and the Holocaust*. Washington, DC: Catholic University of America Press, 2006.

————. "The Hidden Encyclical of Pius XI Against Racism and Anti-Semitism Uncovered—Once Again!" *The Catholic Historical Review* 84 (1998): 63–72.

Cornick, Martyn. *Intellectuals in Politics: The* Nouvelle Revue Française *under Jean Paulhan, 1925–1940*. Paris: Rodop, 1995.

***Correspondance de Georges Bernanos, Tome I, 1904–1934*, ed. Albert Béguin and Jean Murray, O.P. Paris: Plon, 1971.**

***Correspondance Fondane-Maritain: Correspondance de Benjamin et Geneviève Fondane avec Jacques et Raïssa Maritain*, ed. Michel Carassou and René Mougel. Paris: Paris Méditerranée, 1997.**

Corte, Marcel de. "Jacques Maritain et la 'question juive,'" in J. Maritain et al., *L'impossible antisémitisme*.

Cournos, John. "A Catholic to Jews," *New York Times*, September 10, 1939.

Crane, Richard Francis. "Jacques Maritain, the Mystery of Israel, and the Holocaust," *The Catholic Historical Review* 95 (2009): 25–56.

———. "*La Croix* and the Swastika: The Ambiguities of Catholic Responses to the Fall of France," *The Catholic Historical Review* 90 (2004): 45–66.

———. "Surviving Maurras: Jacques Maritain's Jewish Question," *Patterns of Prejudice* 42 (2008): 385–411.

Daniel-Rops, Henri, ed. *Les Juifs*. Paris: Plon, 1937.

Das, A. Andrew. *Paul and the Jews*. Peabody, MA: Hendrickson, 2003.

Davies, Alan T. *Anti-Semitism and the Christian Mind: The Crisis of Conscience after Auschwitz*. New York: Herder and Herder, 1969.

Davies, Brian, and G. R. Evans, eds. *Anselm of Canterbury: The Major Works*. Oxford: Oxford University Press, 1998.

Dietrich, Donald J. "Catholic Theology and the Challenge of Nazism," in Spicer, ed., *Antisemitism, Christian Ambivalence, and the Holocaust*.

Dillistone, F. W. "Atonement," in Richardson and Bowden, eds., *The Westminster Dictionary of Christian Theology*.

Dobry, Michel, ed. *Le mythe de l'allergie française au fascisme*. Paris: Éditions Albin Michel, 2003.

Doering, Bernard E. *Jacques Maritain and the French Catholic Intellectuals*. Notre Dame, IN: University of Notre Dame Press, 1983.

———. "Jacques Maritain and the Spanish Civil War," *The Review of Politics* 44 (1982): 489–522.

———. "The Origin and Development of Maritain's Idea of the Chosen People," in Royal, ed., *Jacques Maritain and the Jews*.

Dougherty, Jude. *Jacques Maritain: An Intellectual Portrait*. Washington, DC: Catholic University of America Press, 2003.

Dwork, Debórah, and Robert Jan Van Pelt. *Holocaust: A History*. New York: W. W. Norton, 2002.

Edelstein, Alan. *An Unacknowledged Harmony: Philo-Semitism and the Survival of European Jewry*. Westport, CT: Greenwood, 1982.

Everett, Robert Andrew. *Christianity Without Antisemitism: James Parkes and the Jewish-Christian Encounter*. Oxford: Pergamon, 1993.

Fischer-Galati, Stephen. "The Legacy of Anti-Semitism," in Braham, ed., *The Tragedy of Romanian Jewry*.

Fisher, Eugene J., ed. *Visions of the Other: Jewish and Christian Theologians Assess the Dialogue*. Mahwah, NJ: Paulist Press, 1994.

Flannery, Edward. *The Anguish of the Jews*. Mahwah, NJ: Paulist Press, 1985.

Fleischner, Eva, ed. *Auschwitz: Beginning of a New Era?* New York: KTAV, 1977.

Floucat, Yves. *Pour une restauration du politique. Maritain l'intransigeant. De la Contre-Révolution à la démocratie*. Paris: Téqui, 1999.

Fourcade, Michel. "Jacques Maritain, inspirateur de la Résistance," *Cahiers Jacques Maritain* 32 (June 1996): 14–57.

———. "Jacques Maritain et l'Europe en exil (1940–1945)," *Cahiers Jacques Maritain* 28 (June 1994): 5–38.

Friedländer, Saul. *The Years of Extermination: Nazi Germany and the Jews, 1939–1945*. New York: HarperCollins, 2007.

Geller, Barbara. "Transitions and Trajectories: Jews and Christians in the Roman Empire," in Coogan, ed., *The Oxford History of the Biblical World*.

Gide, André. "Les Juifs, Céline, et Maritain," in J. Maritain et al., *L'impossible antisémitisme*. (The article originally appeared in the *Nouvelle Revue française* (n. 295) on 1 April 1938.)

Goyet, Bruno. *Charles Maurras*. Paris: Presses de Sciences Po, 2000.

Griffiths, Richard. *The Uses of Abuse: The Polemics of the Dreyfus Affair and its Aftermath*. Oxford: Berg, 1991.

Gross, Jan. *Fear: Anti-Semitism in Poland after Auschwitz*. New York: Random House, 2006.

Guéna, Sylvain. "La Passion d'Israël: Réflexions de Jacques Maritain sur la Shoah," *Istina* 45 (2000): 16–36.

Gutman, Israel. *The Jews of Warsaw, 1939–1943: Ghetto, Underground, Revolt*, trans. Ina R. Friedman. Bloomington, IN: Indiana University Press, 1982.

Halls, W. D. *Politics, Society, and Christianity in Vichy France*. Oxford: Berg, 1995.

Hanna, Martha. "Iconology and Ideology: Images of Joan of Arc in the Idiom of the Action Française, 1908–1931," *French Historical Studies* 14 (1985): 215–39.

―――. *The Mobilization of the Intellect: French Scholars and Writers during the Great War*. Cambridge, MA: Harvard University Press, 1996.

Hellman, John. *Emmanuel Mounier and the New Catholic Left, 1930–1950*. Toronto: University of Toronto Press, 1981.

―――. "The Jews in the 'New Middle Ages': Jacques Maritain's Anti-Semitism in its Times," in Royal, ed., *Jacques Maritain and the Jews*.

―――. "Maritain and Mounier: A Secret Quarrel over the Future of the Church," *The Review of Politics* 42 (1980): 152–66.

Hyman, Paula E. *The Jews of Modern France*. Berkeley: University of California Press, 1998.

Ioanid, Radu. *The Holocaust in Romania: The Destruction of Jews and Gypsies under the Antonescu Regime, 1940–1944*. Chicago: Ivan R. Dee, 2000.

Isaac, Jules. *The Teaching of Contempt: Christian Roots of Anti-Semitism*, trans. Helen Weaver. New York: Holt, Rinehart, and Winston, 1964.

Iswolsky, Helen. *Light before Dusk: A Russian Catholic in France, 1923–1941*. New York: Longmans, Green, 1942.

Jackson, Julian. *France: The Dark Years, 1940–1944*. New York: Oxford University Press, 2001.

Jenkins, Brian. "L'Action française à l'ère du fascisme: une perspective contextuelle," in Dobry, Michel, ed., *Le mythe de l'allergie française au fascisme*.

"Jews Urged to Honor Pius XI and Mundelein: Rabbi S. S. Wise Lauds Their Fight Against Anti-Semitism," *The New York Times*, October 23, 1939.

***Journet-Maritain Correspondance, II, 1930–1939*. Fribourg: Éditions Universitaires, 1997.**

***Journet-Maritain Correspondance, III, 1940–1949*. Fribourg: Éditions Universitaires, 1998.**

Judaken, Jonathan. "Between Philosemitism and Antisemitism: The Frankfurt School's Anti-Antisemitism," in Lassner and Trubowitz, eds., *Antisemitism and Philosemitism*.

Kent, Peter C. *The Lonely Cold War of Pope Pius XII: The Roman Catholic Church and the Division of Europe, 1943–1950*. Montreal: McGill-Queen's University Press, 2002.

Kernan, Julie. *Our Friend, Jacques Maritain: A Personal Memoir*. Garden City, NY: Doubleday, 1975.

Kershaw, Ian. *Hitler, 1936–45: Nemesis.* New York: W. W. Norton, 2000.

Kertzer, David. I. *The Kidnapping of Edgardo Mortara.* New York: Knopf, 1997.

Klarsfeld, Serge, ed. *Il y a 50 ans: Le statut des Juifs de Vichy.* Paris: Centre de Documentation Juive Contemporaine, 1991.

Klenicki, Rabbi Leon. "Jacques Maritain's Vision of Judaism and Anti-Semitism," in Royal, ed., *Jacques Maritain and the Jews.*

Kruger, Steven F. *The Spectral Jew: Conversion and Embodiment in Medieval Europe.* Minneapolis: University of Minnesota Press, 2006.

Kubovy, Aryeh L. "The Silence of Pope Pius XII and the Beginnings of the 'Jewish Document.'" *Yad Vashem Studies* 6 (1967).

Kulka, Otto Dov, and Paul R. Mendes-Flohr. *Judaism and Christianity under the Impact of National Socialism.* Jerusalem: Historical Society of Israel and Zalman Shazar Center for Jewish History, 1987.

Laborie, Pierre. "The Jewish Statutes in Vichy France and Public Opinion," *Yad Vashem Studies* 22 (1992): 88–114.

———. *La France des années troubles: De la guerre d'Espagne à la Libération.* Paris: Desclée de Brouwer, 2001.

LaCapra, Dominick. *Representing the Holocaust: History, Theory, and Trauma.* Ithaca, NY: Cornell University Press, 1996.

Lacouture, Jean. *De Gaulle: The Rebel, 1890–1944,* trans. Patrick O'Brian. New York: W. W. Norton, 1990.

Langmuir, Gavin I. *History, Religion, and Antisemitism.* London: I. B. Tauris, 1990.

Lassner, Phyllis, and Lara Trubowitz, eds. *Antisemitism and Philosemitism in the Twentieth and Twenty-First Centuries: Representing Jews, Jewishness, and Modern Culture.* Newark: University of Delaware Press, 2008.

Lazare, Bernard. *Antisemitism: Its History and Causes*. Lincoln, NE: Bison, 1995.

Levinas, Emmanuel. "L'essence spirituelle de l'antisémitisme d'après Jacques Maritain," in Maritain et al., *L'impossible antisémitisme*.

Libionka, Dariusz. "Antisemitism, Anti-Judaism, and the Polish Catholic Clergy during the Second World War, 1939–1945," in Blobaum, ed., *Antisemitism and its Opponents in Modern Poland*.

Lipstadt, Deborah E. *Beyond Belief: The American Press & the Coming of the Holocaust, 1933–1945*. New York: The Free Press, 1986.

Littell, Franklin H. *The Crucifixion of the Jews: The Failure of Christians to Understand the Jewish Experience*. New York: Harper and Row, 1975.

Lottman, Herbert. *The Left Bank: Writers, Artists, and Politics from the Popular Front to the Cold War*. San Francisco: Halo, 1991.

Loyer, Emmanuelle. "La débâcle, les universitaires, et la Fondation Rockefeller: France/États-Unis, 1940–1941," *Revue d'Histoire Moderne et Contemporaine* 48 (2001): 138–59.

Lubac, Henri de, SJ. *Christian Resistance to Anti-Semitism: Memories from 1940–1944*, trans. Sister Elizabeth Englund, O.C.D. San Francisco: Ignatius, 1990.

———, Joseph Chaine, Louis Richard, and Joseph Bonsirven. *Israël et la foi chrétienne*. Fribourg: Librairie de l'Université, 1942.

Mahoney, Daniel J., ed. *In Defense of Political Realism*. Lanham, MD: Rowman and Littlefield, 1994.

Marino, Andy. *A Quiet American: The Secret War of Varian Fry*. New York: St. Martin's, 1999.

Maritain, Jacques. "À propos de la question juive," in J. Maritain et al., *L'impossible antisémitisme*.

———. "Abraham, hou, hou," in J. Maritain, *Le Mystère d'Israël et autre essais*.

———. *Antimoderne*. Paris: Éditions de la Revue des Jeunes, 1922.

———. "Anti-Semitism as Problem for the Jew," in J. Maritain, *Pour la Justice*.

———. "At the Edith Stein Guild" [untitled manuscript], in J. Maritain and R. Maritain, *Jacques and Raïssa Maritain: Oeuvres Complètes*, vol. 12.

———. "Atonement for All," in J. Maritain, *Pour la Justice*. (This essay was originally published in *Commonweal* on 18 September 1942.)

———. "Blessed are the Persecuted," *Commonweal*, 11 October 1946, http://www2.nd.edu/Departments/Maritain/etext/range17.htm (accessed 23 January 2007).

———. *A Christian Looks at the Jewish Question*. New York: Longmans, Green, 1939.

———. "The Christian Teaching of the Story of the Crucifixion," in J. Maritain, *The Range of Reason*, www2.nd.edu/Departments/Maritain/etext/range10.htm (accessed 30 January 2007).

———. *Christianity and Democracy*, trans. Doris C. Anson. New York: Scribner's, 1944.

———. "The Conquest of Freedom," in Anschen, ed., *Freedom: Its Meaning*.

———. "The Crisis of Civilization," in J. Maritain, *Pour la Justice*.

———. *Distinguish to Unite, or The Degrees of Knowledge*, trans. G. B. Phelan. New York: Scribner's, 1959.

———. "Le Droit raciste et la vraie signification du racisme," in J. Maritain, *Le Mystère d'Israël*.

———. "The End of Machiavellianism," *The Review of Politics* 4 (1942): 1–33.

———. "Europe is Already Saved!" *The Washington Post*, 15 October 1939.

———. "Foreword" to Oesterreicher. *Walls are Crumbling.*

———. *France, My Country, Through the Disaster.* New York: Longmans, Green, 1942.

———. *God and the Permission of Evil*, trans. Joseph W. Evans. Milwaukee, WI: Bruce, 1966.

———. "The Healing of Humanity," undated manuscript, JM 4/02a, Jacques Maritain Center, University of Notre Dame.

———. "L'impossible antisémitisme," in J. Maritain et al., *L'impossible antisémitisme.*

———. *Integral Humanism: Temporal and Spiritual Problems of a New Christendom*, trans. Joseph W. Evans. New York: Scribner's, 1968.

———. "Les Juifs parmi les nations," in J. Maritain et al., *L'impossible antisémitisme.*

———. **"Lettre à la Conférence du Seelisberg," in J. Maritain, *Le Mystère d'Israël.***

———. **"Lettre à un Juif Chrétien (1967)," *Cahiers Jacques Maritain* 23 (1991): 41–42.**

———. **"Lettre de Jacques Maritain à André Chouraqui (1969)," *Notes et Documents* 11 (May–September 2008): 33.**

———. *The Living Thoughts of Saint Paul*, trans. Harry Lorin Binsse. New York: Longmans, Green, 1941.

———. *Man and the State.* Chicago: University of Chicago Press, 1951.

————. "The Menace of Racialism," *Interracial Review* 10 (1937): 70–71.

————. *Messages (1941–1944)*. New York: Éditions de la Maison Française, 1945.

————. "Le mystère d'Israël," in J. Maritain et al., *L'impossible antisémitisme*.

————. *Le Mystère d'Israël et autres essais*. Paris: Desclée de Brouwer, 1965.

————. "The Mystery of Israel," in J. Maritain, *Ransoming the Time*.

————. *Notebooks*, trans. Joseph W. Evans. Albany, NY: Magi, 1984.

————. "On Anti-Semitism," *Christianity and Crisis*, 6 October 1941, in J. Maritain and R. Maritain, *Jacques and Raïssa Maritain: Oeuvres Complètes*, vol. 8. Fribourg: Éditions Universitaires, 1989.

————. *On the Church of Christ: The Person of the Church and Its Personnel*, trans. Joseph W. Evans. Notre Dame, IN: University of Notre Dame Press, 1973.

————. *On the Philosophy of History*, trans. Joseph W. Evans. New York: Scribner's, 1957.

————. *Une Opinion sur Charles Maurras et le devoir des catholiques*. Paris: Plon, 1926.

————. "The Passion of Israel," in J. Maritain, *Messages (1941–1944)*. New York: Éditions de la Maison Française, 1945.

————. *The Peasant of the Garonne: An Old Layman Questions Himself about the Present Time*, trans. Michael Cuddihy and Elizabeth Hughes. New York: Holt, Rinehart, and Winston, 1968.

————. *The Person and the Common Good*, trans. John J. Fitzgerald. London: Geoffrey Bles, 1948.

————. "La persécution raciste en France," in J. Maritain, *Messages*.

————. *Pour la Justice: Articles et Discours (1940–1945)*. New York: Éditions de la Maison Française, 1945.

————. *The Range of Reason*. New York: Scribner's, 1955.

————. *Ransoming the Time*, trans. Harry Lorin Binsse. New York: Scribner's, 1941.

————. "Rapport sur le sionisme addressé à Pie XI (1925)," reprinted in *Cahiers Jacques Maritain* 23 (October 1991): 27–30.

————. "Religion and Peace," in J. Maritain, *Pour la Justice*.

————. "Réponse à André Gide sur les Juifs," in J. Maritain et al., *L'impossible antisémitisme*. (The letter originally appeared in the *Nouvelle Revue française* (n. 297) on 1 June 1938.)

————. *Réponse à Jean Cocteau*. Paris: Librairie Stock, 1926.

————. *The Rights of Man and Natural Law*, trans. Doris C. Anson. New York: Scribner's, 1947.

————. *Saint Thomas and the Problem of Evil*. Milwaukee, WI: Marquette University Press, 1942.

————. *The Social and Political Philosophy of Jacques Maritain: Selected Readings*, ed. Joseph W. Evans and Leo R. Ward. New York: Scribner's, 1955.

————. "Sur l'antisémitisme" [Untitled manuscript], in J. Maritain and R. Maritain, *Jacques and Raïssa Maritain: Oeuvres Complètes*, vol. 16. XVI.

————. "Ten Months Later," in J. Maritain, *Pour la Justice*. (The article originally appeared in *Commonweal* on 21 June 1940.)

————. *The Things That Are Not Caesar's*, trans. J. F. Scanlan. London: Sheed and Ward, 1932.

————. *Three Reformers: Luther, Descartes, Rousseau.* New York: Thomas Y. Crowell, 1970.

————. *The Twilight of Civilization*, trans. Lionel Landry. London: Sheed and Ward, 1945.

————. "La Voix de la Paix," in J. Maritain and R. Maritain, *Jacques and Raïssa Maritain: Oeuvres Complètes*, vol. 9.

————. "World Trial: Its Meaning for the Future," *Contemporary Jewish Record* 6 (August 1943): 339–47.

————, and Raïssa Maritain. *Jacques and Raïssa Maritain: Oeuvres Complètes.* Fribourg: Éditions Universitaires, 1999.

————, et al. *Clairvoyance de Rome.* Paris: Spès, 1929.

————, et al. *L'impossible antisémitisme, précédé de Jacques Maritain et les Juifs par Pierre Vidal-Naquet.* Paris: Desclée de Brouwer, 2003.

————, Etienne Borne, Olivier Lacombe, Yves R. Simon, and Maurice de Gandhillac. "For the Common Good: The Christian's Responsibilities in the Present Crisis," trans. Bernard E. Doering, *Notes et Documents* 20 (July–August 1980): 1–20.

————, P. Doncoeur, V. Bernadot, E. La Jeunie, D. Lallement, and F.X. Marquart. *Pourquoi Rome a parlé.* Paris: Spès, 1927.

Maritain, Raïssa. *Chagall ou l'orage enchanté.* Geneva: Éditions des Trois Collines, 1948.

————. "Il en est temps, Réveillez-vous Seigneur Jésus, venez!" in J. Maritain, *Messages.*

————. *We Have Been Friends Together*, trans. Julie Kernan. New York: Longmans, Green, 1941.

————. *We Have Been Friends Together and Adventures in Grace: The Memoirs of Raïssa Maritain*, trans. Julie Kernan. Garden City, NY: Doubleday, 1961.

Marrus, Michael. "The Ambassador and the Pope: Pius XII, Jacques Maritain, and the Jews," *Commonweal*, 22 October 2004.

———. "French Churches and the Persecution of Jews in France, 1940–1944," in Kulka and Mendes-Flohr, *Judaism and Christianity*.

———. *The Holocaust in History*. New York: Meridian, 1987.

———. "A Plea Unanswered: Jacques Maritain, Pope Pius XII, and the Holocaust," *Studies in Contemporary Jewry* 21 (2005): 3–11.

———, and Robert O. Paxton, *Vichy France and the Jews*. New York: Basic Books, 1981.

Maurras, Charles. *Le Bienheureux Pie X, Sauveur de la France*. Paris: Plon, 1953.

May, Ernest R. *Strange Victory: Hitler's Conquest of France*. New York: Hill and Wang, 2000.

Mazgaj, Paul. *Imagining Fascism: The Cultural Politics of the Young Right, 1930–1945*. Newark, DE: University of Delaware Press, 2007.

McInerny, Ralph. *The Very Rich Hours of Jacques Maritain: A Spiritual Biography*. Notre Dame, IN: University of Notre Dame Press, 2003.

Minerbi, Sergio I. *The Vatican and Zionism: Conflict in the Holy Land, 1895–1925*, trans. Arnold Schwarz. New York: Oxford University Press, 1990.

Molette, Charles. "Jacques Maritain et la Conférence de Seelisberg," *Nova et Vetera* 69:3 (1994): 196–223.

Morgenthau, Hans J. "The Evil of Politics and the Ethics of Evil," *Ethics* 56 (1945): 1–18.

Mougel, René. "A propos du mariage des Maritain: Leur voeu de 1912 et leurs témoignages," *Cahiers Jacques Maritain* 22 (June 1991): 5–44.

———. "Les années de New York, 1940–1945," *Cahiers Jacques Maritain* 16–17 (April 1988): 7–28.

Moyn, Samuel. *A Holocaust Controversy: The Treblinka Affair in Postwar France*. Waltham, MA: Brandeis University Press, 2005.

Munro, Bradley R. "The Universal Declaration of Human Rights, Jacques Maritain, and the Universality of Human Rights," in Sweet, ed., *Philosophical Theory and the Universal Declaration of Human Rights*.

Neher-Bernheim, Renée. *Éclats d'une Amitié: Avshalom Feinberg et Jacques Maritain*. Paris: Éditions Parole et Silence, 2005.

———. "Rencontre de deux personnalités d'Eretz Israël vers 1900–1920: Aaron Aaronsohn et Absalon Feinberg," *Cahiers Jacques Maritain* 23 (October 1991): 2–18.

O'Brien, Nancy Frazier, "Bishops Vote to Revise U.S. Catechism on Jewish Covenant with God," 12 August 2008, http://www.usccb.org/bishopsvotecatec.shtml (accessed 16 September 2008).

Oesterreicher, John M. "Cher ami et maître," in Royal, ed., *Jacques Maritain and the Jews*.

———. "Declaration on the Relationship of the Church to Non-Christian Religions: Introduction and Commentary," in Vorgrimler, ed., *Commentary on the Documents of Vatican II*, vol. 3.

———. *Racisme-Antisémitisme-Antichristianisme*. New York: Éditions de la Maison Française, 1943.

———. *Walls are Crumbling: Seven Jewish Theologians Discover Christ*. New York: Devin-Adair, 1952.

Ousby, Ian. *Occupation: The Ordeal of France, 1940–1944*. New York: St. Martin's, 1997.

Parkes, James. *Anti-Semitism: A Concise World History*. Chicago: Quadrangle, 1963.

————. *The Conflict of the Church and the Synagogue*. London: Soncino, 1934.

Passelcq, Georges, and Bernard Suchecky, *The Hidden Encyclical of Pius XI*, trans. Steven Rendall. New York: Harvest Books, 1997. (The book includes the encyclical reprinted in its entirety.)

Pawlikowski, John T. "The Canonization of Pope Pius XII," in Rittner et al., eds., *The Holocaust and the Christian World*.

————. "Christian Theological Concerns after the Holocaust," in Fisher, ed., *Visions of the Other*.

————. "The Vatican and the Holocaust: Putting *We Remember* into Context," *Dimensions: A Journal of Holocaust Studies* 12 (1998): 11–16.

Peck, Abraham J., ed. *Jews and Christians after the Holocaust*. Philadelphia: Fortress, 1982.

***Péguy au porche de l'Église: Correspondence inedite Jacques Maritain-Dom Louis Baillet*, ed. René Mougel and Robert Burac. Paris: Éditions du Cerf, 1997.**

Pertinax (the pseudonym of journalist André Géraud). *The Gravediggers of France*. Garden City, NY: Doubleday, 1944.

Peschanski, Denis. "Les statuts des Juifs du 3 octobre 1940 et du 2 juin 1941," in Klarsfeld, ed., *Il y a 50 ans: Le statut des Juifs de Vichy*.

Peterson, Erik. *Le Mystère des Juifs et des Gentils dans l'Eglise. Suivi d'un essai sur l'Apocalypse*. Paris: Desclée de Brouwer, 1935.

Peterson, Neil, ed. *From Hitler's Doorstep: The Wartime Intelligence Reports of Allen Dulles, 1942–1945*. University Park, PA: Penn State Press, 1996.

Phayer, Michael. *The Catholic Church and the Holocaust, 1930–1965*. Bloomington: Indiana University Press, 2000.

Pieper, Josef. *The Four Cardinal Virtues*, trans. Richard Winston et al. Notre Dame, IN: University of Notre Dame Press, 1966.

Poliakov, Léon. *The History of Anti-Semitism, Volume Four: Suicidal Europe, 1870–1933*, trans. George Klim. New York: Littman Library of Jewish Civilization, 1985.

―――. *Mémoires*. Paris, Jacques Grancher Editeur, 1999.

Poznanski, Renée. *Jews in France during World War II*, trans. Nathan Bracher. Hanover, NH: University Press of New England, 2001.

Prévotat, Jacques. *Les Catholiques et l'Action Française: Histoire d'une condemnation, 1899–1939*. Paris: Fayard, 2001.

Rebatet, Lucien. "Juifs et Catholiques," in J. Maritain et al., *L'impossible antisémitisme*.

Richardson, Alan, and John Bowden, eds. *The Westminster Dictionary of Christian Theology*. Philadelphia, PA: Westminster, 1983.

Richmond, Colin. *Campaigner against Antisemitism: The Reverend James Parkes, 1896–1981*. London: Vallentine Mitchell, 2005.

Rittner, Carol, Stephen D. Smith, and Irena Steinfeldt, eds. *The Holocaust and the Christian World*. New York: Continuum, 2000.

Rohr, Isabelle. "The Use of Antisemitism in the Spanish Civil War," *Patterns of Prejudice* 37 (2003): 195–211.

Royal, Robert, ed. *Jacques Maritain and the Jews*. Notre Dame, IN: American Maritain Association and University of Notre Dame Press, 1994.

―――. "Péguy, Dreyfus, Maritain," in Royal, ed., *Jacques Maritain and the Jews*.

Ruether, Rosemary Radford. *Faith and Fratricide: The Theological Roots of Anti-Semitism*. New York: Seabury, 1974.

Rutkoff, Peter M., and William B. Scott. "Letters to America: The Correspondence of Marc Bloch, 1940–1941," *French Historical Studies* 12 (1981): 277–303.

Samuel, Maurice. *The Great Hatred*. New York: Alfred A. Knopf, 1940.

Sanchéz, José M. *Pius XII and the Holocaust: Understanding the Controversy*. Washington, DC: Catholic University of America Press, 2002.

Schall, James. *Jacques Maritain: The Philosopher in Society*. Lanham, MD: Rowman and Littlefield, 1998.

Schloesser, Stephen. *Jazz Age Catholicism: Mystic Modernism in Postwar Paris, 1919–1933*. Buffalo, NY: University of Toronto Press, 2005.

Schor, Ralph. *L'Antisémitisme en France dans l'entre-deux-guerres: Prélude à Vichy*. Brussels: Éditions Complexe, 2005.

Schwob, René. "Être Chrétien" in Daniel-Rops, ed., *Les Juifs*.

Shain, Milton. *Antisemitism*. London: Bowerdean, 1998.

Soloveichik, Meier. "No Friend in Jesus," *First Things* 179 (January 2008): 29–32.

Spicer, Kevin, ed. *Anti-Semitism, Christian Ambivalence, and the Holocaust*. Bloomington: Indiana University Press, 2007.

Starobinski-Safran, Esther. "Judaïsme, peuple juif, et état d'Isräel," in Bresolette and Mougel, eds., *Jacques Maritain: Face à la Modernité*.

Stendahl, Krister. *Paul among Jews and Gentiles and Other Essays*. Philadelphia: Fortress, 1976.

Stock, Phyllis H. "Students versus the University in Pre-World War Paris," *French Historical Studies* 7 (1971), 93–110.

Suther, Judith D. *Raïssa Maritain: Pilgrim, Poet, Exile*. New York: Fordham University Press, 1990.

Sutton, Michael. *Nationalism, Positivism, and Catholicism: The Politics of Charles Maurras and French Catholics, 1890–1914*. Cambridge: Cambridge University Press, 1982.

Sweet, William, ed. *Philosophical Theory and the Universal Declaration of Human Rights*. Ottawa: University of Ottawa Press, 2003.

Tester, Keith. "A Theory of Indifference," *Journal of Human Rights* 1 (2002): 173–86.

Theuilloy, Guillaume de. *Le Chevalier de l'Absolu: Jacques Maritain entre Mystique et Politique*. Paris: Éditions Gallimard, 2005.

Tilley, Terence W. *The Evils of Theodicy*. Washington, DC: Georgetown University Press, 1991.

Tracy, David. "Religious Values after the Holocaust: A Catholic View," in Peck, ed., *Jews and Christians after the Holocaust*.

"Ultra-Modernist," *Time,* 31 May 1948, www.time.com/time/magazine/article/0,9171,798708,00.html (accessed 23 July 2008).

Ventresca, Robert A. "Jacques Maritain and the Jewish Question: Theology, Identity, and Politics," *Studies in Christian-Jewish Relations* 2 (2007): 58–69, http://escholarship.bc.edu/cgi/viewcontent.cgi?article=1074&context=scjr (accessed 24 October 2008).

Vidal-Naquet, Pierre. "Jacques Maritain et les Juifs: Réflexions sur un parcours," in Maritain et al., *L'impossible antisémitisme*.

Vorgrimler, Herbert, ed. *Commentary on the Documents of Vatican II*, vol. 3. New York: Herder and Herder, 1967

Weber, Eugen. *Action Française: Royalism and Reaction in Twentieth-Century France*. Palo Alto, CA: Stanford University Press, 1962.

———. *France: Fin de siècle*. Cambridge, MA: Harvard University Press, 1986.

Winock, Michel. *La France et les Juifs de 1789 à nos jours*. Paris: Éditions de Seuil, 2004.

Yerushalmi, Yosef Hayim. "Response to Rosemary Radford Ruether," in Fleischner, ed., *Auschwitz: Beginning of a New Era?*

Zollberg, Aristide R. "The *École Libre* at the New School, 1941–1946," *Social Research* 65 (1998): 921–52.

INDEX